W9-AVG-872

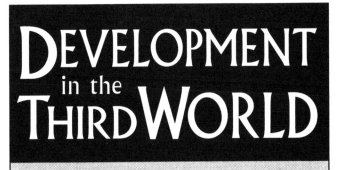

DEVELOPMENT in the THIRD WORLD

FROM POLICY FAILURE TO POLICY REFORM

Kempe Ronald Hope, Sr.

M.E. Sharpe
Armonk, New York
London, England

Library of Congress Cataloging-in-Publication Data

Hope, Kempe R.
Development in the third world: from policy failure to policy reform /
Kempe Ronald Hope, Sr. ; foreword by Rawle Farley.
p.   cm.
Includes bibliographical references and index.
ISBN 1-56324-732-1 (hc : alk. paper).—ISBN 1-56324-733-X (pbk. : alk. paper)
1. Developing countries—Economic policy.
2. Developing countries—Economic conditions.
3. Economic development.
I. Title.
HC59.7.H655   1996
338.9′009172′4—dc20
95-38405
CIP

Printed in the United States of America

The paper used in this publication meets the minimum requirements of
American National Standard for Information Sciences—
Permanence of Paper for Printed Library Materials,
ANSI Z 39.48-1984.

BM (c)   10   9   8   7   6   5   4   3   2   1
BM (p)   10   9   8   7   6   5   4   3   2   1

To the memory of my brother Gordon
and to our inspirational children

Contents

───── List of Tables ─────

Foreword

Professor Kempe Ronald Hope has been a distinguished and continual contributor to relevant and practical thinking and action in the administration and acceleration of economic development of less developed countries. The theoretical underpinnings of his work always remain rigorous. Yet the contributions of Professor Hope, to getting on with the job of making development an ongoing process in Third World countries, are earthily realistic and immediately applicable, given a determination to develop, and given the skills, ingenuities, and the character that the development process requires.

The urgency of the development situation, which Professor Hope advocates, is such that development, in my view, could probably be regarded as making the improbable possible now. Populations explode and the economic and social condition of millions are so desperate that people want development ideals to be satisfied within their lifetime. The pressure is always for development now. Hungry, undereducated, unemployed, underhoused, inequitably taxed, inflation-burdened, and opportunity-constrained people can hardly be told that in the long run all will be well. Dead people in the long run cannot enjoy development, and for obvious reasons. Calculations, however necessary, of where any developing economy will be a hundred years from now do not alleviate the contemporary distress of the marginal millions. These marginal millions, referred to in my *The Economics of Latin America: Development Problems in Perspective* (New York: Harper and Row, 1972, pp. 78–79), remain factored out of organized institutional linkages in their own society and are therefore factored out of contributive economic and social decision making essential for the promotion of economic development.

We have, so far, found no magical, universally applicable model for jump-starting and transforming the behavior of the poor economy. Vocal ideologues on the right assumed that neo–laissez faire was the only essential for economic transformation. Vocal ideologues on the left assumed that neocomplete command approaches would achieve development objectives, while simultaneously introducing purifying ethics into individual and social relationships. In the prevailing passions of the last sixty years or so, the middle-roader was relegated as a development wimp. Emotions became so fierce that in many countries millions of lives were lost, liberty was contemptuously sacrificed, and cooler and constructive reflection hardly ever became the source point of compromise and of the emergence of an unavoidable key requirement for economic advance. That key requirement is simple: *No development can begin to take place, much less be maintained, unless the climate of the particular community decisively inspires, protects, and enlarges private initiative in every sector of the economy.*

I believe that I was almost alone in trying to remind a Third World, emotionally carried away by ideological passion on the left and equally unyielding rigidity on the right, that on the morrow of independence, nationalists and socialists will have to reconcile themselves to private entrepreneurship. The *private* sector, condemned under anticolonial passions, becomes, after independence, the only sector with the skills and ingenuities to build up and enlarge the anemic economies, as envisaged by the public sector, provided the public sector has the common sense to provide essential and appropriate rewards to encourage the required degree of *private* initiative. For future development, ideologues have to give way to technicos, to public-service-driven administrative entrepreneurs, to profit-sector-driven entrepreneurs, to those who could lead, organize, and spread innovation throughout an economy, to those who could bargain, innovate, compromise on realisms, forge self-respecting but practically possible international linkages, and abandon simplistic dependence on parastatism and the easier resort of sacrificing democracy for the illusory possibility of achieving more worthwhile standards of life for all.

The lessons of experience can never be finitely summarized, but some key lessons culled from the development experience of nations can certainly be pinpointed, as Professor Hope has done in this book. Obviously, parastatism for the sake of parastatism has been unsuccessful. Marxism has clearly fallen into disrepute. As a matter of fact, Marxism is irrelevant. Marxist prophecies proved false and, in the process of enforced application, decivilized human existence and wasted the lives of millions of individuals. The market system, despite some of its faults, has produced the more acceptable life consistent with the freedom to choose, a principle that could never be diluted without degrading everyday human relationships.

The realities to be confronted in the development process are simple and eternal. Development will always begin and continue under conditions of uncertainty. Uncertainty remains an eternal challenge to development management. Uncertainty will never disappear. The anxiety over resource shortages will never end. Market uncertainties will never end. Imperfections in the market structure will never end. Competition will never end. Power leveraging is always part of social and economic relationships—local, national, and international. Production will always go up and down, prices will always change, technology will always be a factor, as well as skills and jobs under the threat of change. Discrimination, inequities, and national power imbalances will not go away, authoritarianism—whether fascist, communist, or parastatal—will always be a threat to be resisted. The weather will always be a factor. There will always be shocks, economic and noneconomic. Yet, the development process must continual triumph despite this incomplete range of sources of uncertainty.

Given a recognition that market forces cannot be replaced successfully by rigid ideologies, as Professor Hope points out, what ingenuities will be brought to bear on each development situation will be data-determined. What success is achieved again will differ from time to time and from situation to situation. The rise and fall of nations are historic facts. In the course of history this is not likely to change. Development is not complete in any nation. Development perhaps is never complete given the range of debate over acceptable development objectives. The United States of America, for example, has achieved the highest GNP the world has ever seen. Yet this unique economy, so triumphant a demonstration of mass democracy and of the American development genius, still confronts the problems of the urban ghetto, the Native American reservation, and inevitable debates over economic and social priorities.

The problem of high unemployment and continual adjustment to economic changes remains. Eastern Europe has made open confession to the world that the command system failed and now turns to capitalist methods to secure its development ideals. Yet, capital surplus economies, like Saudi Arabia, which I have called "exceptional economies," cannot be regarded as development models despite their exceptional capital surplus advantage. Evsey Domar's unique emphasis on adequate capital resourcing as the condition for economic development must then be amplified. Britain, despite a continuing flood of innovations and the admirable stability of faith in democracy and private initiative, must deal with development incompletions. Guyana, with the magnificent literacy rate of over 95 percent, a population of under one million, and a land area of over ten times the size of Israel, presents an economy where the per capita GNP in 1993 was only $350 in contrast with $13,920 for Israel. Guyana, a potential El Dorado, remains a peculiar paradox of massive intellectual advantages, yet with a per capita income that was far inferior to that of the small island of Barbados ($6,230) in 1993.

Kempe Ronald Hope has produced a book of fertile development common sense, which I am sure will become a sobering and instructive everyday reference wherever development engineering is an unshiftable priority on the national political agenda.

Rawle Farley
State University of New York at Brockport

Preface

Economic development in the Third World has been elusive for a great many reasons. This book outlines and analyzes what I consider the primary issues pertaining and contributing to such a state of affairs, and then offers some specific policy responses and an optimistic policy-oriented viewpoint on the development prospects of the Third World within the present world economic order. The book argues that development is achievable in the Third World with the continued efforts and assistance of the international development agencies and nongovernmental organizations, coupled with a modified policy framework, implemented by the Third World nations, that emphasizes liberalized economic policies.

The elusiveness of development has been a source of serious economic distress for the great majority of Third World nations. In fact, the ills of many of those countries during the past two decades or so have been related, in one way or another, to their lack of economic development. Such elusive development has resulted in, among other things, tremendous public sector deficits, unmanageable debt, deteriorating physical infrastructure, rapid urbanization, corrupt bureaucracies, high rates of unemployment, widespread poverty, and spiraling inflation. Consequently, a vigorous debate now exists on the development orthodoxy and thinking that prevailed since World War II. The debate centers on the relevance of development economics and the need for alternative frameworks that recognize the limitations inherent in the dogma that was derived from some of the past development formulations.

Economic development in the Third World is a complex process that involves more than just economic factors. Consequently, the choice of policies must, obviously, be based on the particular circumstances of individual countries. Nonetheless, given the generally similar characteristics of the economic problems now faced by the majority of Third World nations, there are some general implications for policy. In any case, the basic thrust of any attempt to make a sustained effort to promote economic development must contain elements of the modified policy framework outlined in this book. The historical record and the lessons learned from the political economy of policy change suggest a wide acceptance, though by no means a universal one, that the starting point for development policy must be increased openness and reduced state intervention. All of the evidence suggests that, to the extent that state interventions are necessary, it is better that they should work with, or through, the market mechanism, rather than against it, since it is unlikely that success will emanate from policies that go against the tide of the marketplace.

The origin of this book goes back to 1988 when, on the occasion of one of my faculty seminars at the University of North Carolina, a debate was triggered between myself and some of my academic colleagues (many of whom were not economists) on the problems contributing to the lack of development in the Third World nations and the then-current state of the debate on development theory and policy. It occurred to me at that time, after some further prompting from my colleagues, that another book would have to be done, following a multidisciplinary approach, to explore the development dilemma in the Third World, in general, and to attempt to provide a cohesive synthesis and point of view on the development prospects for the Third World nations.

Throughout the process of preparing the book I incurred many intellectual, as well as other, debts too numerous to mention here. I am particularly grateful, however, to Professor Rawle Farley of the State University of New York at Brockport, Professor Nathan Rosenberg of Stanford University, and Professor Rudolph Grant of York University for their comments and suggestions on earlier drafts of the manuscript. Of course, neither individually nor collectively do they bear any responsibility for the final product as contained herein. Of Mr. Lennox "Merve" Morgan I am eternally appreciative, for his many engaging and articulate debates on the meaning and the process of development. The significance and impact relevance of those debates—which are ongoing, and which are now dubbed the "Manderly Debates," after their primary geographic location—have been duly incorporated into this book. I also express here a debt of gratitude to Olivia and my secretary, Mrs. Nancy Keirstead, for their word-processing and editing assistance which, appreciably, was above and beyond the call of duty.

Finally, although this book was completed before my current affiliation with the United Nations, its publication while such an affiliation is in effect dictates that I follow the traditional protocol and state that the views and analyses contained herein are entirely my own and not necessarily those of the United Nations or any of its agencies or any other institution with which I am currently affiliated.

DEVELOPMENT in the THIRD WORLD

Chapter 1

Development Theory and Third World Development Policy

Economic development in many Third World countries has been elusive for a great many reasons. Primary among those reasons, however, has been the failure of development theory, and the consequent policy thrusts arising from such theory, to capture the real long-term issues, associated with the economic environment at the time, that ultimately determine the prospects for development. For example, perhaps the two most crucial elements in the quest for development—governance and the development management machinery—have invariably been excluded from the theoretical formulations and from the policy considerations and subsequent policy implementation. However, as will be brought out in this work, governance and the machinery for development management are also critical ingredients for the successful outcome of any development policy thrust in the Third World.

One of the lessons learned from the formulation of postwar development theory and policy and their failure in the Third World is that "new ideas win a public and professional hearing, not on their scientific merits, but on whether or not they promise a solution to important problems that the established orthodoxy has proved itself incapable of solving."[1] Much too much of the work on development theory and policy has technical and scientific merit that makes it appropriate for insertion in professional publications to be read by professional economists. The formulation and implementation of development policy, however, must also entail appropriateness. If development policy has scientific merit but lacks appropriateness, then it is doomed to failure and the process of development will remain elusive in the Third World, ad infinitum.

Postwar Conceptualizations of Development

The concept of economic development has become commonplace in this century, and there is a growing body of literature on its historical development. Moreover, economists have gone to great lengths to differentiate between the terms *economic development* and *economic growth*. It is now recognized that they are two different, but related, processes that are both counterparts and competitors, depending on the time span involved, and that the distinction is important from both theoretical and policy-making standpoints.[2]

In the commonly used meanings of the two terms, they are clearly complementary processes, each with the potential to contribute to the success of the other. But this does not negate their competitive nature. Unusually favorable growing conditions may easily result in impressive growth for a country's traditional outputs or in increased leisure for its population, without much, if any, structural change, as was found to be the case in Liberia,[3] for example. Similarly, development is possible without growth. One sector may grow at the expense of another. Industrial expansion may be matched by a decline in the agricultural sector, for example, as was the case in the Caribbean.[4]

The development–growth distinction is essential in economic thinking. Growth and development are different processes that are considered complementary in the long run but competitive in the short run. Economic growth is regarded as a process of simple increase, implying more of the same, while economic development is a process of structural change, implying something different if not something more.[5]

From the immediate postwar period to the present time, there have been several contrasting perceptions of development.[6] In the 1940s, the less affluent countries, located in Africa, Asia, and Latin America, were usually described as backward. By the 1950s, the term "backward," with its pejorative connotation, had been generally discarded in favor of the term "underdeveloped," which implied the existence of a potential that could be realized and did not suggest directly, at least, an attitude of superiority on the part of the industrialized nations. In the 1960s, these countries began to be referred to as less developed, which was an even more acceptable term, since the countries in question were somehow to be regarded as developed, but only less so than some others. At the same time, the expression "Third World" became prominent and was used to distinguish these nations from the Western industrialized countries (First World), on the one hand, and the Eastern socialist nations (Second World), on the other.

In the 1970s, several new terms came into common use. One was the expression "developing nations," which seemed to remove all implications of inferiority. A distinction was also made between the "oil-producing" and "non-oil-producing" nations. In the 1980s, the term "newly industrializing" countries emerged, referring primarily to four Asian nations—Hong Kong, Korea, Singapore, and Taiwan—that were experiencing sustained industrial growth and economic development. At the present time, the appellations "less developed nations," "developing countries," and "Third World countries" are the most widely used and are commonly used interchangeably.

Through the interwar years, the term "economic development," when used outside the Marxist literature, continued to denote the development or exploitation of natural resources. In the immediate postwar years, economic development became virtually synonymous with growth in per capita income in developing nations.[7] Development meant a rising gross national product (GNP), increasing investment and consumption, and a rising standard of living. A theory was elaborated on the basis of Western experience during the nineteenth century. Accordingly, a developing economy was to have become strong enough and complex enough to take off toward the industrial heights scaled by many countries in the Northern Hemisphere.[8]

The tools of this type of development also were, quite clearly, anything that could help get the engines of investment, production, and consumption moving in the individual poor country, including the inflow of capital goods from the rich nations. At the same time, priority was given to import-substitution policies. Import-substitution industries were to become the key to development. Round and round the system was supposed to go, getting steadily richer, until the poor country could truly be said to be developing. This theory of economic development worked extremely well in some countries. In South Korea and Taiwan, for example, production of goods and services leaped upwards—assisted, of course, by U.S. aid and defense outlays—until the countries genuinely began to leave poverty behind.[9]

However, some flaws appeared in the theory. For one thing, many Third World nations challenged the notion that development could be measured purely in terms of growth in GNP. That challenge resulted in a search for a new meaning and approach to development. "The task was therefore one of finding a new measure of development to replace the growth or national income measure, or, more precisely, to enable the national income to be given its true, somewhat limited, significance as a measure of development potential."[10] The emphasis therefore shifted and development was seen as being brought about not through reliance on external assistance but through national effort. In that regard, in the early 1960s, import-substitution policies were discarded and rapid industrialization for export expansion became the task.

In the mid-1960s, rapid industrialization was regarded as an illusion and rapid agricultural growth became the only road to development. It was felt that, in the debate over industrialization, the relative importance of the agricultural sector in development had been neglected. It was recognized, however, that the agricultural sector still loomed large in the Third World since it was the sector that provided employment for the bulk of the labor force, contained the majority of poor people, and was the birthplace of many of the urban poor. Furthermore, it was generally the foreign-exchange earnings from the agricultural sector that tended to permit or constrain the expansion of industrial output and employment.

Basically, the debate over development strategy then, as now, unfortunately, often swirled around the relative importance to be assigned to agriculture versus industry. Historical evidence, however, suggests that this dichotomy is frequently overstated. Specifically, the notion that rapid industrialization entails a total neglect of agriculture is erroneous; it underestimates the importance of the mutually beneficial links between agricultural and industrial development, and indeed, in most Third World nations, successful industrialization has been supported by sustained and broadly based agricultural growth.

During the mid-1960s also, another conceptualization or line of interpretation of development—more sociological and political—was initiated and became known as "dependency theory." Theorists from Latin America provided the initial impetus for this view, but the ideas were quickly taken up in Africa and Asia. Dependency theory raised the question of why peripheral industrialization did not have its logical effects on the course of development. It identified the problem of dependence with the assumed hegemony of the stronger over the weaker countries, and such a relationship was seen as unilateral and, invariably, negative, and was held responsible for all the ills of the periphery.[11] The dependency perspective assumed that the development of a national or regional unit can only be understood in connection with its historical insertion into the international political-economic system that emerged with the wave of European colonization. Development and underdevelopment were considered characteristics of the global system and were linked functionally, and, therefore, interacted and conditioned each other mutually. This, it was argued, resulted in the division of the world between industrial or "center" countries and developing or "periphery" countries. The center was viewed as capable of dynamic development responsive to internal needs and as the primary beneficiary of the global links. On the other hand, the periphery was seen as having a reflex type of development that was constrained by its incorporation into the global system and that resulted from its adaptation to the requirements of the expansion of the center.[12]

Dependency theory, however, tended to overstate the role of external influences, and consequently minimized the internal factors affecting the development of more equitable domestic economic, social, and political systems. A reduction of dependence on the industrialized nations would have required better management of local resources and significant social and economic changes within the Third World. These issues would be explored in greater detail later on. Suffice to say here, though, that the policy framework to be considered and adapted by the Third World should, of necessity, have been more introspective in nature. The exclusive focus on "dependency" to explain underdevelopment encouraged the evolution of a paralyzing and self-defeating mythology.

In the latter part of the 1960s, the Third World nations began to give priority to population control policies because of the general thinking that all development was likely to be submerged by the population explosion. Direct methods of birth control, such as contraception, became the focus of the early family planning programs. The control of natural population growth has been regarded as the most important form of population planning. However, some of the development problems resulting from population redistribution, especially in the urban areas, have also resulted in some attempts to initiate policies designed to change population distribution. Population policies, while they may have been modestly effective in a few Third World countries, did not help solve the problems of elusive development.

In the 1970s, the general thinking was that the poor masses had not gained much from development. This led to the adoption of policies in favor of distribution and the provision of basic needs for the poor. At the same time, the Third World nations began to clamor for joint action to improve their bargaining position and to protect their economic interests vis-à-vis the industrialized countries. This resulted in a United Nations resolution, on May 1, 1974, for a "Declaration and Program of Action on the Establishment of a New International Economic Order" (NIEO). The concept of the NIEO was intended to embody institutional arrangements that promoted the economic and social progress of the Third World nations in the context of an expanding world economy. It was supposed to be a framework of rules and institutions, regulating the relations among sovereign nations.

The primary elements of the NIEO were considered to be three-fold.[13] First, and foremost, measures were to be sought to reduce, and eventually to eliminate, the economic dependence of Third World nations on industrialized-country enterprises in the production and trade of Third World countries, thus allowing those countries to exercise full control over their natural resources. A second element was to have been promoting the accelerated development of the economies of the Third World on the basis of dependence on their own internal efforts. Third, appropriate institutional changes were to be sought to introduce some measure of global management of resources in the long-term interests of humanity.

The NIEO was intended to stand for a new way of ordering the international economic system to bring about, first, improved terms of trade between the present-day center and periphery countries; second, more control by the periphery over the world economic cycles that pass through them; and, third, increased and improved trade among the periphery countries themselves. The NIEO concept emerged because of what was perceived as defects of the existing international economic order, which, it was argued, had resulted in an economic crisis perpetuating poverty and inequality, both between countries and within each country. Consequently, the NIEO, which the Third World nations sought, was intended to facilitate a direct attack on the central issue of widespread poverty.

With respect to the basic-needs approach, the primary objectives were to provide opportunities for the full physical, mental, and social development of the individual.[14] This approach focused on mobilizing particular resources for particular groups, identified as deficient in those resources, and concentrated on the nature of what was to be provided rather than on income.[15] The basic-needs approach did not rely solely on income generation or transfers; it placed primary emphasis on the production and delivery to the intended groups of the basic-needs basket through supply management and a delivery system.[16]

The basic-needs approach differed conceptually from other poverty-oriented development strategies. In defining the objectives and distinguishing features of the basic-needs policy approach, recognition was given to the fact that countries would have different requirements as a result of their varying economic, political, social, cultural, and technological characteristics. As a result, there were no objective criteria for defining the contents of a basic-needs bundle. It was determined that while certain minimum physiological conditions were necessary to sustain life, basic needs would vary between geographical areas, cultures, and time periods. There was to be no single level of basic needs but instead a hierarchy in which societies could define their own basket of basic goods and services that would, of necessity, differ according to the society's objectives.[17]

Understandably, the conceptualization of the basic-needs approach to development generated a great deal of literature and became the cornerstone of policy for the international development agencies. The basic-needs approach did not call for asceticism or puritanism. It did insist, however, on a certain order, or priorities: First, meet the basic needs of those most in need, and then, and *only then,* go about satisfying any other needs. The basic theoretical and empirical question in connection with the basic-needs approach had to do with the ordering of those pursuits in terms of time. The assumption was that the pursuit of nonbasic needs would stand in the way of meeting basic needs.[18]

During the 1980s to the present period, the focus shifted to private-sector-led development. This not only was the policy thrust emanating from the international development agencies, but also represented an important policy shift for many Third World nations that implemented and are implementing such a policy. After decades of growing state involvement in development, many Third World nations found themselves in the throes of a serious fiscal crisis that necessitated their policy shift from the public to the private provision of goods and services. In essence, the policy shift was an admission by the Third World nations that excessive state involvement was not providing the hoped-for results of growth and development and had, instead, led to economic misery.

The foregoing discussion has been interpreted and placed in historical perspective elsewhere. Griffin, for example, identifies three distinct phases in the evolution of development thought, since the end of World War II, that dominated academic discussion and research and influenced public policy and action in the Third World.[19] He delineates these phases as follows: Phase One was regarded as "The Brave New World of High Theory," where the priority for development was economic growth to stimulate the stagnant economies and traditional societies of the underdeveloped countries, as they were referred to then. Phase Two was considered "The Golden Age of Global Expansion," where the emphasis of thinking on development shifted quite markedly from growth as the priority for development to redistribution with growth. The issues of concern became employment, policies for the direct alleviation of poverty, improving the distribution of income, and the satisfaction of basic human needs. In this era, Griffin argues, central planning ceased to be fashionable and in its place came the advocacy for greater reliance on the market mechanism, which was regarded as superior and more efficient than the planning mechanism. Phase Three was "The Rude Awakening," where the emphasis shifted to economic restructuring and major economic reforms brought on by declining living standards and economic decay in the Third World. Disenchantment with the state as a vehicle for promoting development led to the exploration of possibilities for greater government decentralization and local mobilization for development.

Colin Simmons, on the other hand, postulates that there were two periods in the emergence and development of the modern discipline of development economics since the end of World War II.[20] The first period covers the years 1945–75 and was regarded as the era of "Faith, Hope, and Charity." During that period, Simmons argues, Keynesian economics triumphed and, among other things, legitimized a degree of purposeful state intervention that was consistent with the stated intentions of many Third World governments anyway. This permitted the formation of a "Development Orthodoxy" that essentially emphasized state planning. The second period covers the years 1975–85 and is dubbed the "Decade of Doubt, Dissent, Pessimism, and Retreat." Whereas the first period can be characterized as a time of great expansion, widespread consensus, and reasonably optimistic prognostication for Third World economies, the second period was one of gloom, decline, disagreement, and disparagement. Development theory in this era was found to be drastically wanting and in need of urgent surgery.

The critiques and subsequent reappraisal and reformulation of development theory were centered on the key elements of the development orthodoxy, which included dualism, structuralist-inspired import-substituting industrialization strategies, overvalued currencies, planning, and so on.[21]

Yet another author, Ozzie Simmons, claims that "most classic and neoclassic economic thought, however, from Adam Smith through John Maynard Keynes, has proved to have little relevance for development economics."[22] Simmons argues further that the development field, more than most other areas of human effort, has been subject to many fads and fashions, with a variety of ideas predominating in the mainstream of development thought during the past three decades. This diversity is rationalized on the basis of the many disappointments of development thought and the persistence of the problems of development. The development field was seen as lacking the ability to build a stock of cumulative wisdom on the basis of lessons learnt. Simmons concludes that "the rapidity with which different prescriptions for development came into vogue attests to this lack of cumulativeness."[23] Apart from these latter correct assertions, this work by Simmons, however, provides a very narrow view on development perspectives that is essentially limited to equity-oriented development. For example, the author does not tackle the contemporary issues pertaining to the role of the state in the development process, market-oriented versus non-market-oriented policies, and so on.

A much more complete offering by Ranis and Fei depicts the development debate in terms of the political economy of policy change.[24] They vigorously concur with those who believe that reports of the death of development economics have been greatly exaggerated, and they see the postwar era of development policy as representing a unique period of attempted transition from colonial agrarianism toward the epoch of modern economic growth, emulating the long-run historical experience of the now developed countries. The transition was seen as representing an extremely growth-conscious period during which macroeconomic policy instruments were used to promote growth, thereby resulting in the penetration of the imperfect Third World markets, which had been focused on colonial objectives, by the political forces of nationalism.

The common denominator of Third World development policy was regarded as residing in the recognition that organizational and policy choices are basic to the explanation of developmental success and failure. The authors claim that, "for example, it is now more widely accepted, though by no means universally, that increased openness and reduced government intervention are generally associated with improved development performance. The role of the pursuit of rents has opened up an important related area of inquiry. But what still has eluded observers and constitutes an important field for investigation is just how to endogenize policy change over time."[25] Ranis and Fei argue for the need to include policy convergence, that is, the study of how societies organize themselves as they move into modern growth since such organizational and policy changes are just as important as the statistically observed changes in economic structure and performance. They conclude that "the political process through which policy either accommodates or obstructs the evolution of an economic system toward modern growth lies at the heart of the issue—as do the roles of natural resources and foreign capital."[26]

Development Planning

The concept of development planning has several connotations and forms. In some instances, it has been used to denote a wide range of activities from central management of the economies in communist nations to government-sponsored forecasts by private groups in countries such as Sweden. Most authorities, however, agree that planning refers to the formulation and execution of a consistent set of interrelated measures designed to achieve certain specific economic and social goals. Or, as former Indian Prime Minister Jawaharlal Nehru defined it: "Planning is the exercise of intelligence to deal with facts and situations as they are and find a way to solve problems."[27]

Waterston, on the other hand, concludes that countries were regarded to be engaged in development planning if their governments were making conscious and continuing attempts to increase their rates of economic and social progress and to alter those institutional arrangements that were considered obstacles to the achievement of that aim.[28] He further says that, to plan economically, one need not have a moral purpose; one need only be prudent in the use of scarce resources.[29] Consequently, the use of development planning is not limited to a particular kind of economy or society. It exists under a variety of political systems.

Despite the great variety of forms that it may take, all planning has certain common attributes. These include making choices and, where possible, arranging that future actions for attaining objectives follow fixed paths; or, where this is impossible, setting limits to the consequences that may arise from such action.[30] Basically, the arguments that have been made in support of the case for planning rest on the misplaced notion that the planning calculus is superior to the calculus of the market place. The so-called public interest, as expressed in a development plan, supposedly requires that the market judgment and the decisions reached by individuals and interest groups be more or less subordinated to plan enforcement. Planning, therefore, represents the mechanism through which the state exercises control over an economy.

The theoretical construct giving impetus to development planning can be found in the proposition that the state should initiate activity where the starting costs for the minimum efficient scale of production are high and the cumulative investment large at low rates of return, but the contributory long-term effects are significant. This, ultimately, led to large-scale public investment in power generation, roads, water systems, transportation networks, and so on. Planning was a postwar phenomenon that was intended to lead to capital formation. Planning models proliferated, based originally on the theoretical work of Jan Tinbergen or on adaptations of Harrod–Domar growth models. From the early 1960s, development planning became an accepted practice in most Third World nations based on what came to be called the "conventional approach" to planning. This approach to planning emphasizes the establishment of a state planning agency; the formulation and implementation of global plans into sectoral components; and the introduction of a geographical dimension by assigning responsibilities for projects to regional authorities.[31]

Development planning in the Third World is based on the belief that development can be achieved or enhanced through state intervention. Planning agencies and their officials have steadfastly argued that complete reliance on market forces could *not* be expected to bring about the desired level of economic development and, consequently, that elected governments would have to play a more interventionist role in the development process. Planning is, therefore, regarded as more of a technocratic concept for the fulfillment of specific development goals. Arguments in favor of plan enforcement are thus based on two sets of propositions. Proposition I is that free enterprise resource allocation is ineffective or, to be more precise, it is less effective than planned allocation. Proposition II is that there is a lack of congruence between private interests, expressed in the market system, and public interests. As a consequence, in the absence of the planned channeling of investment, there would be no economic development.

Planning practice in the Third World has been associated with three distinct approaches.[32] The first is denoted as "comprehensive," usually practiced by the centrally planned economies of Eastern Europe and some Third World countries. The second is "indicative," practiced by several South Asian and Francophone African nations. The third approach is called "ritual," as practiced by several sub-Saharan Africa and Caribbean countries. More recently, however, these distinctions have become blurred because the degree of state intervention has varied as a number of countries began switching, in varying degrees, to markets and prices while some others, because of manpower and budgetary constraints, have not been able to produce and publish plans.

Public Enterprises

In concert with development planning, public enterprises were created and became a popular mode of production in the Third World beginning in the 1960s. The rapid expansion of public enterprises in these nations occurred for essentially the same reasons that development planning became a vigorous activity in these countries. The establishment of public enterprises was regarded as a necessary ingredient in the state's arsenal for implementing development policy. Although its proliferation had its origins in the process of nationalization, the public enterprise sector in the Third World has grown through the creation of new entities, the establishment of joint ventures with the private sector and/or other public enterprises, and through acquisition by purchase. It was estimated that the share of public enterprise output in gross domestic product in the 1970s ranged from 1 percent (Nepal) to 14 percent (Taiwan) in Asia, 7 percent (Liberia) to 38 percent (Zambia) in Africa, and 1 percent (Guatemala) to 75 percent (Guyana) in Latin America and the Caribbean. By the early 1980s, however, public enterprises accounted, on average, for 17 percent of gross domestic product in sub-Saharan Africa, for 12 percent in Latin America, 3 percent in Asia (excluding China, India, and Myanmar), and for 10 percent in mixed economies worldwide.[33]

The growth and expansion of the public enterprise sector has been fueled by many factors and multiple considerations. Third World leaders have often attempted to justify the public enterprise mode of production on the need to ensure that their citizens, as opposed to foreigners, made the strategic decisions relating to the development of their individual nation-states; the need to create industries that are deemed to be important for future growth; the need to stimulate a particular sector of the economy; the need to reduce areas of dependency and insulate their economies from external pressures; the need to contribute to stability and employment; the notion that the market was incapable of contributing to social policy goals; and the need to control the "commanding heights" of their economies.

Consequently, the growth of public enterprise in the Third World is reflected in a wide range of public sector activities. These enterprises are no longer restricted to the traditional areas of the infrastructure and public utilities but have moved into virtually every segment of economic activity. It is this range and diversity of public enterprises, and the critical role which they have been asked to play in the process of development, that has brought them under closer scrutiny in recent times and resulted in the current debate on their appropriate role in the process of development. Moreover, critical analyses of public enterprises are now essential to a determination of their viability within the context of restructured economies.

Public enterprises in the Third World, however, have special problems that are not faced by their counterparts in the industrialized nations. These special problems arise from the social, economic, and political environment in which the public enterprises function and from the public enterprises themselves. For example, cultural values and limited work experiences affect attitudes toward work, organizational discipline, an understanding of technical limitations, and the requirements of machines, management style, and so on.[34] Moreover, the desire to maintain or achieve political control appears to be the primary factor in understanding the use of public enterprises by Third World governments as a means for controlling economic activity in their countries. Such control has little to do with the promotion of growth and efficiency.[35]

The use of public enterprises, therefore, as a mode of production in the Third World, like development planning, represented another means through which the role of the state, as a paramount force in economic decision making, was entrenched. Moreover, public enterprises were used, and continue to be used, as instruments of political power and will. This tended to be based on generally socialist orientations and has led to political interference in the administration of the public enterprises, ranging from ill-informed or misguided interventions to outright abuse of the system and the resources and assets of the public enterprises. This, in turn, has affected the financial performance and efficiency of the enterprises and limited their ability to generate economic surpluses and contribute to the development effort. It is in this regard that the view emerged of the state as an economic predator exploiting national resources through parasitic public enterprises and policies.

Where the public enterprise mode of production is dominant, there is a tendency for predatory practices to be entrenched. The availability and control of vast state-owned assets, along with the desire to maximize political and economic power, have created the impetus to use public enterprises for personal and ruling party interests. Most patronage appointments, for example, are made in public enterprises where they are not subject to the rules pertaining to usual civil service appointments. Although patronage appointments, per se, are not bad, in Third World public enterprises these appointments are usually made to satisfy political ends, exclusively, or to guarantee the continued flow of economic benefits from those enterprises to specific individuals or groups: in other words, as discussed further in chapter 6, the use and plunderous abuse of state institutions.

Development Management

Development management applies, primarily, to the activities of governments to facilitate defined programs of social and economic progress through the public administration machinery. It pertains to organized efforts to implement programs or projects considered to serve developmental objectives and, as such, is the bureaucratic process that facilitates or stimulates the achievements of socioeconomic progress through the utilization of the talents and expertise of the bureaucrats. It is the mobilization of bureaucratic skills for enhancing the development process.[36] In contextual and operational terms, development management implies efficient organization and management of the development activities of a nation to attain the goals of development. It is also the process of guiding institutions toward the achievement of progressive economic objectives to promote nation building and socioeconomic development.

Back in 1966, the Nobel Laureate in economics, the late Sir W. Arthur Lewis wrote that the secret of successful development planning lies not only in sensible politics but in good development management.[37] Previous to that observation, Kapp argued that a quantitatively inadequate or qualitatively defective system of development management will not merely retard the development process but may defeat the entire development effort in an even more decisive manner than any temporary shortage of capital or an unfavorable monsoon.[38] Despite such observations, it was not until the 1970s that the international development agencies began to give very serious consideration to the role of development management in the development process.

Prior to the 1970s, much of the thinking on development management was influenced by optimism on the subject of the availability of material, human, and scientific resources for development. Currently, questions are being asked about the capacity of public administration to bring about, effectively, the necessary readjustments and increases in productivity to enhance development.[39] The management of development in the Third World is now receiving just as much scrutiny as the current debate on development theory and policy, and for good reason. Development management has a major role to play in the development effort. It must supply the facts, apply the methods, and evaluate the record. It represents the instrument of implementation and accomplishment. It is fundamental to the economic success of Third World nations.[40]

A Critical Assessment

The mere fact that there have been so many contrasting perceptions, shifting emphases, and development policy frameworks during the postwar period is testament to the fact that applied development theory and development policy have failed to improve living standards and the quality of life in the Third World. Irrespective of how development may be measured and evaluated, it has been elusive in the great majority of Third World nations. Using the extent of poverty as one measure of development, it was determined, in the *World Development Report 1990*, that approximately one-third of the total population of the developing world was poor in 1985, using an upper poverty line of $370. Of that total, approximately 630 million (18 percent of the total population of the developing world) were extremely poor, that is, below the lower poverty line of $275. Close to half of the developing world's poor and close to half of those in extreme poverty live in South Asia. Sub-Saharan Africa has about one-third as many poor, although in relation to the region's total population, its poverty is roughly as high. The nations in Africa, particularly those south of the Sahara, suffer the greatest human deprivation. Africa has the lowest life expectancy of all the developing regions, the highest infant mortality rates, and the lowest literacy rates. Its average per capita income fell by a quarter in the 1980s. Africa contains twenty-eight of the forty-two least developed countries.

Economic development in the Third World has been elusive primarily for two reasons. The first is the legacy of development planning, an approach to economic development that concentrated investment decisions in the hands of the state and negated the role of the market mechanism. The second reason is that development policies, particularly in Africa and the Caribbean, were based on socialist ideology, which was regarded as the automatic alternative to colonialist policies after independence. Many Third World governments somehow regarded socialism and nationalism as one and the same. The consequence of these two notions has been the virtual bankruptcy of the Third World nations and economic deprivation for their citizens, among other things, as will be gleaned in this book.

It has been suggested by Toye that to be critical of development theory and practice that predated the 1970s would cast one as an anti-Keynesian counterrevolutionary or, more precisely, as a development counterrevolutionary.[41] He attributes the development counterrevolution to such prominent economists as the late Harry Johnson, Peter Bauer, Deepak Lal, Ian M.D. Little, and Bela Balassa, whom he identified as "united in opposition to Keynes and neo-Keynesianism, 'structuralist' theories of development and the use of planning for development purposes. On the positive side, they are united by the belief that the problems of economic development can only be solved by an economic system with freely operating markets and a government that undertakes a minimum of functions."[42] However, it is incumbent upon me to point out that it is *not* necessary to wear or be suited in ideological armor to be critical of any aspect of economic theory and policy. Development theory and policy have failed dismally to result in economic progress in the Third World. The evidence and current analyses suggest that this is directly attributable to excessive state intervention in those economies and to other policies that were not an expression of the general good.[43]

A much more balanced work by Killick argues that, while current thinking on development theory and policy offers valuable insights into Third World economic performance and the nature and role of the state, it offers no panaceas or grounds for dogmatism and, in fact, has gone too far.[44] He further states that medium-term development planning in most Third World nations had almost entirely failed to deliver the advantages expected of it. At the same time, however, he suggests that the manner in which the public sector went about its tasks is more important than its absolute size and, consequently, the role of the state should be the incidental outcome of the relative efficiencies of each sector and will vary greatly from country to country but with a major role envisaged for the state.[45]

Killick further believes that, to the extent that policy interventions are necessary, it is better that they should work with, or through, the market mechanism, rather than against it, since it is more than likely that failure will result from policies that seek to swim against the tide of market incentives. "At the same time, however, recognize the limitations of narrowly market-oriented programs; and the potentially wide range of 'market failures' which would justify government intervention, if there is reasonable cause to believe that this will result in a net improvement in welfare."[46] Furthermore, Killick is considerably preoccupied with the possible temptation to exaggerate the appropriateness of policy solutions derived from mainstream theory and the overconfident advocacy of prescriptions that such exaggeration can generate, in particular, the avoidance of simplistic and single-solution responses to complex problems in the Third World.[47]

Hettne, on the other hand, postulates that the crisis in development theory did not result from stalled theorizing but rather from the failure to answer seriously the question of whose development.[48] He contends that, from the very beginning, development theorists—and development economists in particular—were addressing governments on the assumption that national development was to be given the highest political priority. However, planning has now become outmoded and the market for development economists has shrunk drastically, particularly since very few governments in the Third World are concerned with development as a priority.[49] To noneconomists, and perhaps even to some professional economists, these statements may appear at first glance exaggerated. They are not. Rather, they are accurate observations on the current state of development economics and a reflection on some of the contributory factors to the development crisis.

Undoubtedly, the climate of opinion on development theory and policy has changed dramatically in the last decade or so, and for good reason. The state, inevitably, has come to be seen less and less as the basic instrument for national development. It was relatively too easy for Third World governments to use state institutions to pursue purposes other than those they were mandated to pursue. Public enterprises, for example, were forced to set prices below what was required to recover production costs for purely political reasons. The end results were, of course, cumulative deficits that became a burden on the public treasury. Public enterprises, instead of contributing to national savings, became a budgetary burden and a net drain on savings. Appropriately, the state sector became identified with economic inefficiency and tolerated waste. Consequently, whether by choice or by force of circumstances, many Third World governments are now scampering around to attempt to shrink their public sectors and to give a boost to their private sectors. Such a necessary private sector boost will expose once-sheltered parts of Third World economies to market forces and thereby promote greater choice, competition, and efficiency.

The focus on and assessment of macroeconomic variables tend to beg the question as to why and when public enterprises would be of development significance. Generally, public enterprises that are profitable, efficient, and operate in conformity with commonly accepted commercial standards would not result in a drain on financial resources. Rather, their impact would not vary significantly from private sector operations undertaking similar functions.[50] The record of public enterprise performance certainly suggests, however, that many of those enterprises are simply not viable and should be disposed of unless a very strong case, based on social or other noncommercial objectives, can be made for retaining such enterprises in the public sector.[51] That would mean a determination that the public enterprise sector can function in an orderly manner and that, as individual entities and as a group, they could fulfill the mandate and effectuate the purposes for which they were established while also contributing to economic development.

Third World governments must bear in mind, however, that there is overwhelming evidence that increased reliance on markets, combined with other efforts to ensure efficiency, has led to improvements in economic growth and development performance and, over the long-term, to reductions in inequality and poverty. Such pragmatic approaches offer much more hope for furthering progress and development than do utopian planning models and public enterprise production.[52] The quantitative evidence on public enterprise performance in the Third World is provided in chapter 7.

Development planning has been a gigantic disaster and a failed policy framework for promoting development in the Third World. Planning has been disastrous in the Third World for two primary reasons. The first is that current planning, by its very nature, has had to eschew the market mechanism in its implementation. The second is that planning represents what can be termed "crystal ball economics." In other words, it presupposes precise economic forecasting. However, economic performance in the Third World has never been able to achieve or even come close to the aggregates spelled out in the plans. Planning is anticipatory decision making. It is an attempt to bring about predetermined outcomes in an atmosphere of uncertainty and with no ability to control all future events and variables that can influence the planned outcomes. For example, it may not be possible to predict and/or control for changes in export performance that can be severely affected by a natural disaster, or internal mismanagement for that matter.

In spite of the shortcomings and lack of any measurable gains from planning, it became a growth industry in the Third World during the postwar period. Moreover, there continues to be an overwhelming desire in those countries to plan, although the reasons for doing so have not changed significantly since the inception of development planning. However, if some recognition is given to the fact that, in the Third World, resources are scarce and indivisibilities and externalities are present, then some means of ensuring consistency and coordination of allocative decisions must be undertaken. In that regard, a case can be made for planning in the Third World that is short-term in nature, flexible, and market-oriented. In other words, flexible market-oriented planning (FMOP) that is able to adjust to the changing economic environment and current times of uncertainty. It is minimalist planning and can be regarded more as enlightened state intervention. This is explored further in chapter 7.

During the past three decades or so, it became clear that development management had a great part to play in the development effort. More recently, development policy has undergone critical assessment and evaluation that has led to the conclusion, among other things discussed in this work, that development is not the result simply of applying theories, models, or strategies, but is an integral part of the dynamic process of society's growth as a whole. Moreover, managing that development has a direct impact on the nature and structure of the change effected through the development process. However, development management in the Third World has been inept despite the fact that management constraints are as serious a barrier to development as is a shortage of development finance.

Development management capability in the Third World is hampered by a great many factors and major administrative reform is now required, as discussed in chapter 6. Development management is hampered primarily by the transformation of the civil service into a bureaucratic organization where the sovereignty of politics, rather than the supremacy of administration, is emphasized. Politics has become the most important activity, and politicians have come to occupy a position of unquestionable supremacy in matters of decision making. Development management authority is now centralized in the political apparatus, and administrative corruption has reached epidemic proportions (also discussed in chapter 6).

The ultimate result of all of these manifestations is a lack of coordination of policies among government departments, a lack of information dissemination for effective decision making, and a complete breakdown in the structured mechanisms through which the development process is managed. Consequently, development management is now at a crossroads in the Third World. Its traditional role is being challenged as development policy continues to be scrutinized. Some very fundamental questions are now being posed with respect to the proper role and efficiency of development management in the development process. The debate centers around the *justifiable* need to improve the performance of the development management machinery in national affairs. That is, to increase the responsiveness and productivity of the bureaucracy. While the process of change takes place, new problems and needs will arise. However, the role of development management will always be critical. The fundamental issue comes down to promoting the national economic interest, on the one hand, and building management capability for changing needs, on the other.

Concluding Remarks

Development economics has undergone its most thorough evaluation, in its history as a discipline, during the last decade or so. This evaluation was necessitated by the failure of development theory and policy to facilitate the achievement of economic progress in the Third World. Much of the concern has been centered on the reformulation of development thinking and theoretical constructs with much finger-pointing at the prevailing orthodoxy that exists in many of the textbooks and numerous journal articles. What has been severely lacking, however, is criticism of the Third World nations themselves for implementing development policies that were proven failures and did nothing more than enable politicians to maintain political power while their nations went bankrupt. Moreover, development theory has absolutely nothing to do with the fact that a poor Third World nation would, for example, spend enormous sums on such things as helicopters and luxury cars for use by government officials and the ruling party brass, while basic goods are not available for acquisition by the citizenry. Such examples are abundant.

On another level, however, it is also possible to argue that if a particular school of thought is willing to take credit for its good economic results, then it must also accept responsibility for its bad economic results. In that regard, we can attribute the bad results of development policy in the postwar era to the Liberal–Orthodox (state interventionist) framework that dominated development economics from the postwar era until about a decade ago. Indeed, what Toye[53] regards as a counterrevolution in development theory is a logical, and now increasingly accepted, intellectual response to what the late Sir W. Arthur Lewis had acknowledged to be the doldrums of development economics,[54] and to the lack of utility of the Liberal–Orthodox analyses.[55] As a matter of fact, it has been accepted that the standard left view is a static one that assumes that current policies are sustainable indefinitely.[56]

For many Third World nations, in the postwar period, the tremendous "expansion of the government bureaucracy, of the public sector, and of controls on industry, prices, and foreign trade have created a new system of subinfeudation, in which politically created property rights to rents for various groups are financed by implicit or explicit taxation of the general populace."[57] This created a crisis as the existing means of funding those entitlements became nonviable.[58] Moreover, Third World governments have been increasing their fiscal burden in order to subsidize what can be regarded as mistaken development efforts.[59] For sure, this followed from what Lal refers to as *dirigiste* economic policy,[60] a primary feature of which has been the supplanting of the price mechanism through state intervention.

The challenge now facing the Third World is one of moving forward to policy reform for sustainable development. Sustainable development can be defined as development that meets the needs of the present without compromising the ability of future generations to meet their own needs. In other words, it is the management of present activities to ensure that future generations have the natural and other resources necessary to sustain growth and development.

Notes

1. Harry G. Johnson, "The Keynesian Revolution and the Monetarist Counter-Revolution," *American Economic Review, 61* (Papers and Proceedings, May 1971), p. 12. Johnson was arguing here that theoretical developments in economics took place in response to social needs and not as a result of scientific progress in the discipline. More recently, it has been argued that there are limitations imposed by the preoccupation with mathematical methods much to the neglect of historical, institutional, and other qualitative considerations. See S. Rashid, "Economics and the Study of Its Past," *World Development, 16* (February 1988), pp. 207–18. Moreover, it has also been elucidated that "there are no useful propositions in economics that cannot be stated accurately in clear, unembellished, and generally agreeable English." See John Kenneth Galbraith, *Economics in Perspective: A Critical History* (Boston: Houghton Mifflin, 1987), p. 4.

2. Robert A. Flammang, "Economic Growth and Economic Development: Counterparts or Competitors," *Economic Development and Cultural Change, 28* (October 1979), p. 47.

3. See Robert Clower, et al., *Growth without Development* (Evanston, IL: Northwestern University Press, 1966).

4. See Kempe Ronald Hope, Sr., *Economic Development in the Caribbean* (New York: Praeger, 1986), pp. 52–66.

5. Robert A. Flammang, "Economic Growth and Economic Development: Counterparts or Competitors," pp. 50–61.

6. For a more extensive exposition of these contrasting perceptions, see Paul Streeten, "Development Ideas in Historical Perspective" in K.Q. Hill (ed.), *Toward a New Strategy for Development: A Rothko Chapel Colloquium* (New York: Pergamon Press, 1979), pp. 21–52.

7. H.W. Arndt, "Economic Development: A Semantic History," *Economic Development and Cultural Change, 29* (April 1981), pp. 463–65.

8. Among the many expositions on this theory, see, for example, W.W.

Rostow, *Stages of Economic Growth* (Cambridge: Cambridge University Press, 1959), and Harvey Leibenstein, *Economic Backwardness and Economic Growth* (New York: Wiley, 1957).

9. Robert Hunter, *What Is Development* (Washington, DC: Overseas Development Council, 1971), p. 1.

10. Dudley Seers, "The New Meaning of Development," *International Development Review, 11* (December 1969), p. 3.

11. Raúl Prebisch, "Dependence, Interdependence and Development," *CEPAL Review, 34* (April 1988), pp. 197–99.

12. J. Samuel Valenzuela and Arturo Valenzuela, "Modernization and Dependency: Alternative Perspectives in the Study of Latin American Underdevelopment," in Heraldo Munoz (ed.), *From Dependency to Development: Strategies to Overcome Underdevelopment and Inequality* (Boulder, CO: Westview Press, 1981), p. 25:

13. Kempe Ronald Hope, Sr., "The New International Economic Order, Basic Needs, and Technology Transfer: Toward an Integrated Strategy for Development in the Future," *World Futures, 18,* 3 and 4 (1982), pp. 163–76.

14. Paul Streeten, "Basic Needs: Premises and Promises," *Journal of Policy Modeling, 1,* 1 (1979), p. 136.

15. Ibid.

16. T.N. Srinivasan, "Development, Poverty, and Basic Human Needs: Some Issues," *Food Research Institute Studies, 16,* 2 (1977), p. 18.

17. Paul Streeten and Shahid Javed Burki, "Basic Needs: Some Issues," *World Development, 6,* 3 (1978), pp. 411–21.

18. Kempe Ronald Hope, Sr., "Basic Needs and Technology Transfer Issues in the New International Economic Order," *American Journal of Economics and Sociology, 42* (October 1983), pp. 393–403.

19. Keith Griffin, "Thinking about Development: The Longer View," *Development, 2/3* (1988), pp. 5–8.

20. Colin Simmons, "Economic Development and Economic History," in Barbara Ingham and Colin Simmons (eds.), *Development Studies and Colonial Policy* (London: Frank Cass, 1987), pp. 3–99.

21. Ibid., pp. 18–19.

22. Ozzie G. Simmons, *Perspectives on Development and Population Growth in the Third World* (New York: Plenum Press, 1988), p. 5.

23. Ibid., p. 9.

24. Gustav Ranis and John C.H. Fei, "Development Economics: What Next?" in Gustav Ranis and T. Paul Schultz (eds.), *The State of Development Economics: Progress and Perspectives* (New York: Basil Blackwell, 1988), pp. 100–36.

25. Ibid., pp. 102–3.

26. Ibid., p. 130.

27. J. Nehru, "Strategy of the Third Plan," in *Problems of the Third Plan* (New Delhi: Government of India, 1961), pp. 33–34.

28. Albert Waterston, *Development Planning: Lessons of Experience* (Baltimore: Johns Hopkins University Press, 1965), p. 27.

29. Ibid., p. 9.

30. Ibid.

31. Francisco R. Sagasti, "National Development Planning in Turbulent

Times: New Approaches and Criteria for Institutional Design," *World Development, 16,* 4 (1988), p. 432.

32. See Ramgopal Aggarwala, *Planning in Developing Countries: Lessons from Experience,* Staff Working Paper No. 576 (Washington, DC: World Bank, 1983), pp. 5–9.

33. Richard Hemming and Ali M. Mansoor, *Privatization and Public Enterprises,* Occasional Paper 56 (Washington, DC: IMF, January 1988), p. 3; Kempe Ronald Hope, Sr., *An Assessment of the Economic Performance of the Guyana State Corporation Group of Corporations,* report prepared for UNIDO/UNDP, Technical Assistance Project Guy 86/008, October 1988, p. 2; and S. Kikeri, J. Nellis, and M. Shirley, *Privatization: Lessons of Experience* (Washington, DC: World Bank, 1992), p. 15.

34. Victor Powell, *Improving Public Enterprise Performance* (Geneva: International Labor Organization, 1987), pp. 14–15.

35. Edwin S. Mills, *The Burden of Government* (Stanford, CA: Hoover Institution Press, 1986), p. 156.

36. Kempe Ronald Hope, Sr., *The Dynamics of Development and Development Administration* (London: Greenwood Press, 1984), pp. 63–67.

37. W. Arthur Lewis, *Development Planning* (London: Allen and Unwin, 1966), preface.

38. K. William Kapp, "Economic Development, National Planning and Public Administration," *Kyklos, 13,* Fasc. 2 (1960), pp. 172–201.

39. Faqir Muhammad, "Public Administration: Prevailing Perceptions and Priorities," *International Review of Administrative Sciences, 54* (March 1988), p. 5.

40. Joseph C. Wheeler, "The Critical Role for Official Development Assistance in the 1990s," *Finance and Development, 26* (September 1989), p. 38.

41. John Toye, *Dilemmas of Development: Reflections on the Counter-Revolution in Development Theory and Policy* (New York: Basil Blackwell, 1987), pp. 22–44.

42. Ibid., preface.

43. See, for example, Deepak Lal, *The Poverty of "Development Economics"* (London: Institute of Economic Affairs, 1983); and Tony Killick, "Twenty-Five Years in Development: The Rise and Impending Decline of Market Solutions," *Development Policy Review, 4* (June 1986), pp. 99–116.

44. Tony Killick, *A Reaction Too Far: Economic Theory and the Role of the State in Developing Countries* (London: Overseas Development Institute, 1989), pp. 21–32.

45. Ibid.

46. Ibid., p. 63.

47. Ibid.

48. Bjorn Hettne, "Three Worlds of Crisis for the Nation State," *Development, 2/3* (1988), pp. 14–25.

49. Ibid., p. 20.

50. Kempe Ronald Hope, Sr., *An Assessment of the Economic Performance of the Guyana State Corporation Group of Corporations,* p. 48.

51. Richard Hemming and Ali M. Mansoor, *Privatization and Public Enterprises,* p. 19.

52. Johannes F. Linn, review of Pat Devine, *Democracy and Economic Planning* (Boulder, CO: Westview Press, 1988), *Finance and Development, 26* (March 1989), p. 51.

53. See John Toye, *Dilemmas of Development: Reflections on the Counter-Revolution in Development Theory and Policy,* pp. 22–159.

54. See W. Arthur Lewis, "The State of Development Theory," *American Economic Review, 74* (March 1984), pp. 1–10.

55. Walter Elkan, for example, has regarded the intellectual response to the Liberal–Orthodox theory as a "major contribution to the literature on the problems facing Third World countries" and "a brilliant display of theory." See his review of Deepak Lal, *The Poverty of "Development Economics"* (London: Institute of Economic Affairs, 1983) in *Economic Journal, 94* (December 1984), pp. 1006–7.

56. John Toye, *Dilemmas of Development: Reflections on the Counter-Revolution in Development Theory and Policy,* p. 98.

57. Deepak Lal, "The Political Economy of Economic Liberalization," *The World Bank Economic Review, 1* (January 1987), p. 293.

58. Ibid.

59. Colin Simmons, "Economic Development and Economic History," pp. 18–19.

60. See Deepak Lal, *The Poverty of "Development Economics,"* pp. 5–16.

——— Chapter 2 ———

Tax Policy and Savings Mobilization

Tax policy and savings mobilization mechanisms are the two primary sets of internal levers policy makers have at their disposal to influence and control fiscal policy on the revenue side. Fiscal policy is that segment of national economic policy that is primarily concerned with the receipts and expenditures of the central government, with the relation between those two flows, and with the economic effects of those receipts (primarily from taxation) and expenditures, for all the functions in which governments are now engaged.

Third World countries cannot carry out the complex tasks of economic development they face unless they have access to certain levels of funds and maintain a certain level of accumulation. Maintaining such accumulation presumes a transformation of the entire economic structure and increased productivity in the leading sectors of the economy. Only by expanding production can the growth of the national product serve as a source of increased accumulation and contribute to further economic development. Through this accumulation process, additional savings can be mobilized through the tax system.

Tax Policy and Development

The quantity of resources derived from taxation is determined to a large extent by the type of tax system that is introduced. Third World countries differ markedly in the type of tax system that can be implemented. The factors that influence the nature of their tax systems include, but are not limited to, the type of tax system that existed in the past, the political system, the extent of state intervention in the economy, the rate and state of economic development, the inflation rate, and so on.[1]

The most salient characteristic of taxation is its compulsory nature. There is no quid pro quo relationship of taxes paid and benefits received by the citizenry. So far, all attempts to establish a relationship between taxes paid and benefits received by the citizenry have failed. There is no way of "ascertaining the true benefits."[2] Where public goods are relatively "pure" and the exclusion principle does not apply, there are "no discrete outputs that are appropriable by individuals."[3] However, the generally accepted goals of taxation are (1) efficient resource allocation, (2) full employment with price stability, (3) a satisfactory distribution of income, and (4) a highly stable rate· of economic growth. These generally accepted goals of taxation have to be judged by certain criteria as to how they are fulfilled.

Four general criteria can be developed to evaluate taxes: (1) allocational efficiency, (2) equity, (3) administrative feasibility, and (4) revenue productivity. Allocational efficiency is concerned with the economic effects of taxation on the pattern of resource allocation. Equity refers to different taxes and how each tax redistributes income and wealth among the citizens in such a way as to narrow the gap between the poor and the rich. Administrative feasibility encompasses the problems of how efficiently a particular tax can be administered. Finally, revenue productivity deals with the ability of a tax to maximize government revenues. These are standard criteria used in taxation theory for the purpose of evaluating various taxes. However, while the criteria for evaluating various taxes are generally agreed upon, there is no agreement on an ideal tax system for all countries. A country's tax system must be reviewed periodically as development proceeds. Dependence on various taxes for revenues must be modified as a country's economy changes. The aim should always be a tax system that will be adequate, flexible, and in harmony with the emerging pattern of economic activity.[4] Furthermore, these general criteria for appraising a tax system may be in conflict with each other. Neutrality may be in conflict with revenue productivity criteria, and revenue productivity may be in conflict with equity criteria.

In examining the literature on tax structure in Third World countries, one finds that almost all of the authors seem to agree that the tax system must transfer resources from the private to the public sector so that the public sector will have the capability of carrying out those functions that are basic to the role of government, as well as those related to the development of the countries.[5] The tax system must also induce a transfer of resources within the private sector away from low-priority toward high-priority uses. Taxes put resources in the hands of governments, and these resources can be used to carry out certain investment programs that are supposed to be productive to the economy, especially in the long run.

In the early stages of the economic development of the United Kingdom and the United States, their fiscal structure as a whole favored accumulation and capital formation and discriminated against consumption. The economic development of these countries was brought about largely by the efforts of a dynamic private enterprise; and to enable it to plough back its increasing incomes into investment, the structure of taxation was made highly regressive and the fiscal structure as a whole tended to redistribute the national income in favor of investors and savers.

In the Third World, however, as the public sector attempted to play an increasing role in accelerating development, it was not reasonable to finance the development outlay of the public sector by depending entirely upon regressive taxes. In a democratic type of country, such a distribution of tax burden, apart from being, as Kaldor points out, "contrary to the sense of justice and equity of a democratic society,"[6] may also create social discontent, which may hinder the process of economic development itself. Besides, there is a much greater concentration of income and wealth in the hands of a very small proportion of the population in the Third World, and the process of economic development itself tends to magnify these concentrations. Some of these concentrations of income and wealth emanate from nonentrepreneurial sources such as rent and interest, and the persons in possession of such wealth and income have no tradition of saving and productive investment; but they are inclined to dissipate their income into nonfunctional consumption and unproductive investment. Therefore, as noted by Tripathy, tax policy in the Third World, as an instrument of development finance for the public sector, has to be geared effectively to the taxation of nonentrepreneurial incomes, providing, at the same time, adequate incentive to the private sector undertaking useful production and essential investment.[7]

Although in the early stages of the economic development of the United Kingdom and the United States the tax structure was predominantly regressive, with complete dependence of the tax system on outlay taxes, the position has been fundamentally reversed in modern times, and the taxes on income and wealth are more important in their tax structure than the taxes on outlay. As a matter of fact, in the industrial countries, in general, indirect consumption taxes now account for less than one-fifth of total revenue.

Public savings in the Third World nations are bound to remain small if their tax–income ratios are not substantially increased. The existing tax structure in many Third World countries is not conducive to a rapid growth of tax revenues unless there are frequent changes in coverage and rates of taxation. In a 1975 publication, Chelliah found that the average tax ratio in the Third World countries was 15.1 percent, compared with 13.6 percent in his 1971 publication.[8] A 1979 publication disclosed that the average tax ratio had increased slightly to 16.1 percent.[9] In a more recent abstract, the average tax ratio for Third World countries was found to be 20.4 percent.[10] However, in spite of this general increase in tax ratios, the average level of taxation in these countries is still considerably less than in developed countries. The primary reason for this variation is the wide difference in per capita income levels. When the two groups of countries are compared, per capita income differences are clearly associated with tax-level differences.[11]

Tax ratios measure the level of taxation in a country. This is usually judged in terms of the ratio of taxes to some measure of national product. What elements should be included in the numerator and in the denominator of the ratio depends upon what aspect of the governmental role one wishes this ratio to reflect or signify, and on what one intends to show by international comparisons of tax levels. The standard approach has been to use the ratio of all taxes and tax-like charges to gross national product at market prices. Hence, the overall tax ratio shows the proportion of national income that is compulsorily transferred from private hands into the government sector for public purposes. As such, the ratio gives an idea of (a) the division of responsibilities between the public and the private sectors, and (b) the degree of control that the government can potentially exercise over the disposition of purchasing power in the economy.[12] Tax ratios and changes in them over time are subject to control by governments. Nevertheless, the changes in tax ratios brought about in different Third World countries are partly dependent on major characteristics of the economy that have a bearing on taxable capacity.

Tax ratios have been widely regarded as an index of the size of the public sector, and many authors have attempted to explain the variations in the size of the public sector as reflected in tax ratio differences between different countries as well as over time. These studies have tried to discover whether there is any measurable relationship between economic characteristics, including the existing level of development, and tax ratios. The majority of the studies have been in the nature of cross-section analysis. The pioneering study of tax ratio variations, explained by different economic and sociopolitical factors, was done by Sir W. Arthur Lewis and Alison Martin,[13] who concluded that the proportion of national income spent on basic public services varies not so much with income as with the "progressiveness" of the rulers or electorate of the state. Williamson used per capita income as an indicator of the stages of development and fitted an exponential function to data for thirty-three countries. His results showed that there was a distinct positive relationship between the revenue ratio and per capita income. However, the differences in revenue share were found to be less pronounced than those in per capita income.[14]

Plasschaert used per capita income and import/GNP ratio as determinants to explain variations in the ratio of government revenue to GNP.[15] The import ratio turned out to be significant both when used alone and when used in conjunction with per capita income; per capita income itself did not emerge as a significant determinant of the revenue ratio. Hinrichs also found that "openness," as measured by the import ratio, not per capita income, is a major determinant of government revenue shares of gross national product.[16] Lotz and Morss attempted to examine the relationship between the tax ratio differences and differences in per capita income and degree of openness.[17] They used the ratio of the sum of imports and exports to GNP, rather than the import ratio or the export ratio, as the index of openness. They found both income and openness to be significant explanatory variables, positively related to the tax ratio; and together they explained a high proportion of the variance.

In a later work, Lotz and Morss inserted new variables into their analysis. They introduced the monetization factor as an explanatory variable; this resulted in a distinct increase in the explained variance, but lowered considerably the significance of per capita income.[18] While important gaps remain to be covered, their results suggest that the availability of taxable bases is a more important determinant of tax levels in Third World countries than variations in the demand for government expenditures. Their suggestion is based on findings that factors measuring tax administrative capacity, while not very meaningful as indicators of demand for public services, are highly significant in explaining the tax ratios in Third World countries.

It can be claimed that, "conceptually, the tax ratio or share of national income appropriated by the government can be determined by four broad groups of factors."[19] On the side of demand for government services, there may be two groups of factors: (1) the need for services arising out of "objective" conditions, and (2) the preferences of the people and the leaders as between public and private services, including the institutional arrangements arising from them. On the side of raising resources or supply of funds, two operative factors may be suggested: The first is the ability of the people to pay taxes, and the second is the ability of the government to collect taxes.

While a simple comparison of tax ratios gives some indication of relative levels of taxation in various areas, however, any inference on tax performance or effort based merely on such a comparison fails to take into account the fact that some countries are more favorably placed to levy taxes: that is, they can be said to have greater taxable capacity than others. It has been pointed out, though, that the successful measurement of taxable capacity, used in many studies, depends critically on the a priori justification of the explanatory variables as affecting only taxable capacity and not at all on either demands for higher public expenditures or willingness to tax.[20] It is not surprising, therefore, that Bird has argued that the distinction between "capacity" and "willingness" is very fuzzy and, indeed, "it is inherently extremely difficult to specify correctly any model of (usable) taxable capacity to quantify what Musgrave has called the tax handles available to a country."[21]

If we accept, however, that something called "taxable capacity" exists, then the next step is calculation of tax effort. Tax effort is defined as the ratio of the actual tax ratio in a particular country to what would be predicted on the basis of the taxable capacity concept. A tax effort ratio of less than one is usually taken to mean that the country exploits its estimated tax potential less than the average. In other words, it has a preference for a level of taxation below the average, or a low tax effort. Tax effort is a process that may take several forms, including reform of existing taxes, improvement in administration, and introduction of new taxes. The indices of tax effort should not be used in a mechanistic way, but rather should be considered useful additional information in judging the scope for more taxes.[22]

The tax ratio and tax effort concepts discussed above are based on two sets of techniques for comparative analysis. One technique equates tax effort to the ratio of taxes (or revenues) to income. Such a straightforward comparison implicitly assumes that total income is the only relevant indicator of intercountry differences in taxable capacity. The second technique, a stochastic approach, gives markedly different results. It involves the assumption that the tax ratio (T/Y) is an appropriate reflection of taxable capacity if it is adjusted for intercountry variations in factors that are assumed to reflect intercountry differences in the size of the tax base and the ability to collect taxes. While clearly preferable to a straight tax ratio for comparative purposes, the stochastic approach has a number of methodological problems. In general, the aggregative regression approach does not allow a desirable examination of the kinds of explicit relationships between particular taxes and particular economic structure variables that would seem useful for purposes of making intercountry comparisons of taxable capacity and tax effort.

Bearing these facts in mind, Bahl proceeded to develop an alternative method for making intercountry tax effort comparisons in which the tax effort index derived may be related to the intensity of use of specific taxes. He designated his methodology the "representative tax system approach," and it involves application of average effective rates to a standard set of tax bases.[23] This approach does allow an examination of marginal effects. Taxable capacity is defined in this approach as the total tax amount that would be collected if each country applied an identical set of effective rates to the selected tax bases—that is, as the yield of a representative tax system.

The application of the representative tax system approach gave a distribution that did not differ significantly from that obtained in the analyses employing the aggregate regression approach.[24] However, three general observations can be pointed out. First, the level of taxable capacity responds most to changes originating in basic sector income. Second, the yield of a representative system is more responsive to a change in income generated in a particular sector if it is accompanied by a change in total income than if it reflects only a sectoral redistribution of some constant amount of income. Third, the criticism that tax effort indices and rankings vary erratically with changes in the estimating procedure used was not strengthened by the representative approach.

Other studies have attempted other approaches to measure what essentially seems to be tax ratios and tax efforts. Heller developed a utility maximization model of the fiscal behavior of the public sector by assuming that the public sector reflects the actions of a set of public decision makers.[25] His results confirm that only a small proportion of marginal tax increases is allocated to investment, with the bulk used for public consumption. Hence, increases in tax revenue positively influence the expenditure categories, and tend to reduce total borrowing, and vice versa.[26]

Tax effort studies and methodologies, however, have not been immune to criticism. The International Monetary Fund (IMF) itself, where most of these studies were conducted, pointed out that "due caution must be exercised in interpreting the tax effort indices."[27] Tanzi notes, with regard to tax structure development, that clearly up to now the marriage between the general theories and the statistical analysis carried out thus far to verify those theories have not taken place.[28] He further states that "the truth of the matter is that we still do not have an answer to the question of what kind of tax structure a country should have at a given stage of economic development."[29]

Bird, on the other hand, postulates five propositions he considers his basic criticisms of the tax effort studies:[30] (1) There is inadequate a priori justification for the use of the selected variables as measures of taxable capacity. (2) The data are very bad; these data problems are very serious, and no one can truthfully claim to be aware of all the biases they impart to the result. (3) Virtually all of the work that has been done on quantitative international comparisons is cross-sectional in nature, yet the policy inferences drawn from this work invariably concern changes in particular areas. (4) The nature of the norms applied in tax effort analysis leaves them subject to distortions. Further, the implicit norm in the usual use of the tax effort index may also be criticized as being proportional. (5) The conventional tax effort exercise lends itself too readily to misuse to be worth further attention at this stage of our knowledge. Despite these criticisms, however, the general tendency has been to use these studies, particularly in the international development agencies, as the background for policy decisions.

Apart from tax structure, tax effort, and tax ratio studies, a significant amount of work has also been done on tax incidence in developing countries. It seems, though, that the major reason for this amount of work has been "the desire to provide quantitative, and therefore supposedly definitive, support for particular policy positions—which usually means to demonstrate the case for a more progressive tax system."[31] De Wulf has provided a survey and critique of the major studies.[32] The shifting assumptions used in those studies are the traditional ones. Indirect taxes were generally assumed to be shifted forward, and direct taxes unshifted. Corporate profits taxes were assumed to be shifted forward in various proportions, but no backward shifting was considered. The shifting assumptions adopted on property and wealth taxes varied. Some studies assumed no shifting, while others allowed for some forward shifting of the property tax on rental property. The proportion of this tax that is assumed to be shifted forward varies greatly from study to study.

Three major reasons for undertaking tax incidence studies can probably be distinguished. First, most studies wanted to analyze the redistribution of income through the fiscal system and concentrated on the efforts of taxes on different income size classes of the population. They were concerned with vertical equity. A second group of incidence studies concentrated on the differential tax burden between the rural and the urban sectors and on the transfer of resources between these two sectors. This emphasis stems from concern with both horizontal equity and policy for development. The third category of studies was also concerned with the horizontal equity between various geographical areas or between various ethnic components of a country.

All of the studies favored redistribution of income from the rich to the poor. A progressive tax system was also deemed a desirable feature of fiscal policy and, as such, results showing the redistribution effects of fiscal policy were welcomed, even though the lowest-income classes were often found to contribute a considerable fraction of their income in taxes, and those showing regressive taxes led to recommendations for the elimination of the regressivity.

Basically, from both a conceptual and a statistical point of view, tax incidence studies are too questionable to bear the weight of interpretation that is sometimes put upon them. "At most," write Bird and De Wulf, "properly constructed and heavily qualified incidence estimates can be a useful supplement to efforts to appraise and improve tax systems in developing countries: they cannot in themselves provide a road map to the better world, however."[33]

Tax policy in Third World countries and, hence, the relative contributions of the two classes of taxes (indirect and direct) have not changed much during the past two decades, however, despite the proliferation of empirical work done on tax structures in those countries. Because of the nature of the tax bases in the Third World, indirect taxation—customs duties, excises, sales taxes, and some miscellaneous types—remains the dominant form of taxation in those nations. Those taxes provide approximately 60 percent of the tax revenues of the forty-four countries with per capita income below $800 and half of the revenue for the thirty-nine countries with per capita income between $800 and $3,000, while, by contrast, the countries with per capita income exceeding $3,000 received approximately 30 percent of their revenues from indirect taxes.[34] On average, taxes on goods and services account for about half the total government revenue in Third World countries.

The theoretical and practical merits, however, of retaining the present predominant reliance on indirect taxes in Third World countries have begun to be reassessed. In particular, three principles now circulating in the literature are advocated as a useful basis for tax policy.[35] The first is that tax revenues can be increased in an efficient manner by taxing goods and factors with inelastic demand or supply. Second, taxation, concerned with distribution, externalities, or market failure, should go to the root of the problem to avoid distortions resulting from price changes. Third, taxes that seek to counteract problems with distortions or inequities should be carefully examined for possible impacts on other policy objectives. Given the constraints facing Third World nations, however, the dominant use of indirect taxation is likely to persist in those countries for some time into the foreseeable future. Consequently, what needs to be pursued are attempts to maximize other tax revenue sources within the existing constraints and development prospects of the Third World nations.

It may also be possible to improve the efficiency and distributional effects of the indirect taxes. In particular, rate differentiation of varying types may be considered as a means of establishing a system of progressive sales and excise tax rates that can make the incidence of indirect taxes progressive. Such a reform measure, however, as useful and equitable as it may be, has to weigh equity and other gains against increased administrative costs. Also of importance is the requirement that tax administration be improved in Third World nations. Irrespective of the nature of the tax structure, if tax administration is inefficient, then tax compliance and tax revenue collections will also be deficient.

Historically, one of the most significant advantages of indirect taxes is that they can be more effectively enforced than the direct taxes. This is so primarily because the indirect taxes are collected either at importation or from business firms where goods are subject to physical inspection, as opposed to the individual income tax, where compliance requires volunteered declarations, especially by the self-employed. Because of the growth and size of the subterranean sector in the Third World, which is discussed in chapter 5, only about 1 to 3 percent of the total population in those countries complies with the compulsory requirement to pay income taxes.

The low income tax compliance rates in the Third World are also a function of the many opportunities to shelter income in those countries. Such opportunities are not usually available with indirect taxes. One point that needs to be made here, however, is that the low compliance by the self-employed is not just a Third World phenomenon. Compliance by the self-employed is also a problem in the developed countries. In the United States, for example, the compliance rate for informal supplier income is only 20 percent, compared with an overall compliance rate of approximately 80 percent and a wages and salaries rate of approximately 95 percent.

Perhaps the Third World nations need to consider, on a case-by-case basis, the possibility of implementing a program of tax amnesty before giving any further consideration to tax reform. Recent attempts at tax reform have generally not been successful in generating additional tax revenues and growth to justify the cost of the reform exercise. Accordingly, skepticism is justified regarding exaggerated claims made in favor of any particular reform strategy.[36] Under a tax amnesty scheme, taxpayers would be given an opportunity to file delinquent tax returns and be exempt from any penalties for failure to file in the past, and would be required to pay any past taxes owed for a specified past period of time, say five years. Implementing tax amnesty will, undoubtedly, increase the number of tax filers, particularly if the program includes severe penalties for those found not to have complied after the program's expiration date.

The tax base, moreover, will increase and thereby improve future tax collections. A well-regulated tax amnesty program can ensure that those individuals who utilize the amnesty are not only added to the list of taxpayers but also can be audited in the future. Tax amnesties can therefore decrease the need to raise taxes in the future because of the expanded tax base. As a consequence, regular taxpayers may also benefit from tax amnesties as nonpayers are brought onto the tax roster.[37] In Colombia, for example, an estimated US$4 billion flowed back to the country in 1991 as a result of an across-the-board amnesty for tax evaders that was coupled with a law allowing the legal possession of U.S. currency.

It would seem that would-be tax reformers need to heed the advice of Bird, who bluntly states that "too often would-be tax reform-mongers have been led astray in the futile search for the perfect fiscal instrument in theoretical terms," and, as such, "it is no wonder that tax administrators often view would-be tax reformers to be little more than residents of an ivory tower, who descend after the battle is largely over to shoot the wounded."[38] Bird further states that those who would change the world must first understand it, since starting from such a basis appears to offer a better prospect of attaining an acceptably fair and generally efficient tax system than the adoption of the latest up-to-date model of fiscal perfection from the academic drawing board.[39] The message here is as loud and as clear as it was in chapter 1: Reform ideas that have scientific merit but do not promise a solution to the development problems of the Third World are of little use to the process of economic progress required by the citizens of the Third World.

In other words, practical policy relevance, rather than esoteric academic formulations, is of significance to the development process. One of the reasons why development theory has failed to result in economic development, when applied in the Third World, is that it never took into consideration the historical, institutional, and absorptive-capacity elements of the development mandate. In terms of application to tax reform, it is necessary that those who are undertaking such an exercise should both understand thoroughly the existing tax administration and assess realistically the probability of rapid improvement.

Moreover, any changes in tax structure must be closely matched to the economic structure. This requires an even more thorough understanding of national economic conditions and the political and risk factors that impact upon decision making. This is important because of the need to have smooth and ongoing implementation that can easily be affected by redistributive concerns. In the final analysis, implementation is crucial to the successful outcomes of tax reform. Accordingly, all of the obvious factors that can impact upon the implementation process must be considered. Consequently, it is now generally recognized that the key to successful tax reform is to design a tax structure that can be administered adequately with the available resources while at the same time making the best possible use of those resources from a long-term perspective.

Savings Mobilization

Most of the literature on savings in Third World countries has been concerned primarily with the determinants and nature of the savings function, as well as the role and impact of domestic savings in the development process. The rate of savings, historically, has been regarded as a key performance indicator in the development process, and Third World countries have always been encouraged to increase their savings ratio as a necessary step for achieving economic growth. Increases in the savings ratio were, naturally, expected to lead to a reduction in dependence on foreign aid by the Third World countries.

As a result of that somewhat general consensus, the theme of the literature shifted from the necessity for savings to measures for mobilizing domestic savings for productive investment and, hence, economic growth. A 1962 publication of the United Nations indicated that "high rates of economic growth have long been associated with high rates of investment and savings."[40] It further stated that although, theoretically, investment can be financed by any mix of domestic and foreign capital, historically, domestic sources have generally supplied the bulk of savings for rapidly growing economies.[41]

Domestic savings is defined as the sum total of all savings in all sectors for any given country. For some Third World countries, it is possible to arrive at net domestic savings by deducting capital consumption allowances. It is often preferable, however, to contrast countries on the basis of gross savings, since the practices with respect to methods of computing capital consumption allowances vary considerably from country to country. The major categories of savings are (1) savings by households, (2) savings by the business sector, and (3) savings by government. The magnitude of savings in each of the three categories is directly affected by government policies.

There are two basic ways governments can attempt to increase domestic savings rates. First, they can encourage greater savings by the private sector (households and businesses). The success of this approach lies in the incentives provided to induce people to forego consumption. The second approach is for the government to appropriate private sector income directly. This is done primarily through taxation, as explained in the previous section.

Writing in 1952, Adler argued that in order to obtain the desired increase in savings and to direct those savings into the most desired channels, it appears essential that the government curtail, through taxation, the availability of additional output for consumption and utilize the additional income for an increase of development expenditures.[42] Van der Mensbrugghe has argued that savings by households is dependent on a great variety of factors, a number of which can be influenced by government policies.[43] First among the factors that may be influenced is the rate of growth of disposable income. Another factor is the distribution of income.[44] The higher the level of disposable income, the greater the possibility of increased savings. This is very important, since in Third World countries, the level of per capita income is usually low, most of it is required for satisfying the bare necessities of life, and the margin of income available for capital formation is quite low. Thus, the low level of per capita productivity in Third World countries explains the low savings ratios in those countries.[45]

The low savings ratio in Third World countries arises not only because of the independent behavior of the consumption function at low levels of incomes, but also because of the phenomenon characterized by Duesenberry as "demonstration effect," arising out of the tendency to emulate the higher levels of consumption both on the part of the low-income groups within the domestic economy and on the part of low-income countries at the international level.[46] Thus, the demonstration effect operates on both the national and international levels.

The possibility that the demonstration effect may inhibit savings in developing countries cannot be denied, but the importance of the demonstration effect can easily be exaggerated at the international level. Bauer and Yamey have argued that the usual analysis of the international demonstration effect seems to omit certain major considerations that are relevant to the economic problems of Third World countries.[47] The international demonstration effect, for example, may operate to provide incentives for greater productive effort and enterprise in Third World countries. In such circumstances, consumption and investment are complementary; the higher level of consumption induces additional and more productive effort, which serves to generate incomes, which in turn renders possible both increased consumption and increased accumulation of capital.

The accumulation of savings makes possible the release of productive resources from consumption, which may then be utilized to add to the stock of productive capital, thereby promoting the expansion of output. It is for this reason that much has been made of various measures of savings as a key to the self-help performance of Third World countries. A country is considered to be doing well if the ratio of its domestic savings to its total output is high, or at least rising. Conversely, a low or falling savings ratio is often regarded as evidence of insufficient domestic effort.

Inferences along these lines would be reasonable if the efforts to save more were all that was needed to bring about a higher level of investment. In fact, however, attempts to raise the level of savings may be frustrated in a number of ways. For example, a reduction in consumption will help to raise savings only if total output is not adversely affected thereby, and the resources released from consumption are in fact utilized for additional investment. Where the additional savings are generated through higher tax revenues, and are used indirectly by the public sector for stepping up its own investment, no problem would arise. But where there is a spontaneous reduction in private consumption without a rise in public investment, this does not in the least imply that entrepreneurs would thereby be induced to add to their original planned level of investment. And if they did not do so, the effect of the fall in consumption would be to reduce total output and income to the point at which savings were no greater than the original planned level of investment. In these circumstances, the effort to save more would fail.[48]

As such, a marked increase in savings in Third World countries can be ensured in the long run primarily in association with the rise in real income. In the short run, an increase in total savings could perhaps be ensured by a rise in public savings by reducing government consumption or increasing government revenue, provided that no offsetting reactions take place in private savings. Taxation is one of the most powerful instruments for controlling the level and composition of national expenditure and influencing the allocation of real resources.

According to the classical school, the savings behavior of the people depends on the market interest rate. Keynesian economic theory, however, doubts the validity of the market interest rate as a measure of time preference and saving behavior. It suggests that the rate of interest is instead determined partly by the preference of individuals and firms to hold funds and to be liquid. It can be added, as Gianaris has done, that in domestic monetary policies, the ratio of exports to national income and primarily the revenues from exploitation of natural resources, especially oil and metals, plays an important role in the determination of the savings ratio.[49]

In most countries, however, the actual level of domestic savings falls short of the potential level of domestic savings, which might be viewed as the difference between the national product that could be produced, given the full utilization of employable productive resources in a natural and technological environment, and what a policy maker might regard as essential consumption.[50] Wolfson has argued that the potential level of savings is a normative concept, therefore, based on the social valuations of the body politic.[51] Further, particularly in early stages of development, a substantial part of the potential domestic savings may be wasted by idleness and misemployment.[52] It should, therefore, be a prime task of fiscal policy to further savings and to mobilize it into productive channels.

Some economists, notably Shaw, have stated that the most effective steps governments can take to stimulate the mobilization of savings constitute financial liberalization.[53] This means the dismantling of government controls over financial markets. Shaw regards liberalization as the key to "financial deepening," the accumulation of financial assets at a pace faster than the accumulation of nonfinancial wealth. He argues that financial liberalization tends to raise ratios of private domestic savings to income and permits the financial process of mobilizing and allocating savings to displace, in some degree, the fiscal process, inflation, and foreign aid.[54] Furthermore, Shaw indicates that liberalization opens the way to superior allocations of savings by widening and diversifying the financial markets in which investment opportunities compete for the savings flow. In the repressed economy, savings flow mainly to the savers' own investments. In the liberalized economy, savers are offered a wider menu of portfolio choice, and the market for their savings is extended.[55]

Zuvekas, on the other hand, agrees that financial liberalization can make a major contribution to the mobilization of domestic savings but does not endorse the concept with Shaw's enthusiasm. He points out, first, that there are serious social and political constraints to liberalization in many Third World countries, and the objectives of liberalization can easily be thwarted by opponents of measures that suddenly free markets once tightly regulated.[56] Second, while liberalization may have a positive effect on economic growth, measures to reduce inflationary pressures tend to discriminate against the lower-income segments of the population, thus widening income inequalities.[57]

However, many governments have been uneasy or impatient with policies to increase private savings, foreign or domestic. Bhatt and Meerman have observed that some governments have distrusted their ability to steer private capital to socially appropriate investments. As a consequence, many governments have attempted to follow an explicit public savings strategy to draw resources into the public sector by fiscal means and to undertake public investments with these resources.[58] Such efforts usually demand a substantial increase in taxes and, in fact, some of the emphasis on increasing taxes in Third World countries has, as a rationale, the need to increase public savings.[59]

From the foregoing discussion, some broad observations can be made with regard to domestic savings in the development process. One general conclusion that emerges is that aggregate savings is a function of a number of interdependent variables that together with savings propensities determine the course of economic development.[60] Second, maintenance of high investment levels is largely a function of domestic savings performance; capital inflow from abroad serves more as a catalyst and as a factor in relaxing the foreign-exchange constraint than as a major factor in supporting rising levels of investment.[61] Third, the domestic savings rate is positively related to the level of income and its growth rate and also seems to be a function of the size of a country.[62]

The mobilization of savings is an important role of government in the process of development. Increasing domestic savings, however, may often be politically difficult. Since taxes are never popular, those governments whose political base is weak may find it difficult to raise tax rates, introduce new taxes, or even enforce existing tax laws.[63] In general, however, depending on the mobilization means to be used, it may be necessary to influence savings with respect to size as well as composition. This requires optimum use of the existing financial institutions.[64]

Savings determine the rate at which productive capacity and, hence, income can grow. Generally, the more rapidly growing Third World countries have had higher savings rates than the countries with lower growth. Those Third World countries with growth rates below 3 percent (twenty-two countries) had a savings rate of 19 percent for the period 1965–87; for the medium-growth countries (fifty-one countries with a growth rate between 3 and 7 percent), the savings rate for the same period was 18.5 percent; while for the high-growth countries (seven countries with a growth rate exceeding 7 percent), the savings rate was 28 percent for the same period.[65] From the point of view of the relative national income of the countries, the savings rate for the low-income countries increased from 18.3 percent in 1965 to 25.4 percent in 1987; for the middle-income countries the rate increased from 18.7 percent in 1965 to 21.9 percent in 1987; and for the high-income countries the savings rate increased only marginally from 20.8 percent in 1965 to 21.2 percent in 1987.[66] From a regional perspective, however, sub-Saharan Africa has the lowest savings rate, declining from an average of 11 percent of GNP in 1965–73 to approximately 5 percent of GNP in 1982–92, while the East Asian countries have the highest savings rate, increasing from an average of 20 percent of GNP in 1965–73 to approximately 32 percent of GNP in 1982–92.[67]

Undoubtedly, the Third World countries need to improve their efforts at savings mobilization and thereby increase their access to development finance. The key to successful efforts to promote savings for development purposes lies in a reversal of the fiscal and monetary policies currently being pursued in the Third World nations. Excessive state intervention with respect to diminishing interest rates, high reserve requirements, and some credit policies, such as subsidized loan rates for public enterprises, have not only affected savings mobilization but also disrupted the efficient allocation of scarce resources.[68] Despite their intentions, selective credit policies have not had the desired impact on resource allocation and economic growth but, rather, have resulted in negative effects on domestic savings mobilization and financial development. The major beneficiaries of directed credit have been the public enterprises, especially when foreign financing is taken into account.

According to the World Bank's *World Development Report 1989,* the share of public enterprises in nongovernmental borrowing from domestic banks in 1983–85, for example, was 56 percent in Guyana, 43 percent in Mexico, 25 percent in Nepal, and 18 percent in Brazil. At the same time, however, the share of public enterprises in value added was much lower. In Guyana and Mexico it was less than 30 percent, and in Brazil and Nepal it was less than 5 percent. Improving savings mobilization in the Third World countries must include policies that increase interest rates for savings, stabilize prices, increase access to financial institutions, and reform the domestic financial institutions. In general, a liberalization policy to enhance the functioning of the financial system needs to be implemented.

Assurance needs to be given by governments against loss of savings from inflation. Or better still, a significant effort must be made by Third World governments to curb inflation. A most important deterrent to household savings is inflation. Most households, particularly savers of small amounts, have no satisfactory means of protecting their savings from depreciation due to inflation. When prices have steadily increased, the willingness to accumulate savings in the form of deposits, government securities, or life insurance is undermined or eventually destroyed. In Israel, for example, the introduction of special schemes linking the value of savings to the cost of living or the dollar exchange rate attracted a large volume of savings, most of it new. A World Bank study of eighty-one Third World countries, on the other hand, found that the ratio of liquid liabilities to GNP (a measure of financial depth) fell by 1.70 percentage points in response to a 1.0 percentage point increase in the rate of inflation.[69]

The second mechanism relates to the use of the interest rate. The savings rates of interest need to be raised in Third World countries. The low nature of the nominal rate of interest on deposits, relative to the rate of inflation in those countries, lessens the attractiveness of formal savings and the use of formal financial institutions as savings conduits. A disadvantage of a low interest rate is that it results in the withholding of savings.[70] Higher rates of interest will induce the public to increase its savings further in the form of deposits and bonds, rather than divert those savings toward the purchase of gold, jewels, or hoards of foreign exchange. Low interest rates may also divert potential savings toward less useful investments.

In Ghana, for example, it was found that the interest rate was by no means enough to offset triple-digit inflation, and the result was a reduction of bank deposits. Similarly, in Jamaica, the real interest rate in 1978 was −29 percent and the real value of deposits fell by 22 percent. In Brazil, where interest rates had traditionally been adjusted to inflation, a negative real interest rate appeared in 1979–80 because of a break in that tradition, which resulted in a large-scale decrease in the real value of bank deposits.[71] By contrast, the positive effects of higher real interest rates for the mobilization of additional savings can be clearly demonstrated in those nations that have implemented interest rate liberalization policies or more comprehensive reforms of the financial market, for example, Taiwan, South Korea, Indonesia, and Turkey. Another World Bank study using 1985 data found that the ratio of liquid liabilities to GNP rose by 0.75 percentage point in response to a 1.0 percentage point increase in the nominal interest rate paid on deposits.[72]

Overall, higher real interest rates are likely to lead to financial deepening. A stimulation of savings calls for the application of higher interest rates in Third World countries. In those countries that have pursued an active interest rate policy, it has led to significant increases in time and savings deposits and, consequently, to an increase in the credit supply of the financial sector. Households clearly prefer to hold their savings in the form of claims on financial institutions. Hence, any further incentives provided by these financial institutions, in the form of higher interest rates, will tend to increase the volume of household savings. Furthermore, higher interest rates will tend to encourage much more economical use of capital and thus diminish the deficiency of resources for development. In addition, higher interest rates will discourage capital flight and encourage the local accumulation of financial resources.[73]

Since for the great majority of Third World nations capital and foreign exchange are scarce, the outflow of capital on a large scale is very disturbing. Capital flight can be regarded as a diversion of resources from domestic real investment to foreign financial investments. The country of origin loses the associated benefits of such capital even if the yield from such capital were to be repatriated in the future. The loss of benefits include income and tax revenues. Also, there are consequences such as redistribution of wealth from country of origin to country of destination and the inducement of external borrowing.[74] Flight capital is difficult to measure, but economists at J.P. Morgan, a New York bank, estimated that the stock of such wealth (assets held abroad by nonbank private sector residents) of the fifteen largest debtor nations had amounted to $300 billion by the end of 1987.[75] At the time, this was more than half their total foreign debt. However, the Inter-American Development Bank has conservatively estimated the accumulated stock of flight capital from Latin America at $170 billion in 1990. This is the equivalent of approximately one-third of the region's total external debt.[76] This issue is further discussed in chapter 3.

Increasing savings in the Third World necessarily entails improving access to financial institutions. In the Third World, the urban bias in development policy, as discussed in chapter 4, has resulted in a concentration of financial institutions in the urban area, much to the neglect of rural areas. Consequently, and as discussed in chapter 5, there is a greater participation by all classes in informal finance activities in the rural sector. Financial institutions need to "branch" out into the rural areas to allow rural residents access to such institutions. In other words, the rural money markets need to be tapped not only through local branch establishment but also through the offering of appropriate savings and credit instruments suited to the needs of the rural population. The success of savings mobilization through an enlarged branch network would depend on the appropriateness of the financial instruments that are actually offered.

Evidence of the success of financial institutions serving the rural areas can be found, for example, in the innovative approaches undertaken by the Rural Bank of Ghana and the Grameen Bank in Bangladesh. Both of these institutions represent well-documented case studies of successful lending and savings mobilization strategies in the rural areas.[77] These strategies include a convenient location, lending to like-minded individuals and groups of similar economic circumstances, lending based on the borrower's project and reputation rather than on collateral requirements, and the negotiation of loans in the familiar surroundings of potential borrowers, rather than at the desks of bank officers. Also, there are requirements of minimum savings to help develop a savings habit and, as well, the sense of responsibility and repayment morale of borrowers are strengthened by tying lending to savings mobilization.

Concluding Remarks

Tax policy and savings mobilization loom large in the efforts of Third World countries to finance development and, increasingly, both instruments are being scrutinized with an eye to improving and enhancing their contributions within the context of restructured economies. With respect to tax policy, although the relative contribution of indirect and direct taxes has not changed much during the past two decades, it would seem justifiable that Third World countries attempt to broaden their tax base and impose taxes at lower, flatter rates, and thereby increase income tax revenues and improved compliance, while reducing the burden on the poor. Perhaps a program of tax amnesty also needs to be considered.

The significance of savings lies in the further fact that access to foreign funds continues to diminish from both the supply point of view and the deteriorating capacity of the Third World nations to borrow. Faster growth, more investment, and greater financial depth all come partly from higher savings. The evidence suggests that higher real interest rates are associated with increased financial deepening and an increase in savings and investment. Also, the growth rates of those countries with positive real interest rates were found to be considerably higher, on.average, than those of the others. Third World countries must therefore continue to strive toward greater savings mobilization.

Notes

1. Ian Wallschutzsky, "Achieving Compliance in Developing Countries," *Bulletin for International Fiscal Documentation, 43* (May 1989), p. 234.
2. R. Musgrave, *The Theory of Public Finance* (New York: McGraw Hill, 1959), p. 134.
3. Jesse Burkhead and Jerry Miner, *Public Expenditure* (Chicago: Aldine, 1971), p. 196.
4. Robert B. Bangs, *Financing Economic Development: Fiscal Policy for Emerging Countries* (Chicago: University of Chicago Press, 1968), pp. 145–46.
5. Vito Tanzi, "The Theory of Tax Structure Development and the Design of Tax Structure Policy for Industrialization," in David T. Geithman (ed.), *Fiscal Policy for Industrialization in Latin America* (Gainesville: University of Florida Press, 1974), p. 50.
6. N. Kaldor, *Indian Tax Reform: Report of a Survey* (New Delhi: Government of India, Ministry of Finance, 1956), p. 1.
7. R.N. Tripathy, *Public Finance in Underdeveloped Countries* (Calcutta: World Press Private Limited, 1964), p. 96.
8. See Raja Chelliah, "Trends in Taxation in Developing Countries," *IMF Staff Papers, 18* (July 1971), pp. 254–331; and Raja Chelliah, et al., "Tax Ratios and Tax Effort in Developing Countries, 1969–71," *IMF Staff Papers, 22* (March 1975), pp. 187–205. The 1971 publication covers the period 1953–55 to 1966–68 while the 1975 publication covers 1969–71.
9. See Alan A. Tait, et al., "International Comparisons of Taxation for Selected Developing Countries, 1972–76," *IMF Staff Papers, 26* (March 1979), pp. 123–56.
10. International Monetary Fund, *Government Finance Statistics Yearbook, 11* (Washington, DC: 1987), p. 88.
11. Raja Chelliah, "Trends in Taxation in Developing Countries," pp. 280–81.
12. Ibid., p. 258.
13. Alison Martin and W. Arthur Lewis, "Patterns of Public Revenue and

Expenditure," *Manchester School, 24* (September 1956), pp. 203–244.

14. J.G. Williamson, "Public Expenditure and Revenue: An International Comparison," *Manchester School, 29* (January 1961), pp. 43–56.

15. See S. Plasschaert, *Taxation Capacity in Developing Countries*, Report No. EC–103 (Washington, DC: World Bank, 1962).

16. H.H. Hinrichs, "Determinants of Government Revenue Shares among Less-Developed Countries," *Economic Journal, 75* (September 1965), pp. 546–56.

17. J.R. Lotz and E.R. Morss, "Measuring 'Tax Effort' in Developing Countries," *IMF Staff Papers, 14* (November 1967), pp. 478–497.

18. J.R. Lotz and E.R. Morss, "A Theory of Tax Level Determinants for Developing Countries," *Economic Development and Cultural Change, 18* (April 1970), pp. 328–41.

19. Raja Chelliah, "Trends in Taxation in Developing Countries," p. 292.

20. R.W. Bahl, "A Regression Approach to Tax Effort and Tax Ratio Analysis," *IMF Staff Papers, 18* (November 1971), pp. 571–73.

21. R. Bird, "Assessing Tax Performance in Developing Countries: A Critical Review of the Literature," *Finanzarchiv, 34, 2* (1976), p. 253.

22. Kempe Ronald Hope, Sr., *Development Finance and the Development Process* (London: Greenwood Press, 1987), p. 6.

23. R.W. Bahl, "A Representative Tax System Approach to Measuring Tax Effort in Developing Countries," *IMF Staff Papers, 19* (March 1972), pp. 97–122.

24. Ibid., p. 119.

25. Peter Heller, "A Model of Public Fiscal Behaviour in Developing Countries: Aid, Investment and Taxation," *American Economic Review, 65* (June 1975), pp. 429–45.

26. Ibid., p. 441.

27. *IMF Survey* (June 3, 1974), p. 164.

28. Vito Tanzi, "The Theory of Tax Structure Development and the Design of Tax Structure Policy for Industrialization," pp. 62–63.

29. Ibid., p. 63.

30. R. Bird, "Assessing Tax Performance in Developing Countries: A Critical Review of the Literature," pp. 257–58.

31. R. Bird and Luc De Wulf, "Taxation and Income Distribution in Latin America: A Critical Review of Empirical Studies," *IMF Staff Papers, 20* (November 1973), p. 664.

32. Luc De Wulf, "Fiscal Incidence Studies in Developing Countries: Survey and Critique," *IMF Staff Papers, 22* (March 1975), pp. 61–131.

33. R. Bird and Luc De Wulf, "Taxation and Income Distribution in Latin America: A Critical Review of Empirical Studies," p. 677.

34. John F. Due, *Indirect Taxation in Developing Economies* (Baltimore: Johns Hopkins University Press, 1988), p. 208.

35. N.H. Stern, "Optimum Taxation and Tax Policy," *IMF Staff Papers, 31* (June 1984), pp. 368–69.

36. Malcolm Gillis, "Tax Reform: Lessons from Postwar Experience in Developing Nations," in Malcolm Gillis (ed.), *Tax Reform in Developing Countries* (Durham, NC: Duke University Press, 1989), pp. 492–520.

37. Elliot Uchitelle, "The Effectiveness of Tax Amnesty Programs in Selected

Countries," *Federal Reserve Bank of New York Quarterly Review, 14* (Autumn 1989), pp. 48–53.

38. Richard M. Bird, "The Administrative Dimensions of Tax Reform in Developing Countries," in Malcolm Gillis (ed.), *Tax Reform in Developing Countries* (Durham, NC: Duke University Press, 1989), pp. 330, 319.

39. Ibid.; and Richard M. Bird, *Tax Policy and Economic Development* (Baltimore: Johns Hopkins University Press, 1992), pp. 210–14.

40. United Nations, "Measures for Mobilizing Domestic Savings for Productive Investment," *Economic Bulletin for Asia and the Far East, 13* (December 1962), p. 1.

41. Ibid.

42. John H. Adler, "The Fiscal and Monetary Implementation of Development Programs," *American Economic Review, 42* (May 1952), pp. 584–611.

43. Jean van der Mensbrugghe, "Domestic Savings in Developing Countries," *Finance and Development, 9* (March 1972), pp. 36–39.

44. Ibid.

45. R.N. Tripathy, *Public Finance in Underdeveloped Countries*, p. 8.

46. J.S. Duesenberry, *Income, Saving and the Theory of Consumer Behavior* (Cambridge: Harvard University Press, 1949), p. 27.

47. P.T. Bauer and B.S. Yamey, *The Economics of Underdeveloped Countries* (Chicago: University of Chicago Press, 1957), pp. 137–42.

48. United Nations Conference on Trade, Aid and Development, *Problems and Policies of Financing* (New York: United Nations, 1968), pp. 160–61.

49. N.V. Gianaris, *Economic Development: Thought and Problems* (North Quincy, MA: Christopher Publishing House, 1978), p. 172.

50. R.J. Chelliah, *Fiscal Policy in Underdeveloped Countries with Special Reference to India* (London: George Allen and Unwin, 1960), p. 64.

51. Dirk J. Wolfson, *Public Finance and Development Strategy* (Baltimore: Johns Hopkins University Press, 1979), p. 124.

52. Ibid.

53. Edward S. Shaw, *Financial Deepening in Economic Development* (New York: Oxford University Press, 1973), pp. 9–12.

54. Ibid., pp. 9–10.

55. Ibid., p. 10.

56. Clarence Zuvekas, Jr., *Economic Development* (New York: St. Martin's Press, 1979), pp. 325–26.

57. Ibid., p. 326.

58. V.V. Bhatt and J. Meerman, "Resource Mobilization in Developing Countries: Financial Institutions and Policies," *World Development, 6* (January 1978), pp. 45–64.

59. Ibid.

60. R.F. Mikesell and J.E. Zinser, "The Nature of the Savings Function in Developing Countries: A Survey of the Theoretical and Empirical Literature," *Journal of Economic Literature, 11* (March 1973), pp. 1–26.

61. V.V. Bhatt and J. Meerman, "Resource Mobilization in Developing Countries: Financial Institutions and Policies," p. 48.

62. Ibid.

63. C. Zuvekas, Jr., *Economic Development*, p. 333.

64. W.T. Newlyn, *The Financing of Economic Development* (New York: Oxford University Press, 1977), p. 326.

65. World Bank, *World Development Report 1989* (New York: Oxford University Press, 1989), p. 27.

66. Ibid.

67. K. Schmidt-Hebbel, L. Serven, and A. Solimano, *Saving, Investment, and Growth in Developing Contries: An Overview* (Washington, DC: World Bank Policy Research Working Paper 1382, November 1994), p. 5.

68. Bernard Fischer, "Savings Mobilization in Developing Countries: Bottlenecks and Reform Proposals," *Savings and Development, 13,* 2 (1989), p. 117.

69. World Bank, *World Development Report 1989,* p. 27.

70. Sándor Ligeti, "Savings and Interest Rates in Developing Countries," *Savings and Development, 13,* 1 (1989), pp. 45–63; and Biswa Bhattacharyay, "Development of Financial Infrastructure: An International Comparison," *Savings and Development, 12,* 4 (1988), pp. 307–18.

71. Anthony Lanyi and Rúsdu Saracoglu, *Interest Rate Policies in Developing Countries,* Occasional Paper 22 (Washington, DC: IMF, October 1983), pp. 23–24.

72. World Bank, *World Development Report 1989,* p. 27.

73. Jacques J. Polak, *Financial Policies and Development* (Paris: OECD Development Centre Studies, 1989), pp. 86–87; and Bijan B. Aghevli and others, *The Role of National Savings in the World Economy,* Occasional Paper 67 (Washington, DC: IMF, March 1990), pp. 46–48.

74. Ibid.; and Miguel A. Rodriguez, "Consequences of Capital Flight for Latin American Debtor Countries," in Donald R. Lessard and John Williamson (eds.), *Capital Flight and Third World Debt* (Washington, DC: Institute for International Economics, 1987).

75. Reported in *The Economist,* August 12, 1989, p. 16.

76. Inter-American Development Bank, *Economic and Social Progress in Latin America: 1991 Report* (Baltimore: Johns Hopkins University, 1991), p. 19.

77. See, for example, World Bank, *World Development Report 1990* (New York: Oxford University Press, 1990), pp. 66–99; and Tyler S. Biggs, Donald R. Snodgrass, and Pradeep Srivastava, "On Minimalist Credit Programs," *Savings and Development, 15,* 1 (1991), pp. 39–52.

——— Chapter 3 ———

Foreign Aid and Foreign Debt

The inability of Third World nations to mobilize financial resources in sufficient volume to undertake the development effort has resulted in an increasing demand by those countries for foreign economic assistance in the form of aid and loans. The traditional sources of finance—tax revenues, mobilized savings, and surplus hard currency earnings—have not been able to keep pace with the required expenditures of Third World nations. Consequently, there are enormous budget and balance-of-payments deficits and external payments requirements that necessitate the need for greater reliance on foreign aid and foreign borrowing.

As shown in chapter 1, the debate over approaches to development includes a number of issues that may never be conclusively resolved but will certainly increase the intellectual exercise and volume of literature pertaining to development policy. Naturally, the debate has also spilled over into consideration of the role and impact of foreign aid and foreign (external) debt. Also, some concern has been expressed about the deteriorating terms of trade faced by the Third World nations, which have affected their ability to earn foreign exchange to the maximum possible. Without earnings from trade, the ability to finance development programs and to meet previous debt obligations is considerably diminished or terminated altogether. However, the deteriorating terms of trade faced by some Third World nations is only partly to blame for reductions in their foreign-exchange earnings. Also affecting those earnings is the rapidly declining volume of exports from those countries due to production bottlenecks and other inefficiencies.

Foreign Aid and the Development Process

Foreign aid refers to flows of resources made on concessional terms to foreign governments either directly on a bilateral basis or indirectly through multilateral organizations. Foreign aid developed for at least three reasons. The first reason was a general concern for the well-being of the world's poor and the promotion of growth and development in the poor nations. The second reason was the fear on the part of the United States and the then Soviet Union of each other's international influence. The final reason was European imperial politics. In the latter two cases, the ultimate intent was to promote a particular ideological and political framework in the hope that the granting of aid might encourage the recipients to become friendly with and accept the ideological and political stance of the donors, who, in turn, would maintain a position of influence and control over the recipient countries.

Foreign aid programs began after World War II with the launch of the Marshall Plan by U.S. Secretary of State George Marshall. Through the Marshall Plan the United States was able to help restore economic growth to Europe in the years following the war. The first assistance for specific projects in the Third World was offered to three Latin American countries in 1948 and 1949.[1] Third World countries supplement savings by obtaining foreign aid. These resource inflows permit a Third World country to undertake more investment than would be possible if it had to rely on domestic savings alone. It was generally advocated that the effectiveness of aid was measured usually in terms of its effect on growth, which was expected, subsequently, to become self-sustaining. Chenery and Strout argue that their examples support the theoretical conclusion that the achievement of a high rate of growth, even if it had to be initially supported by large amounts of external capital, was likely to be the most important element in the long-term effectiveness of assistance. The substantial increases in internal savings ratios that had been achieved in a decade of strong growth demonstrated the rapidity with which aid-sustained growth could be transformed into self-sustained growth once rapid development had taken hold.[2]

Griffin and Enos, on the other hand, suggest that, if anything, aid may have retarded development by leading to lower domestic savings, by distorting the composition of investment and thereby raising the capital–output ratio, by frustrating the emergence of an indigenous entrepreneurial class, and by inhibiting institutional reforms.[3] Instead of obtaining evidence for growth induced by aid, they observe that the opposite hypothesis was closer to the truth and that, in general, foreign assistance was not associated with progress and, indeed, may have deterred it. If the growth that a nation achieved, or failed to achieve, was related to the assistance it received, then there could be no support for the view that aid encourages growth.[4]

Public opinion about foreign aid has fluctuated considerably during the past three decades. In 1969, a Commission of International Development, chaired by former Canadian Prime Minister Lester B. Pearson, noted that the development efforts of the Third World nations, as a group, were more constrained by the conditions that determined the size of their balance-of-payments gap and aid bill than by the factors that affected the generation of their domestic surplus.[5] The availability of foreign assistance was, in the opinion of the Pearson Commission, an important factor influencing growth. The commission laid primary emphasis on the aid effort, arguing that the gap between the rich and poor countries would continue to widen unless the rich nations substantially increased the volume of assistance being given to poor nations. Further, they stated that if adequate aid were forthcoming for the next forty or fifty years, most of the Third World countries would be in a position to earn their keep, as it were, by about the year 2000.

Several criticisms were hurled at the Pearson Commission report. The rationale of the commission's case for aid was regarded as both a theoretical and a historical concept. Onyemelukwe, for example, reasoned that the historical concept was derived from the success of the first-ever aid program, the Marshall Plan, while the theoretical concept was based on a kind of regional idea of development and arose also because of the success of the Marshall Plan.[6] Other economists argued that it was necessary for the whole attitude toward the problem of international assistance to be fundamentally altered. A group of economists meeting at an International Development Conference at Columbia University in 1970 viewed, with apprehension, the Pearson Commission's suggestion that aid should be regarded merely as a means of achieving a 6 percent growth rate in the Third World countries and should cease when those countries became capable of financing and sustaining such a growth rate themselves.[7] The economists stated that the gap between the rich and poor countries would increase to four times its present size if the Third World countries were to grow at a 6 percent rate from then until the year 2000. It was considered an unrealistic assumption that the relative bargaining strength of the poor nations vis-à-vis the rich would have improved by that date. On the contrary, the international economy would then consist of countries that would, in relative terms, be four times as rich or four times as poor as they were then.[8]

Two arguments have usually been advanced in support of foreign aid. One argument is based on the economic and strategic self-interest of the donor nations; the second is based on the ethical and/or moral responsibility of the residents of wealthy countries toward the residents of poor countries.[9] Both arguments, however, have been subjected to many challenges over the years. Yet, the empirical evidence suggests that donor self-interest plays a relatively larger role in bilateral assistance, while recipient need plays a larger role in multilateral assistance.[10] At the same time, both the popular and official sponsors of foreign aid have regarded the ethical basis for foreign aid as obvious.[11]

Further empirical evidence has emerged recently to support the view that the combined per capita allocations of the multilateral agencies outperformed those of the Development Assistance Committee (DAC) member nations, conforming to the popular view that the aid agencies of donor nations are not entirely free to base their allocations on purely developmental criteria. McGillivray, for example, constructed an aid index that measured the relative performance of donors in terms of aid distribution.[12] He defined donor performance as the extent to which a donor bases its aid allocation on the relative needs of recipient countries. The closer a donor's aid reflects these needs, the greater is its performance. Donor performance was measured by an income-weighted per capita index, and it was determined that Belgium, Finland, Denmark, and Norway outperformed the rest of the DAC member nations. The United States was found to be the poorest performer.[13] These results are not surprising; in fact, they are consistent with the ranking of these countries in terms of the proportion of their GNP devoted to official development assistance (ODA).

Notwithstanding the recent empirical studies, it was already assumed in the past that aid allocation did not seem to be primarily determined by economic considerations. In examining the pattern of aid allocation, Piatier came to the conclusion that aid was not adjusted to the population size of the recipients; it was by no means adjusted to the situation of the beneficiaries; its effectiveness seemed to bear no relation to the efforts made; and the political factor explained certain concentrations of resources.[14] Further, Piatier states that no aid or as little as possible was donated to those countries that were politically, emotionally, or ideologically at odds with the donor. Also, very often, nothing, or as little as possible, was donated to poor but politically reliable countries. Instead, resources were withheld to be used elsewhere.[15] He further states that the maximum aid was earmarked for actual or potential allies whose political situation was unstable and where it was hoped that a little economic well-being would restore internal equilibrium and confirm loyalty.[16] Griffin and Enos observe that foreign aid tended to strengthen the status quo; it enabled those in power to evade and avoid fundamental reforms; it did little more than patch plaster on the deteriorating social edifice.[17]

Banfield suggests, furthermore, that there was no connection between U.S. aid and national interests. He concludes that the popular appeal in the United States of generalizations about foreign aid resulted above all from the nation's self-righteousness and from the impulse to convert others to the American truth: "The same old zeal to make the world safer for democracy is expressed anew [in foreign aid]."[18] The practice of providing or withholding aid for political reasons seems considerably to weaken its usefulness in advancing development. The danger is that donors may pursue their self-interest under the rubric of aid even if it harms the recipient country.[19] Joan Nelson concludes that, unfortunately, U.S. aid was not distributed among countries in such a way that it could provide a strong incentive for effective self-help measures. Because aid was used for security and political purposes, as well as to promote development, the pattern of U.S. aid allocations did not favor good performers clearly enough to induce them to maintain their efforts, or to encourage other nations to improve on poor past records.[20]

Essentially, what aid critics have said, and continue to say, is that aid was used as an instrument for domesticating the Third World countries; that it was seriously ill-conceived, but contained the strategy for maximizing the self-interests of the United States and other Western countries; and that the multilateral agencies had exercised leverage. The radical literature extends the criticism further by pointing out that the aid policies of the international agencies perpetuated and sometimes increased the existing severe inequalities in the distribution of income and power in Latin America, and that, generally, aid had a negative impact on political and economic development in poor countries. It was additionally argued that, for the countries that had recently attained their independence, the greatest threat was the subtle method of neocolonialism, which, even while giving economic aid to those countries, developed new ways of penetrating their economies for the monopolies.[21]

The result of this, argues Johnson, was a strengthened system of imperialism, because the day-to-day administrative influence that the United States wielded in Third World countries was greater than ever before, particularly in Latin America, and because built into the system was a set of ideas—a complex of doctrines that served rather effectively, in most cases, to rationalize and legitimize the structure.[22] He further states that ideology was a distinguishing feature of the system and that new face might, justifiably, be termed "welfare imperialism."[23]

Bauer, while agreeing with the harmful effects of aid on political and economic development, offers the alternative view, that foreign aid could not achieve its declared objectives because foreign aid itself was a distortionary government intervention.[24] Moreover, it was further argued that foreign aid was wasted, and not legitimate, within the framework of Western political philosophy, for government to force-fully extract resources from its citizens in order to transfer them to foreigners.[25] The contention was that government may take from citizens and give to foreigners when doing so serves the common good of the citizens, but it may not do so if all advantages will accrue to foreigners and none to citizens.[26]

In addition, Bauer argues that "many taxpayers in donor countries are far poorer than many people in Third World countries where, moreover, aid often benefits the prosperous rather than the needy and where the governments who demand international redistribution do not practice it at home."[27] All of this boils down to advocacy for the dismantling of aid programs. Furthermore, the basic contention in this line of argument is that foreign aid is simply not required for development because it obstructs development more than it can promote it. In essence, foreign aid hurts rather than helps the Third World nations. It is regarded as involving a transfer of income between governments and, consequently, is interventionist in character while providing no positive results.

The arguments for and against foreign aid and its structure are many and varied. Aid, however, seems to be a permanent feature of the process of international resource assistance. The extent to which it is distributed in accordance with the true principles of equity and efficiency would reflect, to some extent, the contribution of the well-to-do members of the international community toward eliminating the imbalances and inequalities within the world economic system. Recently, the focus of the aid debate came to center on three interrelated themes.[28] One is the effectiveness of aid: that is, to what extent has aid contributed to development? The second theme is the support for aid in donor countries among both the general public and the politicians. The third theme deals with the volume of aid: that is, how much is required to meet the developmental needs of recipients?

The conclusions derived from this recent debate suggest the increasing politicization of aid and the mixing of aid with the foreign policy and commercial objectives of donors. Also, aid was found to be productive and helpful to development; without it, a number of countries would not have been able to graduate from the ranks of poor to middle-income countries, and the countries that remain poor would have been still poorer.[29] Important links were found between the effectiveness of aid, political support for aid, and the volume of aid flows. For example, if aid is demonstrated to be effective, it might increase public support for it and thereby contribute to increases in its volume.[30]

Despite much that was found to be laudable in the recent analyses of foreign aid, there was also much to be criticized. For example, donors usually fail to consider the probable distribution of benefits in projects that are not directly poverty-oriented; they do little to coordinate poverty issues with recipients; their collective efforts do not usually make a coherent contribution to poverty alleviation; and their activities have affected the poor on occasion through the displacement of labor with machinery supplied for some projects.[31]

In spite of its increasing effectiveness, the level and outlook for aid is cause for some serious concern in the Third World countries. The economic difficulties and budgetary deficits of some donor nations are placing limits on their current foreign aid programs. In the United States, for example, which already donates the least in terms of proportion of GNP, new budget proposals indicate that future aid will be lower than in previous years. In comparative terms, Germany contributes less than 0.5 percent of its GNP, the United Kingdom less than 0.4 percent, Japan a little over 0.3 percent, and the United States 0.2 percent. In aggregate, only five of the industrialized nations—Denmark, France, the Netherlands, Norway, and Sweden—have reached and/or surpassed the 0.7 percent of GNP target set by the United Nations for the Second and Third Development Decades. The Development Assistance Committee (DAC) group of countries (made up of OECD mem-

Table 3.1

Net Receipts of Aid from Major Sources by Region, 1981–91

	Billions of U.S. dollars					Per capita dollars	Percent of GNP
Region	1981	1985	1987	1988	1991	1991	1991
Sub-Saharan Africa	6.9	9.0	12.5	14.1	16.2	32.9	9.3
East Asia and Pacific	3.5	3.6	5.5	6.4	7.4	4.6	0.6
South Asia	4.8	4.7	5.6	6.6	7.5	6.5	2.1
Europe, Middle East, and North Africa	7.3	5.0	5.2	4.3	11.2	62.2	3.2
Latin America and Caribbean	2.0	3.3	4.1	4.2	5.0	11.4	0.4

Sources: Organization for Economic Cooperation and Development, *Development Cooperation Reports* (Paris: OECD, several years); and World Bank, *World Development Reports* (New York: Oxford University Press, several years).

bers) still continues to contribute the majority of foreign aid (averaging 80 percent in the 1980s). OPEC's share, which increased during the 1970s, began to decline during the 1980s. The total net receipts of overseas development assistance (foreign aid) from major sources, by region, are displayed in Table 3.1.

The majority of foreign aid goes to middle-income countries. Aid to these countries is heavily biased toward three groups of countries. U.S. aid goes primarily to Egypt and Israel; OPEC's aid is heavily concentrated in contributions to Jordan and Syria; while French aid goes to its overseas territories in the form of technical assistance. More than 30 percent of U.S. nonmilitary aid goes to Israel and Egypt, while 75 percent of the United Kingdom's official bilateral aid is tied to the purchase of British goods and services.

As a whole, over half of all bilateral aid from the Western industrialized nations is now tied to the purchase of goods and services from the donor country; less than 25 percent of the aid given goes to the forty least developed nations; less than 15 percent goes to the agricultural sector, which has the majority of the Third World's poor; less than 11 percent goes to education; and less than 5 percent goes to health and birth spacing combined. Two notable exceptions to these trends are Norway and Sweden, 75 percent of whose donated aid has no strings attached.[32]

The aid reliance ratios (foreign aid as a percentage of a recipient's GNP) indicate that the sub-Saharan Africa countries have the heaviest reliance on foreign aid, with a ratio of 9.3 percent in 1991, while the South Asian nations are in third place, with a reliance ratio that is approximately one-fifth that of the sub-Saharan Africa countries. However, a significant contrast, in comparing these two regions, is that in sub-Saharan Africa there is a greater reliance on foreign aid by the low-income countries. Aid reliance, however, does not necessarily translate into aid effectiveness. Although, as mentioned before, the majority of aid is successful in terms of its own objectives, aid has not necessarily gone where it is most effective. In Africa, where foreign aid works relatively less well than in South Asia, for example, foreign aid receipts increased by a greater proportion than in South Asia through the early 1990s. The primary explanation for this state of affairs is that the DAC donors were responding to the problems of famine and other economic distortions in Africa in a more generous fashion than had been the case before.

In the Japanese view, in particular, aid should be differentiated along the lines of the particular socioeconomic circumstances and other conditions of a recipient country in order to meet its special development needs. In a speech given in Tokyo on April 19, 1989, Takashi Koezuka, Director for Multilateral Cooperation of Japan's Ministry of Foreign Affairs, noted that Japan will enhance its country-specific approach to development aid in the 1990s by giving priority to balanced economic growth accompanied by appropriate poverty alleviation measures to compensate for any social cost to the poorest and the weakest, to economic infrastructure development, and to strengthened disaster prevention with sufficient attention to the protection of the environment.

The Foreign Debt Problem

When foreign borrowing occurs, a foreign debt instrument is created. Whereas taxation constitutes a method of forced internal savings, foreign borrowing is a device to utilize a part of the foreign voluntary savings for financing the development effort of the public sector and functions as an instrument of resource mobilization.

Perhaps the most popular works on the debt problem of Third World nations were those written by Avramovic.[33] What was made clear in those studies, and is still the case, is that the debt of Third World nations had been increasing steadily. The general consensus at the time, however, was that there was no general problem of Third World countries' inability to service their debt, though some individual countries may run into liquidity problems for reasons within or beyond their control.

A similar view emerged from a conference held in Mexico in 1977 to discuss the external public debt of the Third World nations. The participants in that conference felt that the Third World nations had established a very good record of debt servicing in the decade previous to their meeting and that any major defaults were highly unlikely because of the mutual interest of lenders and borrowers in continuing financial relations.[34] These views were reiterated by the World Bank in its 1978 *World Development Report*.[35] As we shall see here, however, Third World debt is now a serious problem and has created an international economic crisis whose impact is going to be with us for a long time.[36]

Borrowing and lending across political borders date back to the ancient civilizations of the Mediterranean and probably much further into the past, to tribal societies.[37] In arguing against the accumulation of public debt, the classical economists assumed the existence of full employment, inelasticity of money supplies, and unproductiveness of public expenditure for purposes other than defense, justice, and so on. Therefore, it was thought that government borrowing involving taxation to defray interest payments deprived the economy of cash and capital, and the government's use of resources was less productive than that of private enterprise.[38] However, this view of public debt is not relevant in the context of a Third World country. In such an economy, public debt, if prudently and skillfully operated and managed, can become an important instrument of economic development.[39]

Some of the debate on the foreign debt issue has focused on the measurement of debt-servicing capacity. The original position on this question was, as Basch points out, to assess the export prospects of groups of major commodities entering the world market and to relate the value of such exports to the existing debt.[40] This is the crude index used to measure the incidence of debt service. This debt-service ratio is used to measure the liquidity problem that may arise from fixed debt-service obligations.

In recent years, however, this so-called crude index has been under attack as an irrelevant and improper measure of the debt-servicing capacity of Third World countries. For example, Ohlin refers to the crude index as a poor measure.[41] Furthermore, he states that what one would like to have is an index summarizing at least three things: (1) the risk of sharp declines in any kind of foreign-exchange inflows, including credit; (2) the risk of sudden increases in import needs due to such things as inflation, harvest failure, and the like; and (3) the offsetting possibility of meeting such disruptions by compressing import rapidly, by compensatory finance, or by drawing down reserves. The debt-service ratio says nothing about any of these things, although it obviously tells us something about the general magnitude of the changes.[42] Similar sentiments are echoed by Islam, who states that the debt-service ratio does not fully convey the implications of debt burden for the balance of payments of a country over the long-run future.[43]

The basic problem in estimating debt-servicing capacity is recognition that increases of external indebtedness and of debt-service liabilities, even when large, do not necessarily imply difficulties for borrowers. Increase of service payments has to be measured against the strengthening that may have occurred in the borrower's economy. Consideration must be given not only to economic, but to the social and political factors that may have a significant impact on the framework through which debt servicing takes place. Further arguments against the debt-service ratio are echoed by Hughes, who asserts that the debt-service ratio is very deficient as a measure of either the borrowers' or the creditors' risk. She further points out that countries with similar debt-service ratios may vary widely in their ability to service their debts, whether that ratio is 10 percent or 40 percent; conversely, countries with widely divergent debt-service ratios may have similar debt-service capacities.[44]

The crystal-clear point that appears to emerge from the debate is that the evaluation of future debt-service burdens must also take into account the interrelationship among such variables as balance of payments, the amount of external liabilities, new external liabilities, gross and net repayments, the amount of external assets, and changes in external assets.[45] These variables, and changes in them, may result from, or be amenable to influence by, the country's own choice of policies and its success in implementing them, but the pattern of future developments in a given country will also depend on some factors outside its sphere of control or direct influence. All of the arguments have led to the use of another measure for determining creditworthiness and the burden of external debt. The suggested measure is that of the ratio of total external debt to GDP. The primary reasons in support of this measure are: (1) a country's creditworthiness and its attractiveness to international lenders are determined not only by its income levels but also by its growth potential; (2) the majority of Third World countries have highly open economies; and (3) external public debt constitutes only a part of the total external debt for a number of them, and thus in some cases may considerably understate the extent of indebtedness.

Within the limits of a country's international creditworthiness, foreign debt provides an opportunity to spend more than the national product and to borrow against the future. Judicious use of this opportunity may raise the rate of growth and provide the scope to meet the future burden without undue stress. Any analysis of the Third World countries' indebtedness over time, however, is beset by the difficulty of taking account of currency realignments and inflation. Currency realignments as well as the floating of currencies have had complex repercussions on the value of debt outstanding, the cost of debt service, the value of reserves, and trade relations in general. Even if we allow for an increase in dollar prices of Third World countries' exports, the real effect of most currency realignments has been a reduction in the debt outstanding.[46]

Related to the effect of currency realignments is the effect of inflation on indebtedness, and this too must be taken into account. To the extent that the inflation rate is not fully reflected in setting the interest rate of a loan, inflation is beneficial to the debtor because the debtor services the debt with money that is worth less than it was when contracting the debt. The effect of inflation is of course more complicated, depending on how the prices of Third World countries' exports and imports are affected, as reflected in their terms of trade. The recent disturbances resulting from higher prices for oil, food, and other primary products have added a further dimension to the complications of debt comparisons over time.[47]

As in other fields of debt analysis, the global picture masks considerable differences among individual countries. The beneficial effect of inflation on their debt service is especially pronounced for those countries whose export prices have risen sharply so that they need to employ that much less in terms of real debt service. On the other hand, this result may be nullified as higher import prices reduce the real value of imported goods.[48]

Finding a means through which debt-servicing problems can be avoided is the most important task facing creditor and debtor countries. The avoidance of debt-servicing problems under conditions that are consistent with an orderly development process in Third World countries is in the interest of both sets of countries. The avoidance of debt-servicing problems will require appropriate policies by both debtor and creditor countries. These policies have substantial areas of overlap, and a broad measure of understanding and complementarity should be promoted in order to achieve a fruitful rapprochement with respect to matters on which divergences may exist. It must be understood, however, that Third World countries bear the responsibility to take all reasonable measures within their means to ensure that debt-servicing problems are avoided, and domestic policies designed to avoid these problems can only be fully successful in a suitable and favorable external environment characterized by frank cooperation between debtor and creditor countries.[49]

Avoiding debt-servicing problems requires, among other things, policies with regard to the mobilization of domestic savings, which have an important bearing on investment programs and therefore on rates of growth of output. Policies with regard to the allocation of new investments are of special significance and can in many cases be improved through more efficient use of project evaluation.[50]

Because of the importance of export earnings in determining total foreign-exchange availabilities in debtor countries, policies in creditor and debtor countries regarding trade have an important bearing on the capacity of the latter to service debt. In this case, appropriate exchange rate and export promotion policies in debtor countries, including, when necessary, the prompt adjustment of exchange rates, will play an important role in fostering an expansion in export earnings. Also of importance is the link between external debt management and other policies. Loser has pointed out that management of external debt should aim at providing the maximum possible net resource transfer that can be sustained over time, while other policies must provide for a sustainable current account outcome consistent with access to foreign borrowing over the medium term.[51]

The Third World debt problem has been a central topic of international concern from around the early 1980s. As a matter of fact, the gestation of the debt problem took place in the period between the first and second oil price shocks (1974–79) occasioned by the emergence of the OPEC cartel and the desire to increase oil earnings. At the end of 1979 the economic situation left the economies of the developing countries vulnerable. However, formal declaration of the debt crisis did not occur until one of the major Latin American countries indicated it was experiencing serious economic problems, although in 1981 Costa Rica had already declared a moratorium on payments. In August 1982, Mexico declared its inability to service its debt. Shortly thereafter, in November 1982, Brazil found itself in a similar situation. Emergency financial packages were put together by the monetary authorities of some developed countries. Since that time many treatments have been recommended. The problem, however, is far from being solved, although there has been much progress in the right direction.

Polak has argued that the origins of the debt crisis can be traced to four successive, sharply adverse changes in the world economy.[52] First was the second oil shock, which raised the world petroleum price by more than 100 percent from 1978 to 1980, and a total of 150 percent from 1978 to 1981. Second was the contractionary monetary policy adopted by the industrial countries to contain the inflationary impact of the rise in petroleum prices that increased the London Interbank Offered Rate (LIBOR) for dollar-denominated credits in 1981. Third was a significant decline in the terms of trade of the Third World nations on goods other than oil, primarily during 1981–82. The last change was an abrupt cessation of the supply of foreign bank credit.[53]

Significantly, some Third World countries do not currently have serious debt problems as commonly understood. Those countries may be struggling with serious development problems, but they are able to meet their debt-servicing obligations. The magnitude of the debt problem is seen in Table 3.2. The long-term debt of the Third World is now over $1,300 billion. In many of those countries, annual repayment of interest and capital still amounts to more than the total of all new aid and loans being received each year. On average, repayments are now responsible for 16 percent of the Third World's export revenues. The long-term Third World debt now represents about 32 percent of their aggregate GNP and more than 150 percent of their export earnings. At the beginning of the 1980s, in contrast, those ratios were 33 percent and less than 85 percent, respectively.

Table 3.2

Low- and Middle-Income Economies: Long-Term Debt and Debt Service, 1985–92 (billions of U.S. dollars and percent)

Item	All low- and middle-income economies			Sub-Saharan Africa		
	1985	1989	1992	1985	1989	1992
Debt outstanding	767.8	958.8	1,308.2	76.1	124.6	155.5
Official (%)	38.3	47.4	51.0	60.1	70.1	73.0
Private (%)	61.7	52.6	49.1	39.9	29.9	27.0
Debt as percentage of GNP	· 37.4	34.9	29.6	42.6	83.3	55.8
Debt service	105.2	115.3	155.3	9.1	6.7	12.0
Interest payments	53.4	51.9	57.1	3.4	3.3	5.6
Official (%)	21.1	32.1	39.3	34.1	52.1	32.9
Private (%)	78.9	67.9	60.7	65.9	47.9	67.1
Principal repayments	51.9	63.4	98.2	5.7	3.4	6.4
Official (%)	24.5	33.9	30.3	25.2	45.5	30.3
Private (%)	75.5	66.1	69.7	74.8	54.5	69.7
Debt-service ratio	24.0	18.8	16.3	23.1	16.9	14.5
Disbursements	84.7	85.7	160.0	8.3	9.0	8.5
Official (%)	36.9	46.1	31.2	53.1	66.6	77.2
Private (%)	63.1	53.9	68.8	46.9	33.4	22.8
Net resource flows on long-term lending	32.9	22.3	61.8	2.6	5.6	2.1
Net transfers on long-term lending	−20.5	−29.6	4.7	−0.9	2.3	−3.5

Source: World Bank, *Annual Reports* (Washington, DC: World Bank, several years). The data cover 129 countries in the World Bank Debtor Reporting System. The debt-service ratio is debt service as a percentage of exports of goods and services. Net resource flows on long-term lending refers to disbursements minus (actual) principal repayments on long-term lending. Net transfers on long-term lending refers to net resource flows minus (actual) interest payments on long-term debt.

There are various reasons why some Third World countries found themselves with excessive debt burdens and others did not. The evidence suggests five primary factors.[54] The first is that it takes time for an excessive debt burden to accumulate; the second is the readily expanded, and highly elastic, supply of credits; third was a shared expectation by borrowers and lenders that capacity to pay would not have deteriorated in the future; fourth was a lack of national official accounting and control of the aggregate of foreign obligations; and the fifth factor, and perhaps the most important, was that some borrowing countries received no comparative benefit in terms of growth from the larger debt they had incurred owing to the fact that investment declined while borrowing increased. Specifically, some nations of Latin America and the Caribbean had shifted somewhat to an economic strategy of sustaining growth by using foreign credits to maintain domestic consumption.[55] This sharp increase in the supply of credit from abroad permitted some governments to avoid hard domestic policy choices.

The debt ratios of the Third World nations indicate that the overall debt has become so large relative to economic size and relative to export earnings that it would be impossible to repay a significant part of it in the short run without imposing what would amount to an impossible burden on those nations. Problems with timely debt servicing seem to have been concentrated in the Western Hemisphere and Africa. However, the circumstances contributing to such a state of affairs are different for each of the two regions. The large debt-service ratio of the countries in the Western Hemisphere reflects the fact that a considerable share of their debt was held by commercial lenders, while the magnitude of the debt-service ratio for the countries in Africa is more a reflection of the large absolute size of their debt relative to their export performance. Given the slow growth in export earnings in Africa, the rise in the debt-servicing ratio was almost inevitable.

Perhaps the most striking feature in the development of the Third World foreign debt problem during the 1980s was the decline in private lending to those countries. Private lending after 1981 declined the most for those countries that experienced debt-servicing problems. Most major banks, particularly in the United States, increased their loan/loss reserves to minimize their exposure to Third World loans, beginning in the latter part of the 1980s. In addition, new financial instruments were also put in place that had the effect of reducing the face value of commercial-bank debt in Mexico, Costa Rica, Venezuela, and the Philippines, for example.

Despite the decline in private capital flows to the Third World in the 1980s, their previous growth gave rise to the Syndicated Eurocurrency Credit Market. Syndicated Eurocredits are loans in which a group of financial institutions make funds available on common conditions to a borrower. They emerged as a popular vehicle for international lending because they offer advantages from the point of view of both lenders and borrowers. For lenders, the syndication procedure is a means for banks to diversify some of the unique risks that arise in international lending while allowing different-sized banks to function in the market simultaneously. From the point of view of the Third World nations, syndication allows for the efficient arrangement of a larger amount of funds than any single lender can feasibly supply.

Moreover, the syndication process is generally free of restrictions and therefore allows a greater degree of policy independence. It also can usually be negotiated fairly quickly and drawn on without delay. Interest on syndicated loans is usually computed by adding a spread to LIBOR, which is the rate at which banks lend funds to other banks operating in the Euromarket. The LIBOR changes continuously. The rate on any particular loan, however, is readjusted only every three or six months. Recently, the LIBOR has been increasing in real terms, with adverse consequences for the majority of Third World countries.

Undoubtedly, some Third World nations have encountered serious economic problems as a result of their debt crisis, and vice versa. Currently, the international concern has shifted to debt reduction policy as a precondition for economic recovery and renewed development. The radical literature, however, marginal as it is, seems anachronistic and is limited only to sweeping statements suggesting, for example, that "the debt crisis is a symptom—one among many—of an increasingly polarized world organized for the benefit of a minority that will stop at nothing to maintain and strengthen its control and privilege."[56] Presumably, the minority here is the industrialized nations. This is "the Conspiracy Theory of History." It lacks credibility. Perhaps, the very nature of radical thought makes it capable only of extremist criticism and devoid of the insight to provide consistent policy solutions.

Policies to Relieve Third World Debt

Various solutions to the debt problem have been, and are being, attempted through innovations in debt restructuring based on initiatives originating primarily in the industrialized nations. Moreover, there is now both intellectual acceptance and practical implementation of the concept of debt reduction. Furthermore, there is now general agreement among all concerned that no one global solution to the debt problem will work for everyone. Cases are different and the solutions would have to be different. In this regard, Claude Cheysson identified the categories of debt cases as: (1) the poorest in the Third World, mostly in Black Africa; (2) the heavily indebted middle-income countries; and (3) the most advanced countries, the four "tigers" of East Asia and those that will soon be in a similar position. For countries in this latter category, growing out of debt is not regarded as a problem.[57]

The major initiatives that have been undertaken include the "Baker Initiative," the "Lawson Plan," the "Brady Plan," the "Miyazawa Plan," the "Mitterand Proposal," and the actions of the international agencies. In addition, several features have been added to the menu of options available to the Paris Club.[58] All of these initiatives gave supreme recognition to the need for renewed and enduring growth in the Third World. The prevailing view that Third World debt would prove manageable with reasonable growth in the industrialized nations, reasonable adjustment policies in the indebted nations, and good intentions all around to keep some capital flowing began to diminish in the mid-1980s when, instead, the realization emerged that unless dealt with up-front, through the creation of the conditions necessary for economic growth, the debt crisis would remain both a major international issue and a problem for the Third World nations.

The "Baker Initiative," so named after its proponent, the then–U.S. Secretary of the Treasury, James Baker, was unveiled in October 1985 in a speech to the IMF–World Bank Annual Meeting in Seoul. This initiative aimed to keep payments from the fifteen major debtors to the creditor banks current by pledging a new and larger infusion of capital.[59] It was backed by stabilization programs of the IMF and adjustment programs of the World Bank. The target of this initiative implied a need for bank exposure to grow by at least 2.5 percent per annum.[60] The strategy envisaged that banks would supply sufficient funds not only to avoid driving debtors into default in the short term but also to strengthen their debt-servicing capacity in the longer term. The total amount of credit to be made available for the fifteen countries was US$20 billion. The Baker Initiative failed, however, for several reasons. Senator Bill Bradley pronounced that the Baker Initiative was "wrong."[61] Basically, the initiative did not achieve its objectives, partly through lack of resources. The initiative expected an increase in private capital flows during a period when commercial bank lending was declining.

Moreover, the Baker Initiative failed to stop a net resource outflow. The fifteen countries paid out more in interest alone, as well as transferring net resources to the creditor nations far in excess of new capital inflows. In addition, the initiative stimulated capital flight as the confidence of domestic investors was undermined with the increasing rather than declining debt burden.[62] Also, the Baker Initiative paid little attention to the debt problem of the poorest countries, particularly in Africa, whose debts were mainly owed, and whose debt service was mainly flowing back, to the governments and international financial institutions that were giving them aid, rather than to the banks.[63] Essentially, the Baker Initiative failed, in addition to the reasons given above, because it prescribed the same solution for all of the countries without taking into consideration the diversity of their economic circumstances and future economic prospects.

The "Lawson Plan," named after the Right Honourable Nigel Lawson, then Chancellor of the British Exchequer, was launched in April 1987[64] within the framework of the United Kingdom's full support of the IMF's Structural Adjustment Facility, which provides cheap loans for poorer countries undertaking agreed-upon economic adjustment policies. The United Kingdom also pledged full support for the World Bank's Special Program of Assistance for Africa, implemented in December 1987.

The Lawson Plan had three parts, the first two of which were somewhat related: (1) the writing off of old loans, and (2) more generous rescheduling terms. As a result of these two initiatives, more aid loans were being written off and longer repayment periods with generous grace periods were allowed when other official loans were rescheduled, within the Paris Club. The third part of the Lawson Plan was a proposal to reduce the burden of interest payments. This was to be accomplished through a choice of three routes. The first route was reducing the interest rates charged on loans from export credit agencies by 3.5 percentage points (or by one-half the rate in those cases where it is below 7 percent). The loans were to be rescheduled over fourteen years, with a grace period of eight years. This was the route adopted by the United Kingdom and some other creditor nations. The second route allowed creditors to write off altogether one-third of the debt service falling due in the period in question, and to reschedule the remainder of the debt over fourteen years with an eight-year grace period, but at market rates of interest. The third route was allowing countries that were unable to accept either of the previous two routes to reschedule their debts, at market rates, over twenty-five years with a fourteen-year grace period.

The "Brady Plan," named after the then–U.S. Treasury Secretary, Nicholas Brady, replaced the Baker Initiative in March 1989. Unlike the Baker Initiative, this plan did not target only the largest debtors, and it also took the position that some debts have already been lost and will have to be written off. The plan assumed about 20 percent debt reduction and it used the secondary market in debt. It called for negotiations between a given country and its creditor banks, utilizing a market-based menu of options so that a balance can be reached between the specific needs of the country and the diverse interests of its creditor banks. Under the Brady Plan, Mexico, Venezuela, Uruguay, and the Philippines, for example, signed deals that showed encouraging early results. It is now up to these countries to make a serious effort to avoid policy reversals.

The "Miyazawa Plan," proposed in 1988 by Japan's former finance minister, Kiichi Miyazawa, who later became prime minister, had three main elements and combined a menu of options and interest reduction. First, debtor countries would "securitize" part of their debt, with guarantees on the principal through liens on their exchange reserves and on the proceeds of the disposal of state-owned assets. Second, the remaining unsecuritized debt was to be rescheduled with grace periods of up to five years during which interest payments could be lowered, suspended, or forgiven. Finally, multilateral and bilateral agencies were to increase their lending to countries that had taken the first two steps.

The "Mitterand Proposal," named after the former French President François Mitterand, advocated that a fund be created in the International Monetary Fund for the middle-income indebted nations. This fund was to guarantee the payments of interest charged on certain commercial loans converted into bonds. The fund was to help lower the finance charges payable by debtor nations. In order to finance it, the industrialized countries were to set aside their share of a new issue of Special Drawing Rights (SDRs) for use by Third World nations.

The international agencies have also been doing their bit with respect to debt relief for Third World nations. The International Monetary Fund, for example, through its Structural Adjustment Facility (SAF) and its Enhanced Structural Adjustment Facility (ESAF), has become an aid donor. The European Community has also been doing its part for the African, Caribbean, and Pacific (ACP) countries under the Lomé Convention, by shifting some of the formal grants money to the support of adjustment policies.[65] The IMF has also devised a special scheme to rescue the poorest and worst off countries. Under the scheme, the Group of Seven (G–7) countries[66] provide special help for countries in arrears with their creditors if those countries agree to follow an IMF economic reform program. Each G–7 country is to undertake to coordinate support for at least one debtor nation. In 1989, Guyana became the first Third World nation to be rescued under this scheme through coordination provided by the Canadian government.

The World Bank executive directors have also approved procedures and guidelines for the use of Bank resources to support debt reduction and debt-servicing reduction. Eligible for such help are all member countries that have a clear need for debt reduction or debt-service reduction in order to achieve reasonable medium-term economic growth objectives and that have adopted a sound medium-term economic policy framework. Bank resources under this program would be provided over a three-year period. In addition, the World Bank transfers some of its net income to the International Development Association (IDA)—the Bank's affiliate that lends to the poorest countries—to facilitate commercial debt reduction in countries that borrow from the IDA alone.

In addition, to the above debt-relief strategies, the commercial banks have also engaged in some novel ideas of relief, ably supported by information provided by the Institute of International Finance (IIF).[67] Included in those novel ideas are debt-equity swaps, buybacks, and debt–debt swaps. The debt-equity swap has so far been the principal novel idea employed. It typically involves the exchanging of a loan for equity in a domestically registered company, often a foreign firm or even a subsidiary of the lending bank's own holding company. In some cases, the swap may be more complicated than just described. It may involve a bank selling debt on the secondary market to a foreign company, which in turn sells the debt to the central bank of the debtor country in return for local currency with which it makes an equity investment in the local economy. In the 1980s, more than US$16 billion was swapped for equity. By 1990, however, only US$9 billion had been swapped for equity.

Buybacks involve the repurchase of bank debt by the debtor governments at a steep discount. For example, in 1988, Bolivia was able to buy back over $300 million of its debt at 11 percent of face value and waive the interest and charges in arrears. Debt–debt swaps involve the swapping of debt for other debt, usually in the form of bonds called exit options. Argentina, Brazil, and Mexico, for example, have all issued exit bonds for some of their debt. This trend in financial innovation has been encouraged by creditor governments, which see it as a convenient means of providing funds from the private sector to debtor countries without committing public monies or providing official guarantees. It must be pointed out, however, that these devices and techniques have not yielded a major increase in the flow of resources to debtor countries.

Concluding Remarks

All of the evidence seems to suggest that low capital flows to the Third World nations will continue into the immediate future and beyond. This requires, therefore, that these countries adopt adjustment policies in an attempt to increase domestic savings and to stave off balance-of-payments crises, while at the same time meeting debt obligations, maintaining essential imports, and struggling to return to economic growth.

It was determined that foreign aid has been effective in attaining its objectives, though its effectiveness can be improved. Given the current state of aid politics, giving more of it where it is most effective may not always be feasible. In fact, given that foreign aid is a tool of foreign policy, there is merit not only in the political and security uses of foreign aid but also in using it as a tool for economic development. However, the fact that a country may be poor and in economic distress and, therefore, in need of help does not automatically qualify it for foreign aid. Other considerations, such as the knowledge that the country's government is notoriously inept and chronically corrupt, may disqualify the country from consideration for aid. On the other hand, other strategic motives (security, economic, political) may result in a decision to provide foreign aid even though the government is inept and corrupt.

To the critics of foreign aid, it needs to be pointed out that greater harm would be done if foreign aid programs were abandoned altogether. The poor would suffer and donor interests would not be served. Given what is known about the inefficiency of Third World governments, it would seem wise that an increased allocation of aid be diverted toward private sector organizations and other nongovernmental organizations making use of the market mechanism, and/or that the flow of aid be increased to those governments making efforts at privatization and moving toward market-oriented policies.

In terms of the debt problem, there is still a long way to go to significant relief, although much progress has been made in the recent past. However, one lesson to be learned from the debt crisis is that some Third World countries, and almost all commercial banks, were overly optimistic in their assessments of future Third World economic performance and creditworthiness. Also, it is now abundantly clear that commercial bank lending at floating rates is not the ideal form of financing for long-term development. It exposes the borrower to interest rate and exchange rate fluctuations, and it does not tie the borrower's payment to the outcome of the investment. Economic theory, on the other hand, suggests that the cost of borrowing money for development is equal to the interest rate on those loans.

Consequently, if the expected yield of the investment financed with the loans is higher than the interest to be paid, then the investment financed by the loan should be profitable. By the same token, investment financed by foreign borrowing should proceed until its marginal product equals the interest rate prevailing on the international capital market. Probably the most significant factor affecting the performance of sovereign borrowing in the Third World was the large part of the loans taken up by public enterprises. Many of those loans had no direct link to specific investment projects. As a matter of fact, the primary reason for contracting some of the loans was to finance deficits.

Also of significance and concern is the continued flight of capital, particularly from the Latin American countries, where it has increased from a trickle to a flood. The estimated more than $170–300 billion in assets held abroad is more than one-third to one-half of the total foreign debt of the fifteen largest debtor nations. Clearly, this trend has to be reversed. Mexican residents alone have $84 billion stashed abroad, equivalent to four-fifths of the country's debt; Argentina's $46 billion is over three-quarters of its debt; Brazil's $31 billion flight capital is more than a quarter of its foreign debt, while Venezuela's $58 billion flight capital exceeds its foreign debt by more than 70 percent.[68] Policies to influence the return of some or all of this flight capital must be given priority.[69] This issue is explored further in chapter 7. Also explored further in chapter 7 is the need for Third World countries to reduce their military expenditures in order to reduce their debt obligations.

Notes

1. Stephen Hellinger, Douglas Hellinger, and Fred M. O'Regan, *Aid for Just Development: Report on the Future of Foreign Assistance* (Boulder, CO: Lynne Rienner Publishers, 1988), pp. 14–15.

2. H.B. Chenery and A.M. Strout, "Foreign Assistance and Economic Development," *American Economic Review, 56* (September 1966), pp. 679–733.

3. Keith Griffin and John Enos, "Foreign Assistance: Objective and Consequences," *Economic Development and Cultural Change, 18* (April 1970), p. 326.

4. Ibid.

5. See Lester Pearson, et al., *Partners in Development* (New York: Praeger, 1969).

6. C.C. Onyemelukwe, *Economic Underdevelopment* (London: Longman, 1974), pp. 101–5.

7. See Barbara Ward, et al., *The Widening Gap* (New York: Columbia University Press, 1971).

8. Ibid.

9. Vernon W. Ruttan, "Why Foreign Economic Assistance," *Economic Development and Cultural Change, 37* (January 1989), pp. 411–24.

10. Alfred Maizels and Machiko Nissanke, "Motivations for Aid to Developing Countries," *World Development, 12,* 9 (1984), pp. 879–900.

11. Roger C. Riddell, "The Ethics of Foreign Aid," *Development Policy Review, 4* (March 1986), pp. 24–43.

12. Mark McGillivray, "The Allocation of Aid among Developing Countries: A Multi-Donor Analysis Using a Per Capita Aid Index," *World Development, 17* (April 1989), pp. 561–68.

13. Ibid.

14. A. Piatier, "The Transfer of Development Resources," in P. Lengyel (ed.), *Approaches to the Science of Socio-Economic Development* (Paris: UNESCO, 1971).

15. Ibid.

16. T. Melady and R. Suhartono, *Development* (Maryknoll, NY: Orbis Books, 1973), p. 73.

17. Keith Griffin and John Enos, "Foreign Assistance: Objectives and Consequences," p. 325.

18. Edward C. Banfield, *American Foreign Aid Doctrines* (Washington, DC: American Enterprise Institute for Public Policy Research, 1963), p. 60.

19. Vernon W. Ruttan, "Why Foreign Economic Assistance," p. 414.

20. See Joan Nelson, *Aid, Influence and Foreign Policy* (New York: Macmillan, 1968).

21. See Teresa Hayter, *Aid as Imperialism* (London: Penguin, 1971); Francis M. Lappé, *Aid as an Obstacle: Twenty Questions about Our Foreign Aid and the Hungry* (San Francisco: Institute for Food and Development Policy, 1980); and Robin Jenkins, *Exploitation* (London: MacGibbon and Kee, 1970).

22. Dale L. Johnson, "Dependence and the International System," in J.D.

Cockroft, André Gunder Frank, and Dale L. Johnson (eds.), *Dependence and Underdevelopment* (New York: Anchor Books, 1972), pp. 71–111.

23. Ibid.

24. Peter T. Bauer, *Reality and Rhetoric: Studies in the Economics of Development* (Cambridge: Harvard University Press, 1984), p. 60.

25. See, for example, Graham Hancock, *Lords of Poverty: The Power, Prestige, and Corruption of the International Aid Business* (New York: Atlantic Monthly Press, 1989); and Peter T. Bauer, *Equality, The Third World, and Economic Delusion* (Cambridge: Harvard University Press, 1981).

26. Ibid.

27. Peter T. Bauer, *Equality, the Third World, and Economic Delusion,* pp. 116–17.

28. Shahid Javed Burki and Robert L. Ayres, "A Fresh Look at Development Aid," *Finance and Development, 23* (March 1986), pp. 6–10.

29. Ibid.

30. Ibid.

31. Robert Cassen, "The Effectiveness of Aid," *Finance and Development, 23* (March 1986), pp. 11–14; and Robert Cassen and Associates, *Does Aid Work?* (New York: Oxford University Press, 1989), pp. 27–32.

32. James P. Grant, *The State of the World's Children 1989* (New York: Oxford University Press, 1989), pp. 27–32.

33. See Dragoslav Avramovic, *Debt Servicing Capacity and Postwar Growth in International Indebtedness* (Baltimore: Johns Hopkins University Press, 1958); and *Economic Growth and External Debt* (Baltimore: Johns Hopkins University Press, 1964).

34. See Miguel S. Wionczek, "Possible Solutions to the External Public Debt Problem of the Developing Countries: Final Report," *World Development, 7* (February 1979), pp. 211–23.

35. See World Bank, *World Development Report 1978* (Washington, DC: World Bank, 1978), p. 24.

36. Nigel Lawson (Right Honourable and former Chancellor of the Exchequer), "International Debt: The Way Forward," in Adrian Hewitt and Bowen Wells (eds.), *Growing out of Debt* (London: Overseas Development Institute, 1989), pp. 7–13; and Stuart K. Tucker, *The Legacy of Debt,* Policy Focus no. 3 (Washington, DC: Overseas Development Council, 1989).

37. Helen Hughes, "Debt and Development: The Role of Foreign Capital in Economic Growth," *World Development, 7* (February 1979), pp. 95–112.

38. S.E. Harris, *The National Debt and the New Economics* (New York: McGraw-Hill, 1947), p. 4.

39. R.N. Tripathy, *Public Finance in Underdeveloped Countries* (Calcutta: World Press Private Limited, 1964), p. 173.

40. A. Basch, *Financing Economic Development* (New York: Macmillan, 1964), p. 267.

41. Goran Ohlin, "Debts, Development and Default," in G.K. Helleiner (ed.), *A World Divided: The Less Developed Countries in the International Economy* (New York: Cambridge University Press, 1976), pp. 207–23.

42. Ibid.

43. Nurul Islam, "The External Debt Problem of the Developing Countries

with Special Reference to the Least Developed," in G.K. Helleiner (ed.), *A World Divided: The Less Developed Countries in the World Economy* (New York: Cambridge University Press, 1976), pp. 225–47.

44. Helen Hughes, "The External Debt of Developing Countries," *Finance and Development, 14* (December 1977), pp. 22–25.

45. Ibid.

46. Kempe Ronald Hope, Sr., *Development Finance and the Development Process* (London: Greenwood Press, 1987), p. 14.

47. Organization for Economic Cooperation and Development, *Debt Problems of Developing Countries* (Paris: OECD, 1974), p. 10.

48. Ibid., pp. 10–11.

49. Kempe Ronald Hope, Sr., *Development Finance and the Development Process*, p. 15.

50. Ibid.

51. Claudio M. Loser, "External Debt Management and Balance of Payments Policies," *IMF Staff Papers, 24* (March 1977), pp. 168–92.

52. Jacques J. Polak, *Financial Policies and Development* (Paris: OECD Development Center, 1989), p. 32.

53. Ibid.

54. The first four factors discussed here are derived from United Nations, *World Economic Survey 1988* (New York: United Nations, 1988), p. 59.

55. Thomas O. Enders and Richard P. Mattione, *Latin America: The Crisis of Debt and Growth* (Washington, DC: Brookings Institution, 1984), p. 7.

56. Susan George, *A Fate Worse than Debt* (New York: Penguin Books, 1988), p. 263.

57. Claude Cheysson, "Global Solutions to a Global Problem: The Role of the European Community," in Adrian Hewitt and Bowen Wells (eds.), *Growing out of Debt* (London: Overseas Development Institute, 1989), pp. 67–75.

58. The "Paris Club" is a representative group of major creditors established in 1956 as the instrument of multilateral debt renegotiations. The club meets in Paris and is chaired by a senior official of the French Treasury. The governments of the major creditor countries and the government of the debtor country, whose foreign debt is being renegotiated, are represented at the club meetings. Representatives of the IMF, World Bank, OECD, and UNCTAD, as well as the regional development banks, attend with observer status. Debt renegotiations under the auspices of the Paris Club are usually conducted within the setting of an economic stabilization program initiated by the IMF.

59. The fifteen countries originally associated with the initiative were Argentina, Bolivia, Brazil, Chile, Colombia, Côte d'Ivoire, Ecuador, Mexico, Morocco, Nigeria, Peru, Philippines, Uruguay, Venezuela, and Yugoslavia. See United Nations, *World Economic Survey 1988,* p. 52, n. 1. Subsequently, Costa Rica and Jamaica were added to the list, thereby identifying the countries as the group of seventeen most indebted Third World nations.

60. United Nations Conference on Trade and Development (UNCTAD), *Trade and Development Report 1988* (New York: United Nations, 1988), p. 105.

61. Bill Bradley, "Debt, Trade and the Dollar," in Adrian Hewitt and Bowen Wells (eds.), *Growing out of Debt* (London: Overseas Development Institute, 1989), pp. 62–66.

62. Ibid.

63. Adrian Hewitt and Bowen Wells, "Introduction," in Adrian Hewitt and Bowen Wells (eds.), *Growing Out of Debt* (London: Overseas Development Institute, 1989), p. 2.

64. Most of the information on the nature and structure of the "Plan" is derived from Nigel Lawson, "International Debt: The Way Forward," pp. 7–13.

65. Claude Cheysson, "Global Solutions to a Global Problem: The Role of the European Community," p. 68.

66. The members of the G–7 group of countries are Canada, France, Italy, Japan, United Kingdom, United States of America, and Germany. The G–7 appellation has been maintained even though the summit meetings of the group are now also attended by the president of the Commission of the European Community, the president of the European Community Council of Ministers (whenever that post is held by a country that is not a regular member of the G–7), and the president of Russia.

67. The Institute of International Finance (IIF) was formally constituted in January 1983 on the initiative of a group of leading European, U.S., and Japanese bankers to improve the availability and quality of financial and economic information of major country borrowers, to provide that information to IIF members on matters relating to international lending, and to create a forum for discussion of current issues. The IIF is located in Washington, DC. Coincidentally, with the creation of the IIF, in which Japanese banks participated, the Japanese government established its own Japanese Center for International Finance (JCIF).

68. Derived from *The Economist,* August 12, 1989, p. 16, and September 23, 1989, p. 94.

69. Stanley Fischer, "Recent Debt Developments," in Rudiger Dornbusch and Steve Marcus (eds.), *International Money and Debt: Challenges for the World Economy* (San Francisco: ICS Press, 1991), pp. 19–26.

Chapter 4

Urbanization and the Urban Bias

During the past three decades, there has been rapid urbanization in much of the Third World due primarily to development strategies that emphasized urban growth at the expense of agricultural and rural development. Consequently, the rate of increase in the size of the nonagricultural population now exceeds the rate of increase in meaningful nonagricultural employment opportunities, leading to what has come to be known as "overurbanization." Urbanization is conventionally defined as the process of growth in the urban proportion of a country's entire population, rather than merely in the urban population per se. If urbanization is so defined, then the appropriate measure of the rate of urbanization is the difference between the growth rates of the urban population and the national population.[1]

Current Trends in Third World Urbanization

Current urbanization rates in the Third World are unique in the sense that these trends now result in some global concern. Today, a mere 1 percent shift of the world's population from rural to urban areas represents approximately 44 million people.[2] Estimates of the United Nations suggest that during the period 1980–2000 there will be a 1.4 billion person increase in population in urban centers worldwide, as shown in Table 4.1, of which 1.2 billion people will be in the Third World.

By the year 2000, the majority of the world's urban population (66 percent) will reside in the Third World. Between 1950 and 2000, it is anticipated that the urban population of the Third World will grow by a factor of 7.7, or factors of 10.9 in Africa, 6.9 in Latin America, 9.2 in East Asia (excluding Japan), and 7.5 in South Asia. In comparison, the urban population of the more developed regions is expected to grow by a factor of only 2.4 during the same period. Seventy-four percent of the

Table 4.1

Total Urban Population and Proportion of Population Living in Urban Areas by Major Areas and Region, 1960–2000 (millions and percentages)

Region/component	1960	1970	1980	1990	2000
World total					
Total urban	1,012.1	1,354.4	1,806.8	2,422.3	3,208.0
Percentage in urban areas	33.9	37.5	41.3	45.9	51.3
Less developed regions					
Total urban	439.4	651.5	972.4	1,453.1	2,115.6
Percentage in urban areas	21.9	25.8	30.5	36.5	43.5
Africa					
Total urban	49.5	80.4	132.9	219.2	345.8
Percentage in urban areas	18.2	22.9	28.9	35.7	42.5
Latin America					
Total urban	106.6	162.4	240.6	343.3	466.2
Percentage in urban areas	49.5	57.4	64.7	70.7	75.2
Caribbean					
Total urban	7.7	11.1	15.7	21.6	28.8
Percentage in urban areas	38.2	45.1	52.2	58.7	64.6
East Asia					
Total urban	194.7	265.2	359.5	476.5	622.4
Percentage in urban areas	24.7	28.6	33.1	38.6	45.4
South Asia					
Total urban	146.9	217.3	329.8	515.7	790.7
Percentage in urban areas	17.8	20.5	24.0	29.1	36.1
Oceania					
Total urban	10.4	13.7	17.8	22.6	27.1
Percentage in urban areas	66.2	70.8	75.9	80.4	83.0

Sources: United Nations, *Patterns of Urban and Rural Population Growth*, Population Studies no. 68 (New York: United Nations, 1980); and United Nations, *World Population Trends and Policies*, Population Studes no. 103 (New York: United Nations, 1988).

anticipated growth in the global urban population between 1950 and 2000 is expected to occur in the Third World, with a breakdown of 13 percent in Africa, 16 percent in Latin America, 18 percent in East Asia, and 28 percent in South Asia.[3]

The average annual growth rates of total, rural, and urban population are presented in Table 4.2. The urban growth rates of the Third

Table 4.2

Average Annual Growth Rates of Total, Urban, and Rural Population by Region, 1960–2000 (percentages)

Component	1960	1965	1970	1975	1980	1985	1990	1995	2000
Total population									
World total	1.89	1.96	1.92	1.93	1.97	1.98	1.91	1.86	1.76
More developed regions	1.28	1.22	0.88	0.88	0.87	0.85	0.76	0.67	0.62
Less developed regions	2.18	2.31	2.39	2.36	2.39	2.37	2.29	2.22	2.08
Urban population									
World total	3.47	3.02	2.93	3.05	3.05	3.02	2.91	2.81	2.69
More developed regions	2.40	2.18	1.96	1.76	1.69	1.61	1.45	1.29	1.18
Less developed regions	5.01	4.09	4.07	4.38	4.29	4.15	3.39	3.76	3.53
Rural population									
World total	1.14	1.42	1.36	1.25	1.25	1.22	1.12	1.02	0.88
More developed regions	−0.18	−0.20	−0.93	−0.84	−0.94	−1.05	−1.21	−1.36	−1.47
Less developed regions	1.50	1.81	1.86	1.65	1.62	1.55	1.42	1.30	1.11

Source: United Nations, Population Division, *Urban–Rural Projections from 1950 to 2000*, Working Paper no. 10 (New York: United Nations, October 9, 1974).

World countries have been and are projected to continue to be twice as high as the urban growth rate of the more developed nations and three times as high by the last decade of the century. By the end of the century, the world urban population is projected to be in the neighborhood of 3.3 billion, an increase of approximately 145 percent.[4] During the period 1950–2000, world population is projected to grow by 160 percent and the urban population by 375 percent.[5] In the 1950s, Latin America and East Asia were the regions that experienced the most rapid urban growth. They have now been replaced by Africa. Urban areas in Africa were estimated to have grown during the period 1980–92 at an annual rate of 5 percent, compared with 4.4 percent during 1970-75.[6] This high growth rate may persist to the end of the century, and is expected then to decline slowly as both the total population growth and the rate of urbanization start to decline.

Components of Urbanization

The significant growth of the urban population in the Third World today is the direct result of a shift in balance between the rural and urban sectors. This shift is closely linked to economic growth and to the changing patterns of employment: in other words, it is linked to the urban bias in development strategies which has resulted in the development of commerce and industry, and the growth of transportation, communication, education, and other types of infrastructure in the urban areas. It is usually recognized in the industrialized nations that the concentration of a large percentage of the total urban population in the largest city (primacy) and the existence of a very large surrounding urban center are not necessarily found together.

In the Third World, however, they are usually found together. Capital cities dominate in the Third World for purely historical economic reasons. During the colonial era, European imperialist powers established all commercial and administrative activities close to the port areas, where raw materials were exported and consumer goods imported. With the end of the colonial era, and despite some attempts by the postcolonial governments to influence the population to settle elsewhere, the prime city in the Third World remains the focal point of both governmental and private sector activities and, as such, the rational settling place for the population.

Natural Population Increase

Despite the much larger pool of potential rural–urban migrants in the Third World, the rate of urban in-migration, on the whole, differs very little from that of the more developed countries. It is therefore fair to conclude that the causes of rapid urban growth in the Third World are closely linked to the causes of rapid natural increase, particularly in the Latin American and South Asian countries.

Demographers have shown that the proximate cause of today's rapid urban population growth in those countries with large natural increases of the urban population has been the postwar decline in mortality rates, which increased the gap between fertility and mortality. There is a broad geographical association in the Third World countries among high age-specific mortality rates, high infant mortality rates, and low life expectancy. It would be erroneous, however, to assume that mortality rates or life expectancy is a direct function of standards of living, since in many Third World countries, where there are sustained negative growth rates, there have been substantial declines in mortality rates and increases in the average life expectancy at birth.

The primary factors in the decline in world mortality have been well documented and are better understood than the factors in the decline of fertility. The decrease in mortality was in large part the unanticipated and unplanned byproduct of social, technological, economic, and political change.[7] The decrease in mortality was disproportionately achieved by lower infant and child mortality. Whereas expectation of life at birth has greatly increased, doubling and more than doubling, that at age sixty has gone up relatively little. The reduced death rates in the Third World were also partly achieved exogenously as the result of technology and technical know-how imported from abroad. Thus, although it took the United States the first half of this century to cut its death rate in half, it took Sri Lanka, for example, less than a decade to do the same after World War II.[8]

Yet, despite the continued rapid decline in mortality in the Third World, there is alarming evidence that some causes of death believed to have been subjected to control have reappeared. For example, deaths attributed to malaria have increased as this disease has again become a health problem in a number of Third World nations in Asia and Africa.[9] The main reason for this state of affairs can be traced to the persistent poverty of those nations, which has resulted in the reemergence not only of malaria but also of other diseases attributable to poor nutrition, poor sewage systems, and inadequate and polluted water supplies.

Mortality is the result of the interaction of three sets of factors affecting an individual's physical well-being: (1) public health services, such as immunization, which affect mortality regardless of individual behavior; (2) health and environmental services (for example, clean water), which reduce the costs of health to individuals but require some individual response; and (3) an array of individual characteristics, including both income, which affects health through food consumption and housing, and education, which affects the speed and efficiency with which individuals respond to health and environmental services.[10] It has been argued that of these three sets of factors affecting mortality, the benefits of the first have been more or less fully harvested.[11] Further mortality declines depend therefore on changes in individual behavior that are facilitated by increasing income and education and better access to health services.

Mortality, however, continued to decline in the Third World during the last decade, though not as quickly as it did during the previous twenty years. The Third World has now reached mortality rates ranging from about 7 per 1,000 in the upper-middle-income countries to about 10 per 1,000 in the low-income countries. These are declining rates, which the developed countries did not attain until about 1900 and, in some instances, not until 1925.[12]

With the possible exception of Africa, the Third World has entered a phase of demographic transition. After significant reductions in mortality following World War II, many Third World countries are now experiencing a decline in fertility that may eventually lead to a new state of stationary population.[13] However, since the developed world reached replacement fertility in 1975 and its population is expected to grow very little, almost all future population growth will be contributed by the Third World. The size of the future population depends, therefore, upon future fertility changes in the Third World.

Fertility declines in the Third World began in the 1950s in a small group of countries including Barbados, Guadeloupe, Mauritius, Puerto Rico, Singapore, Sri Lanka, and Trinidad and Tobago. In the early 1960s these were joined by another set of countries including Chile, Costa Rica, Guyana, Malaysia, and South Korea. During the period 1965–75, fertility began to decline rapidly in a wide range of Third World countries, including Colombia, El Salvador, Indonesia, Jamaica,

Table 4.3

Total Fertility Rate in Selected Third World Nations, 1975–92

Country	Total fertility rate			
	1975	1980	1987	1992
Bangladesh	6.6	6.0	5.5	4.0
Myanmar	5.5	5.3	4.3	4.2
India	5.7	4.9	4.3	3.7
Sri Lanka	4.2	3.6	2.7	2.5
El Salvador	6.2	5.7	4.9	3.8
Peru	5.8	5.0	4.1	3.3
Jamaica	5.4	3.9	2.9	2.5
Hong Kong	3.0	2.2	1.8	1.4
Venezuela	5.3	4.5	3.8	3.6
Singapore	2.8	1.8	1.7	1.7
Brazil	5.2	4.1	3.5	2.8
Philippines	6.4	4.6	3.9	3.9
Colombia	5.9	3.8	3.2	2.7
Mauritius	3.1	2.7	2.2	1.9

Sources: World Bank, *World Development Reports* (New York: Oxford University Press, several years); and World Bank, *World Tables* (Baltimore: Johns Hopkins University Press, several editions).

Mexico, Panama, Thailand, Tunisia, and Venezuela.[14] More recently, there were further declines in several countries, as shown in Table 4.3.

The timing of child bearing, as measured by current fertility rates for women in specific age groups, shows considerable variation in the Third World nations. In those countries where women marry young, fertility rates are high for women aged fifteen to nineteen. Among women aged forty to forty-four and forty-five to forty-nine, low fertility rates exist in several Asian countries, including those with high overall fertility, such as Pakistan. This may be explained in part by the fact that in much of Asia there is a stigma attached to women who continue to have children after their own children have started child bearing; these older women have traditionally controlled their fertility through abstinence.[15] A few nations that show substantial fertility declines, but still have a low age at marriage, tend to have peak fertility at ages twenty to twenty-four; such countries include the Dominican Republic, Guyana, Jamaica, and Panama. In contrast, some high-fertility countries, such as Jordan, Lesotho, and Syria, have high fertility rates over a wider range, generally twenty to thirty-four.[16]

Fertility rates tend to be higher in rural than in urban populations in the Third World. The differential is more pronounced and universal in Latin America. In Africa, Asia, and the Pacific, the differences are smaller and less widespread. When education is taken into consideration, the fertility differentials are much wider. In general, the average number of children per woman declines as the woman's level of education increases. Female education bears one of the strongest negative relationships to fertility. In the poorest countries, women with some primary schooling have slightly higher fertility than women with no education at all. Women who have completed primary schooling, however, virtually always have lower fertility than those with no schooling at all, and fertility declines monotonically as a mother's education increases above primary schooling.[17]

Higher levels of educational attainment in the Third World also tend to reflect higher levels of economic well-being, which in turn influence and result in lower rates of fertility. Urban incomes are generally higher than rural incomes, often by a factor of three or more, and a number of studies have shown that a wife's education level is a better predictor of fertility than that of her husband. In general, married women who work outside the home have smaller families than women who do not. According to data from the World Fertility Survey, as well as other sources, women who work for nonfamilial employers have the lowest fertility, followed by women who work for their family and then those who are self-employed; unemployed women have the highest fertility. Nonfamilial employment has a stronger effect on recent marital fertility in Latin America than it has in Asia and the Pacific.[18]

There are three key demographic factors that make for future natural urban population increase in the Third World. First is the expected and continuing drop in mortality levels, which will in turn result in a substantial increase in life expectancy. These will largely offset fertility declines. The second factor is the very high proportion of children and youth in the general population, particularly in Latin America, where 40 percent or more of the population is fifteen years of age and younger. In the industrialized nations, between 22 and 25 percent of the population is fifteen years old or younger. Thus, when those in this age group in Latin America enter their reproductive period of life, their sheer numbers will represent an awesome potential for further large population increases, regardless of the fact that the rate of increase may be diminishing. The third and final factor is time itself. A lengthy period is needed for a population structure to mature and attain a balance, which occurs when the death rate has passed through its transition period (from high to low levels), and the birth rate has done likewise. In time, the age structure will also evolve so that a larger proportion of the population is adult. Latin America, for example, finds itself near the midpoint in this process.[19] Decades must elapse, however, before the transition is completed in the Third World.

Rural–Urban Migration

Internal migration is the other important determinant of urban population growth. The usual focus is on the net migration from rural to urban areas, but also important are the urban-to-urban migration flows that take place in the Third World. The latter phenomenon is particularly important from the perspective of the smaller towns and intermediate-size cities that may be facing a net migration outflow.[20]

In Tables 4.4 and 4.5 we see the share of net migration in urban growth by region and selected countries, respectively. In sub-Saharan Africa, where most of the cities are relatively small, but growing very rapidly, migration from rural areas is the primary influence on urban growth. However, even in those nations where natural increase is the major source of urban growth, rural–urban migration makes a heavy contribution as well. Because the vast majority of migrants are young adults in the peak productive age groups, with higher fertility than the urban population as a whole, the long-term contribution of internal migration to urban population growth is actually much greater.[21]

There are basically two models of the migration process. In the first, migration is regarded as a purposeful and rational search for a better place to live and work. In the second, migration is viewed as a response to conditions that push the migrant into moving, perhaps without a rational weighing of alternatives. The theoretical literature on migration determinants is well publicized and need not be reviewed in detail here.[22] It is important, however, to discuss what the evidence from that literature suggests.

The various theories have stimulated considerable empirical activity and the results seem to be consistent. Although people migrate for a variety of reasons, the empirical evidence suggests very clearly that the primary factor determining migration is economic betterment. People migrate from rural to urban areas in response to perceived differences

Table 4.4

Average Annual Rate of Rural–Urban Transfers and Rural–Urban Transfers as a Percentage of Urban Growth for Major Regions and Subregions, 1950–60, 1970–75, and 1980–90

Region	Rural–urban transfers per 1,000 urban population			Rural–urban transfers as percent of urban growth		
	1950–60	1970–75	1980–90	1950–60	1970–75	1980–90
World total	16.7	9.3	9.3	48.7	32.5	33.0
Developed countries	12.1	9.3	7.3	48.8	46.2	49.7
Developing countries	29.2	17.1	16.4	59.3	42.0	42.2
Africa	28.6	21.9	18.1	56.3	45.2	38.7
East Africa	34.7	29.3	24.7	61.5	51.7	45.5
Middle Africa	70.3	35.7	25.3	78.7	61.1	48.8
North Africa	21.3	17.2	13.9	45.5	58.0	32.9
South Africa	13.4	10.6	10.9	36.2	28.3	28.0
West Africa	28.9	24.5	22.0	57.8	48.7	43.1
Latin America	17.1	11.6	8.6	38.4	29.5	24.1
Caribbean	5.7	9.4	8.9	19.5	28.4	28.0
Tropical America	23.1	14.4	10.0	44.2	33.1	26.5
East Asia	39.6	14.4	13.7	71.7	46.6	52.1
China	51.9	16.0	17.1	76.5	49.1	57.2
Japan	21.3	10.6	6.3	63.3	45.7	46.7
Other East Asia	25.5	21.1	13.9	47.9	49.5	41.2
South Asia	15.6	17.1	17.3	43.1	40.0	41.0
Southeast Asia	24.0	19.5	18.7	52.0	42.0	42.3
Middle Asia	9.7	14.8	16.6	32.6	37.5	40.2
West Asia	28.7	19.1	12.6	52.7	40.0	69.5
Oceania	8.7	8.1	6.0	35.7	34.3	27.8
Melanesia	81.3	64.1	41.3	82.0	72.7	61.0
Micronesia	21.2	17.4	13.6	46.9	40.6	35.4

Source: Sally Findley, *Planning for Internal Migration: A Review of Issues and Policies in Developing Countries* (Washington, DC: U.S. Government Printing Office, ISP-RD-4, 1977), p. 36.

in economic opportunities between their original location and their final destination. Migrants tend to move from low- to high-income regions, and survey after survey finds that economic factors are most frequently cited as reasons for moving. These economic motives fall into two classes: the search for employment and the search for the higher urban incomes. In most Third World countries, urban income per person can run as much as 50 percent to 100 percent higher than

Table 4.5

Percentage Share of Net Migration in Urban Growth in Selected Nations, 1975–90

Country	Share of net migration
Kenya	64.2
Bangladesh	77.8
Puerto Rico	61.0
Senegal	75.2
Thailand	69.4
Tanzania	85.0
Panama	30.7
Honduras	50.3
Peru	61.8
Indonesia	61.6
Brazil	59.4
Philippines	49.7
Cuba	89.5
Costa Rica	52.6
Guatemala	34.3
South Korea	72.8

Source: Sally E. Findley, "The Third World City: Development Policy and Issues" in J.D. Kasarda and A.M. Parnell (eds.), *Third World Cities: Problems, Policies, and Prospects* (London: Sage Publications, 1993), p. 15.

rural incomes. The differences are particularly large in Africa. In Nigeria, the average urban family income in 1978–79 was 4.6 times the rural, and in Sierra Leone, the average urban income was 4.1 times the agricultural income for the same period; in 1985, the ratio of nonagricultural to agricultural wage rates was 5.21 in Swaziland, 3.57 in Malawi, 3.51 in Zimbabwe, and 2.32 in Zambia.[23] In addition, the expectation of better education facilities for children is usually cited as a major reason for migration to the urban areas.

In addition to the predominant economic factors, there are some demographic factors that tend to influence migration selectivity. Migrants are relatively young; they tend to be between the ages of fifteen and thirty. In Latin America, migration is predominantly female, while in Africa and South Asia it appears to be predominantly male.[24] Female migration to cities in Latin America is encouraged by the multitude of jobs available for women in domestic and other service activities. This age and sex selectivity reflects the life-cycle factor influencing migration. At certain stages in an individual's life there is a high likelihood of changing households and communities at the same time. Examples of such points in the life-cycle are when youth first leave the parental home in search of employment, upon marriage or divorce, and upon retirement.

Another factor in migration selectivity is education. Migrants tend to be well educated and highly motivated relative to the population at the point of origin. Individuals with formal education, especially at the secondary level or higher, can obtain good jobs in government or commerce. These jobs are located in major urban centers and hence aspiring employees must migrate to these cities. Cities that receive migrants thus are not, on balance, burdened with a flood of uneducated, unskilled, and unmotivated individuals and households, although there is little doubt that rural–urban migration tends to keep urban wages at lower levels than would prevail in the absence of migration.[25]

Rural–urban migration continues to be the dominant net migration flow in nearly all Third World nations. Rapid rural–urban migration in the Third World presents both obstacles and opportunities to Third World cities. More than 3 billion people live in the poor countries of Africa, Asia, and Latin America. Of these, about 800 million to 1 billion people are the truly poor. From one-fourth to one-half or even more of these people live in the slums, shanty towns, and streets of the Third World's cities—Lima, Georgetown, Bombay, Bogota—giving rise to what is now regarded as the "urban dilemma."

Consequences of Urbanization

Until a few years ago, economists, demographers, and urban planners alike regarded urbanization as positively associated with higher productivity and industrialization. Proponents of the thesis that large cities have a positive role in development pointed to the advantages for firms or businesses from access to larger markets for their products, as well as for labor and other inputs; they also pointed out the advantages that urban residents enjoy in terms of access to better social services, and the value of the more organized participation in the political process that comes with increased urbanization.[26]

In contrast, however, it is now persuasively clear that there are negative effects and some costs associated with the concentration of economic activity and population in the urban areas of the Third World. The "overurbanization" that results is associated with widespread unemployment and underemployment, in addition to all of the problems of inadequate housing, inadequate access to urban services, traffic congestion, and environmental pollution.

The principal measurement of how well urban areas in Third World countries have absorbed the rapid population growth is estimates of urban unemployment. One of the major consequences of the rapid urbanization experienced by Third World nations in the past two decades has been the increasing supply of urban job seekers. In many countries the supply of job seekers far exceeds demand; this situation results in extremely high rates of unemployment and underemployment in the urban areas. When account is taken of the underemployment rate, which exceeds 25 percent in Latin America, Asia, and Africa, then the overall figure for urban surplus labor well exceeds 30 percent in many Third World nations.[27]

Some research further points out that open unemployment in urban areas is a more serious problem for those fifteen to twenty-four years old than for the total labor force, for females than for males, and, at least up to a postsecondary level of education, for the more educated than for the less educated.[28] This situation, however, has been changing somewhat with the growth of the subterranean sector, as discussed in chapter 5.

Some studies have shown that the migrant group of the urban population tends to have lower rates of unemployment than the natives, possibly because they accept jobs that natives will not take. Low unemployment rates among migrants may or may not lead to increased unemployment among natives. If the jobs are really ones that natives do not take, the natives' unemployment levels may be unaffected.[29] This is an important issue, however, since it brings into question the popular assumption that migrants raise urban unemployment levels either through their own unemployment or by taking jobs away from natives.

Despite the fact that average household incomes tend to be systematically higher in urban than in rural areas and tend to be positively associated with city size, in the cities underemployment and unemployment have a negative income impact on the family and often contribute to its instability. Since the mother and other family members leave home to work, this creates a situation in which children and young people lose some adult supervision. Often the children themselves must find work, and if they do, they also leave home at an early age, which in turn contributes to the disintegration of the family unit. One effect of urbanization has too often been the abandonment of children as traditional value systems erode. Employment and poverty in urban settings clearly have different effects on family structures from those found in rural areas.[30]

The rapid process of urbanization in the Third World has given rise to concern regarding the costs of urbanization. Uncontrolled and unplanned urban growth makes it difficult for cities to provide residents with the services they desire, despite the current urban bias with respect to development expenditures and strategies. Urbanization is divisive because it is expensive. The difference between the costs of urban development and rural development turns on infrastructure. Urban housing, for example, is much more expensive than rural housing. The proportion of urban children for whom schooling is provided is always much higher than in rural areas. Moreover, rural residents do more for themselves with their own resources than do urban residents.[31]

There are four common, but distinct, reasons for concern over the costs of urbanization in the Third World:

1. Fiscal—Urbanization places a heavy burden on governments as they have to meet the rapidly rising demand for urban services.
2. Financial—The high financial costs of urbanization are believed to be the prime cause of the heavy and growing international indebtedness of Third World nations.
3. Efficiency—The economic costs of urbanization (including congestion and pollution costs) are taken to exceed those of rural growth; this in turn is taken as a basis for judging urban development excessive in terms of economic efficiency.
4. Equity—Rural households are thought to subsidize high urbanization costs.[32]

The conclusions on these four considerations, as determined by Linn,[33] are: It is impossible to derive an overall judgment about how aggregate public service costs vary with settlement size. Despite the fact that urbanization imposes a rapidly growing fiscal burden on Third World governments, there is little reason to suspect that reducing the urbanization process per se will reduce this burden unless it is accompanied by reduced rates of industrialization or reduced population and income growth. With respect to financial considerations, it was found that rapid urbanization was not the primary cause of international indebtedness of the Third World nations. There is simply no statistical correlation between urbanization rates and debt ratios. In terms of efficiency considerations, costs alone were found not to influence the optimum degree of urbanization or optimum size of cities. Benefits have to be taken into consideration also.

Moreover, many of the apparent symptoms of urban inefficiency, in particular congestion and pollution, are due to inappropriate policies within the city rather than the result of inefficient city size or inefficiently high rates of urbanization. Finally, with respect to equity considerations, it was found that rural dwellers do not necessarily subsidize urbanization costs. Where this may be the case, the cause was found to be inequitable public pricing and tax policies.

The above conclusions notwithstanding, other evidence suggests that the rapid growth of urban areas has far outpaced the ability of Third World governments to provide adequate services.[34] There is evidence that air pollution, noise levels, congestion, crime, and health problems tend to increase more than proportionately with the size of urban centers.[35] Urban living has increased both the quantity and the quality of the economic needs and desires of the population. Such changes are very important since they raise individual expectations and impose added constraints on the economic policies of governments, thereby reinforcing the urban bias in the use of resources.

Pollution, congestion, lack of adequate services, and urban sprawl are experienced by urban centers in both developed and Third World nations. There is a fundamental difference, however, based on degree. Urbanization in the Third World has occurred at a much more rapid pace, and most of the cities have been unable to meet the growing demand for housing and urban services. Such urban growth is expected to continue into the foreseeable future, even if national policy biases favoring urbanization are corrected. Consequently, the degree of efficiency with which Third World nations allocate their resources will increasingly determine their overall economic performance.

From a quantitative standpoint, using data from the *Human Development Reports* of the United Nations Development Programme, and as shown in Table 4.6, it is possible to demonstrate examples of the degree to which the rural areas lag behind the urban areas. In terms of infant mortality, for several Central American countries the rate is 30 percent to 50 percent higher in rural than in urban areas. For about thirty-one Third World countries, data on the nutritional status of children indicate higher rates of malnutrition in rural areas, 50 percent

Table 4.6

Rural–Urban Disparities: Percentage of Population with Access to Social Services in Selected Countries[a]

Country	Health		Water		Sanitation	
	Rural	Urban	Rural	Urban	Rural	Urban
Argentina	21	80	17	63	29	100
Bolivia	36	90	27	77	10	33
Mozambique	30	100	9	38	12	53
Pakistan	35	99	27	83	6	51
Somalia	15	50	22	58	5	44
Algeria	80	100	55	85	40	80
Costa Rica	63	100	86	100	94	100
Honduras	65	85	45	56	34	24
Korea, Rep.	100	100	79	97	100	100
Tanzania	72	99	42	90	58	93
All Third World countries	45	88	62	85	45	75

Source: United Nations Development Programme, *Human Development Reports* (New York: Oxford University Press, several years).
[a]Based on the most recent estimate.

higher on average. Rural illiteracy rates for selected countries in Africa and Asia are generally twice the urban rates—and for women in Latin America the rural rates are three times higher than the urban rates, and for men, four times higher.

For health care, access is better in urban areas than in rural areas in every Third World country. In about twenty Third World countries, the percentage of the population covered by health facilities in urban areas is more than twice that covered in rural areas. The rural–urban differences in water and sanitation facilities are even greater. Less than 50 percent of the rural population is covered in several of the Third World countries; in some, less than 30 percent of their rural dwellers have access to water. In Mali, access to sanitation facilities in urban areas was nineteen times that in rural areas, while in Guatemala the urban estimate was as much as twenty-four times higher than the rural figure.

Some Policies to Manage Rapid Urbanization

Third World governments have not succeeded in planning urban growth, which has taken place more or less spontaneously. The solution to this urbanization problem requires the adaptation of current Third World urban growth to the limitations imposed by each country's available resources. This type of adaptation ought to result in an "appropriate" city. Such appropriateness implies that the development of urban strategy should be designed to cover the maximum number of the existing population.

Despite the fact that it may be very late to bring about important changes in larger cities, the inevitable urban growth that will be affecting the cities of all sizes in the next two or three decades means that there will be repeated opportunities for doing better before patterns become irreversible. As such, appropriate national urbanization policies must be given priority in the Third World and must include four major objectives: full development of the national resources of the country; maintenance of national cohesion among various regions, particularly in the case of very large disparities in per capita output among regions; prevention or correction of excessive concentration of economic activities within the urban regions; and more efficient and more equitable growth management within cities.[36]

National urbanization policies will be influenced from country to country by the economic, social, political, and cultural characteristics that exist within each country. Countries differ widely with respect to their national urban systems, and these differences imply dissimilar urbanization policies. For example, the strategy to combat a high primacy pattern, such as in Thailand, would be inappropriate for a country with a more balanced spatial structure, such as Malaysia. Also, policies would vary between high-urbanization regions and low-urbanization regions. In general, the lower the current level of urbanization, the greater the scope for a national urbanization policy in the sense of flexibility in changing the urban size distribution.[37]

It follows, then, that national urbanization policies must include elements that reduce urban unemployment and narrow the rural–urban wage gap, increase the relative disposition of the public services in the urban centers, and foster integrated rural development.

Urban Job Creation and the Elimination of Urban Biases

The primary cause of urban poverty in the Third World is the severely limited income earned by the poor through gainful employment. Policies designed to increase the employment and wages of the urban poor must therefore be given most attention. The basic issue to be dealt with therefore is how the urban labor supply can be absorbed at decent wages without further increasing the urban–rural wage differential.

Perhaps the most powerful stimulus to job creation, and hence labor demand, is economic growth. Economic growth leads to rapid labor absorption throughout the economy in both urban and rural areas. Conversely, when economies stagnate, as is currently the case in the Third World, unemployment is a much more pressing problem. Policies aimed at improving the economic growth of a nation are therefore very important elements of any employment strategy. However, such macroeconomic policies by themselves cannot eliminate the general employment problem in the Third World. Clearly, supplementary policies will be needed that bring about the growth of the manufacturing and service activities sectors. Policies designed to generate rapid and sustainable growth in these sectors will therefore also lead to rapid growth in the demand for urban labor.

With respect to urban wage biases, wage rates have consistently been higher in the urban areas. Wage rates in rural areas are usually thought to be determined either by subsistence or nutritional requirements or by the forces of supply and demand, the latter entailing competition, dualism, and monopsony. Efforts to narrow the rural–urban wage gap usually involve income policies to keep urban wage rates from rising and price supports for agricultural products to raise incomes, as in Kenya. Some nations, such as Singapore, have also exercised wage restraint by curtailing the power of the trade unions. Since 1953, India has sought to moderate wage demands through labor courts, wage boards, and industrial tribunals. Other countries, such as Tanzania, have used public sector wage scales. But perhaps what is needed is a freeze on urban wage rates, particularly in the public sector, either through a modification of civil service salary scales or by allowing urban prices and taxes to accelerate disproportionately to rural prices and taxes.[38] Unless such concrete efforts are made to moderate the rural–urban wage differential, then migration from the rural to the urban areas will continue to be a rational decision for achieving economic betterment.

Improving Urban Public Services

Rapid urbanization in the Third World has made it difficult for governments to provide all of the public services urban residents need in a timely and efficient manner. The combination of urban congestion and inadequate services generates health, education, transportation, and housing problems.

Education and Health Policy

Government involvement in the provision of social services such as education and health has been a longstanding practice in the Third World. On average, urban households are more educated, healthier, and better served by education and health facilities than their rural counterparts. The urban poor, however, usually have limited access to the better health care centers and schools in the urban areas because of the prohibitive costs. To combat this situation, a number of countries, notably in the Caribbean, have implemented systems of universal education and health care to ensure access for everyone, regardless of income level or social stratum. These countries must be commended, and such a universalized system of education and health care ought to be attempted in other Third World nations as an effort toward meeting basic human needs in those nations. Such attempts ought to be implemented, however, through a decentralized framework that entails private sector participation: that is, allowing private schools and private provision of health care.

Every individual is born with a collection of abilities and talents. Education, in its many forms, has the potential to help fulfill and apply them, while the widespread provision of basic, preventive, and curative medical services is essential to the life expectancy of all individuals.

Recognition of the link between education and development has made public expenditures on education very important in many nations when measured in relation to gross national product. For a number of Third World nations, education absorbed more than a quarter of all public expenditures. More and more, education is being placed in the overall context of development objectives as one of the many important policy instruments to alleviate the problem of rapid urbanization and national development.

Three separate but related perspectives illustrate the significance of education to development.[39] First, education is a basic human need. It provides people with fundamental knowledge, skills, values, and attitudes, while enhancing their capacity to change and their willingness to accept new ideas. In the Third World, education is becoming increasingly necessary for survival. It assists people in understanding and benefiting from change and helps them to persevere in attaining their economic rights. Second, education is a means of meeting other basic needs, mainly because it provides the necessary knowledge for change in current practices and skills to better use the services provided. Increased productivity and greater longevity arising directly out of education raise the demand for better housing, more food, cleaner water, and more educational and health facilities, while enabling society as a whole to better satisfy such needs. The relationship is reciprocal. Third, education plays a critical role in development by providing individuals with the ability to change their culture and to seek constructive roles in society that promote development.

Improving health in the Third World requires efforts far beyond medical care. It is closely linked with food and nutrition, with employment and income distribution, and with the international economy. In general terms, the determinants of health have long been well known. One is people's purchasing power over certain goods and services, including food, housing, fuel, soap, water, and medical services. Another is the health environment—climate, standards of public sanitation, and the prevalence of communicable diseases. A third is people's understanding of nutrition, health, and hygiene.[40]

The 1970s witnessed the evolution of a much broader approach to health policy, including attempts to implement universal low-cost basic health care. Primary and preventive health care, however, is still not a nationwide reality in most Third World nations. In fact, public health expenditures in the Third World are heavily biased in favor of curative care, and within this category the emphasis is on in-hospital rather than outpatient care, despite the prevalence of diseases whose incidence could be greatly reduced by preventive measures. In 1990, the amount of public health expenditures on preventive and cost-effective health care was estimated to be only a little more than $1 per person.[41] The diversion of public resources to hospitals that provide high-quality care for relatively few people rather than environmental sanitation and mass immunization is a costly social waste at the expense of the poor. There is a long list of diseases to which the poor are particularly susceptible and that can be prevented by the better provision of environmental sanitation projects, piped water, and insecticides.[42]

Health policy in the Third World should therefore reverse existing priorities; indeed, there is some indication that this is beginning to take place. In Indonesia and the Philippines, for example, recent health care projects have emphasized comprehensive preventive care. But perhaps the framework of the basic health care system in Jamaica provides the best example for Third World nations of a comprehensive primary health care system. The system operates out of community-based health centers in locations easily accessible to the poor; it relies primarily on outpatient treatment; it emphasizes preventive health care and education (focused particularly on the needs of such vulnerable groups as pregnant mothers, infants, and children), improved sanitation, maternal and infant care, immunization, family planning, and nutrition programs; and it is supported by a relatively inexpensive but effective paramedical staff.[43]

Transportation Policy

Transportation is typically a means to other ends, in both its passenger and freight aspects. As the essential link between producers and users of goods and services, it plays a central role in the development of urban areas. Traffic congestion inevitably occurs as urban areas grow because transport facilities cannot be expanded enough to maintain mobility, in part because of resource limitations, and in part because urban transport demand is not curtailed by pricing or regulation. The private automobile takes roughly nine times more road space per passenger than does a bus. The explosive increase in automobiles in the urban areas of the Third World, at rates two to five times those of urban populations, therefore exerts tremendous demands on the existing urban road space, and is a major cause of severe congestion and pollution problems, especially in the cities of the middle-income countries.[44]

The poor are mostly affected by the transportation dilemma in the Third World in terms of both the cost and their dependence on it for access to employment and services. As such, disruptions in transportation service create severe hardships for this already hard-pressed group. Considerable scope therefore exists for revising current transportation policies and replacing them with policies that would, inter alia, emphasize mass transit facilities, help conserve energy and foreign exchange, improve access for the poor, impose user fee charges for cost recovery of existing public transportation investments, encourage private service provision and/or denationalize mass transit facilities, and enforce national regulations that maintain order and accountability.

Housing Policy

The need for housing is fundamental. But many Third World nations have not been able to give it priority. However, the high concentration and visibility of deficiencies in urban housing make this one of the most urgent problems facing Third World nations in their transition from rural to urban societies, ultimately resulting in a shortage of adequate housing, which leads to overcrowding, squatter settlements, and steeply climbing housing prices. For example, in Kumasi, Ghana, three of every four households live in only one room. Half of the population of Calcutta, one-third of the urban population of Mexico City, and most people in urban Africa live in similar conditions.

Many Third World nations have developed public housing programs including sites and services schemes. Most of these efforts, however, have failed because they were poorly located, poorly built, or poorly designed, and were often too costly for the poor.[45] Furthermore, there can be no serious housing policy for the poor without a bold land policy, and such a land policy faces grave political obstacles. Often, construction of public housing has been combined with slum clearance programs. This is usually regarded as the solution to the slums' social byproduct by doing away with them easily and quickly. Yet, in most cases, slum clearance is of little help, and is even detrimental to efforts to provide housing.

Several countries have constructed residential estates located some distance from the urban centers. These housing estates help decongest the city and take advantage of lower land prices outside the city. Yet, housing estates suffer from many of the ills of public housing—namely, poor transportation links, inappropriate design, and high rents.[46] Other countries have attempted to cope with housing shortages by promoting cooperative schemes, as was the case in Guyana during the 1970s. This option is not without its problems, however. This type of construction is dependent on mutual cooperation and the participatory process, which cannot be guaranteed for the duration of the construction. Moreover, there is considerable dependence on the government for permits, licenses, and foreign-exchange releases to acquire materials, all of which are subject to bureaucratic discretion and tend to be under the control of corrupt officials who have to be bribed.

Housing policy in the Third World must contain elements that eliminate obstacles to private construction and provision efforts, result in the availability of housing finance, and encourage the upgrading of slums by private developers.

Developing the Rural Sector

The bulk of the poor in the Third World live in rural areas. Urban poverty, however, is more obvious—the slums and degradation of some cities in the Third World force themselves upon the notice of the richest citizen and upon the most casual visitor. But most of the slum inhabitants and squatters on the streets have migrated to towns because they are pushed out of the rural areas by landlessness, joblessness, and hopelessness. It is therefore in the rural areas that the long-term problems of urban poverty can be tackled most effectively. Trying to confront mass poverty by only improving conditions and providing work in the urban centers simply attracts more people from the depressed rural areas.[47]

The development of the rural sector is therefore essential not only in terms of local improvement but also as a part of the overall national economic policy. Rural development is taken here to mean the far-reaching transformation of social and economic institutions, structures, relationships, and processes in any rural area. It conceives of the cardinal aim of rural development not simply as agricultural and economic growth in the narrow sense, but as balanced social and economic development—including the generation of new employment, the equitable distribution of income, widespread improvement in health, nutrition, and housing, greatly broadened opportunities for all individuals to realize their full potential through education, and a strong voice for all the rural people in shaping the decisions and actions that affect their lives.[48]

For rural development to be successful, it must be integrative in nature. Integrated rural development, as a concept, was first introduced by the donor agencies in the 1960s, referring to particular types of projects designed to meet the requirements of simultaneous and comprehensive action in such areas as water, power, extension, credit, roads, and storage. The idea was that the various complementary activities of rural development required a single administrative framework, rather than being implemented by a variety of separate agencies. The success of such projects in raising productivity and incomes in particular areas helped popularize the slogan of integrated rural development, which became the subject of a number of international conferences and seminars in the 1960s and 1970s.

The essential thrust of rural development is action to raise the level of living of the rural poor. Specific means for doing so encompass a wide range of approaches, which, if they are to be successful, must be adapted to the existing country situation; must be realistic in terms of implementation; and must be supported by the policy makers. To achieve all of these goals, particular attention must be given to all aspects of the population situation, since it is only through balanced and coordinated efforts to increase production and services, and to control population growth, that significant improvements in living standards can be achieved in the Third World. Such integrated development is particularly important since much of the unemployed and underemployed rural labor force, together with substantial new additions to the labor force, must be retained in rural areas if the problems of the urban areas are not to be exacerbated through uncontrolled migration.

Rural development strategies focus particularly, but not exclusively, on the agricultural sector since agricultural activity is the major economic activity in the rural areas of the Third World. Debates over development strategy have often swirled around the relative importance to be assigned to agriculture versus industry. The historical evidence suggests that this dichotomy is frequently overstated. Specifically, the notion that rapid industrialization entails a total neglect of agriculture is erroneous; it underestimates the importance of the mutually beneficial links between agriculture and industrial development, and, indeed, in most Third World nations, successful industrialization has been supported by sustained and broadly based agricultural growth. The major issues in agricultural development in Third World nations are how to sustain a rate of growth that allows for a balanced expansion of all parts of the economy, and how to ensure that the pattern of agricultural growth is such as to make a strong and direct impact on rural poverty and, indirectly, on the reduction of migration of the poor to urban areas.

In the struggle toward industrialization, it has been relatively easy to overlook the importance of the agricultural sector in development and to neglect the necessary harmony between policies to encourage the growth of industry and the performance of agriculture. But, despite the recent rapid rise of industry and the growing urbanization, the agricultural sector still looms large in the Third World since it is the sector that provides employment for a large section of the labor force, contains the majority of poor people, and is the birthplace of many of the urban poor.[49]

Realization of the objectives of a broad-based integrated rural development strategy, however, hinges on national commitment and on the translation of that commitment into three areas of action. First, there must be the necessary policy changes, including more equitable distribution of land rights and market pricing for crops produced by subsistence farmers, in particular for cash crops. Second, resources must be allocated on a priority basis to increase the productivity of the subsistence rural sector to develop agricultural technology, effective extension, and transportation networks. Third, an adequate effort must be geared to developing institutional capability in the rural agricultural sector to maximize the use of existing resources and thus to ensure effective implementation of the policies directed at the unemployed.[50]

Fundamental to any process of organized rural development is the active and willing participation of rural peoples in the development of the area where they reside.[51] Such participation requires not only that these people share in the distribution of the benefits of development—be they the material benefits of increased output or other benefits considered enhancing to the quality of life—but that they also share in the task of creating these benefits. Participation may be regarded as a substitute for political mobilization. It is, in that sense, therefore, the antithesis of politicization. It provides, optimally, political legitimation for institutional programs without significant conflict.[52] This then serves to enhance the viability and success of the program or programs.

Former Tanzanian president Julius Nyerere argues that "if the people are to be able to develop they must have power. They must be able to control their own activities within the framework of their village communities. The people must participate not just in the physical labour involved in economic development but also in the planning of it and the determination of priorities."[53] Projects of genuine social and economic value are most likely to be identified, planned, and built if rural people are able to play a decisive role in choosing them. One author argues that optimum participation must be included among development's strategic principles because, unless efforts are made to widen participation, development will interfere with man's quest for esteem and freedom from manipulation.[54]

That higher levels of participation of the poor should and do generally have positive effects on socioeconomic equality in the Third World is a foregone conclusion. More particularly, widespread participation generally means wider access to power, and those who gain access to power will insist on actions to broaden their share in the economic benefits of society. In Jamaica, for example, participation of the poor in a rural development project was closely linked to the benefits that the members derived therefrom.[55] There are also large and growing numbers of peasant community organizations in such countries as Paraguay and Peru through which the rural poor are striving to improve their situations, and their endurance, in the face of great odds, suggests the importance of the participatory process to them and their communities.[56]

But, despite the advocacy of the participatory process in the development literature, and notwithstanding its successful implementation in some countries, a number of obstacles to participation of the poor in the rural development process persist in the Third World. The obstacles faced vary and are found within the implementing agencies, within the rural communities themselves, and also within the broader institutions of the society.[57] Within the implementing agencies, the primary problem is their centralized nature, which does not lend itself to participation in decision making by others. Moreover, these agencies tend to be located at some distance, in national or regional capitals, which keeps them out of touch with the rural communities they are intended to serve.

In the rural communities themselves, the major problems are a lack of appropriate local organization and corruption on the part of the more powerful community individuals who take personal advantage of any latitude for influence available, thus corrupting the purpose of the participatory approach and destroying the spirit of cooperative effort. Within the broader society, the basic problem is that participation is generally pursued as a way of reaching the poorer elements of a society'to increase their welfare. This involves a societal change process, however, which tends to conflict with the status quo.[58]

It follows, therefore, that for the participatory process to be effective, both political and economic power must be held by the people within their communities. The rural residents are in the best position to choose which organizations they will participate in.[59] Experience shows that effective participation cannot be commanded by policy makers, but must instead be induced through the advocacy of projects that offer sufficient incentives to attract the personal resources of time, energy, and freedom of action away from other urgent and competing tasks of the poor.

Concluding Remarks

Urban populations in many Third World nations are growing at rates far in excess of current labor absorption rates. The primary factors influencing the decision to migrate are jobs and wages. However, economic betterment is not necessarily sufficient cause for migration. Social, educational, and some personal factors may also play a strong role in determining the incidence and timing of migration.

Unquestionably, an urban bias exists in the Third World. The urban sector in the Third World receives a disproportionately large share of government expenditures and capital investments. Also, the bulk of the Third World's social services are located in the cities, particularly in the large metropolitan areas, although such things as public transportation fares are subsidized by the entire population out of general revenues. This type of differential treatment, in turn, confirms and strengthens the reality of the city as the dynamic sector of the Third World nations.

Underlying these facts are the unresolved rural development problems. A brief list of them would include the low wages paid to rural workers; the repeated periods of unemployment and underemployment; the lack of agricultural credit for small landowners; and the isolation of some rural communities without potable water, electricity, or medical, educational, or other services considered essential by urban residents. For the Third World countries as a whole, people in urban areas have twice the access to health services and safe water and four times the sanitation services that people have in rural areas.

Urbanization can be regarded as both a contributor to and the result of elusive development in the Third World. It contributes to elusive development by placing inordinate demands on the scarce resources of governments. It is the result of elusive development, in turn, because scarce resources are not being used to develop rural areas. Such rural development would contain the rural population and diminish their desire to migrate to the urban areas, thereby reducing both the rate and the negative effects of urbanization. If rural standards of living can be generally improved for the majority of the rural population, then rural–urban migration can be checked. But the growth of the urban centers will not automatically stop. However, with a serious movement away from strategies with an urban bias and a concentrated effort toward rural development, urban growth in the Third World could become manageable and national development less elusive.

Finally, Third World nations need to move further in the direction of encouraging a more intensive commercialization of agriculture—that is, the production of cash crops not only to increase rural incomes and thereby discourage migration, but also as an integral part of the national development strategy. While cash crops can include food crop production ·surpluses that are sold locally, they are generally understood to be exclusively for sale and, in many instances, for export. This commercial orientation identifies a cash crop, whether or not the cash crop is a food crop.

Cash crops play an important part in producing higher incomes in the Third World and, thus, in increasing food availability. Food security can only be achieved when people have adequate income.[60] Accordingly, a long-term solution to the problem of world hunger requires higher levels of income in the Third World, which can be accomplished through the commercialization of agriculture. Moreover, much needed foreign exchange can also be earned for the Third World nations where the crops are exported. Such commercialization is not, however, inconsistent with increased food crop production. Countries that have done well in cash crop production have also been among the most successful in expanding food production.[61] There is a positive relationship between commercialization of agriculture and national development which needs to be seriously taken into account by Third World governments.

Notes

1. United Nations, *Patterns of Urban and Rural Population Growth*, Population Studies no. 68 (New York: United Nations, 1980), pp. 33–34.

2. Kathleen Newland, *City Limits: Emerging Constraints on Urban Growth* (Washington, DC: Worldwatch Paper 38, Worldwatch Institute, 1980), p. 7.

3. United Nations, *World Population Trends and Policies,* Population Studies no. 103 (New York: United Nations, 1988), p. 179.

4. Bertrand Renaud, *National Urbanization Policy in Developing Countries* (New York: Oxford University Press, 1981), p. 15.

5. Ibid.

6. United Nations, *Patterns of Urban and Rural Population Growth*, pp. 12–13; and World Bank, *World Development Report 1994* (New York: Oxford University Press, 1994), p. 223.

7. United Nations, *The Determinants and Consequences of Population Trends* (New York: United Nations, 1973), chap. 5.

8. Philip M. Hauser, "Introduction and Overview," in P. Hauser (ed.), *World Population and Development* (Syracuse: Syracuse University Press, 1979), p. 15.

9. See Rafael M. Salas, "The State of the World Population, 1978," *Annual Report on UNFPA Activities and Plans to the Governing Council* (New York: United Nations, 1978).

10. Nancy Birdsall, *Population and Poverty in the Developing World*, Staff Working Paper no. 404 (Washington, DC: World Bank, 1980), p. 16.

11. See Jacques Loup, *Can the Third World Survive?* (Baltimore: Johns Hopkins University Press, 1983), pp. 61–65.

12. Ibid., p. 4.

13. Ibid., p. 62.

14. William W. Murdoch, *The Poverty of Nations* (Baltimore: Johns Hopkins University Press, 1980), p. 87.

15. R. Lightbourne, S. Singh, and C.P. Green, "The World Fertility Survey: Charting Global Childbearing," *Population Bulletin, 37* (March 1982), p. 20.

16. Ibid.

17. See Susan H. Cochrane, *Fertility and Education: What Do We Really Know?* (Baltimore: Johns Hopkins University Press, 1979).

18. R. Lightbourne, S. Singh, and C.P. Green, "The World Fertility Survey: Charting Global Childbearing," pp. 23–24; and M. Mhloyi, *Status of Women Population and Development* (Liège: International Union for the Scientific Study of Population, 1994), pp. 8–10.

19. Inter-American Development Bank, *Economic and Social Progress in Latin America 1979* (Washington, DC: IDB, 1979), p. 127.

20. Johannes F. Linn, *Cities in the Developing World: Policies for Their Equitable and Efficient Growth* (New York: Oxford University Press, 1983), p. 44.

21. Michael P. Todaro, "Urbanization in Developing Nations: Trends, Prospects, and Policies," *Journal of Geography, 79* (September–October 1980), p. 169.

22. See for example, Michael P. Todaro, *Internal Migration in Developing Countries* (Geneva: ILO, 1976); Lorene Y.L. Yap, "The Attraction of Cities: A Review of the Migration Literature," *Journal of Development Economics, 4* (September 1977), pp. 239–264; and Sally Findley, *Planning for Internal Migration: A Review of Issues and Policies in Developing Countries* (Washington, DC: U.S. Government Printing Office, ISP-RD-4, 1977).

23. United Nations Development Programme, *Human Development Report 1990* (New York: Oxford University Press, 1990), p. 30; and ILO, *Yearbook of Labour Statistics* (Geneva: ILO, several years).

24. Bryan Roberts, *Cities of Peasants: The Political Economy of Urbanization in the Third World* (Beverly Hills, CA: Sage Publications, 1978), p. 100.

25. Johannes F. Linn, *Cities in the Developing World: Policies for their Equitable and Efficient Growth*, p. 44.

26. Carmen A. Miro and Joseph E. Potter, *Population Policy: Research Priorities in the Developing World* (New York: St. Martin's Press, 1980), p. 124.

27. Michael P. Todaro, "Urbanization in Developing Nations: Trends, Prospects, and Policies," p. 169.

28. Lyn Squire, *Employment in Developing Countries: A Survey of Issues and Evidence* (New York: Oxford University Press, 1981), pp. 66–69.

29. Sally Findley, *Planning for Internal Migration: A Review of Issues and Policies in Developing Countries,* p. 41.

30. Inter-American Development Bank, *Economic and Social Progress in Latin America 1979,* p. 138.

31. W. Arthur Lewis, *The Evolution of the International Economic Order* (Princeton, NJ: Princeton University Press, 1978), pp. 39–40.

32. See Johannes F. Linn, "The Costs of Urbanization in Developing Countries," *Economic Development and Cultural Change, 30* (April 1982), pp. 625–48.

33. Ibid.

34. Michael P. Todaro, *City Bias and Rural Neglect: The Dilemma of Urban Development* (New York: Population Council, 1981), p. 27.

35. See, for example, Irving Hoch, "Urban Scale and Environmental Quality," in R.G. Ridker (ed.), *Resources and Environmental Implications of United States Population Growth* (Baltimore: Johns Hopkins University Press, 1973); and Inter-American Development Bank, *Economic and Social Progress in Latin America 1979,* p. 135.

36. See Bertrand Renaud, *National Urbanization Policy in Developing Countries,* p. 7.

37. Harry W. Richardson, "National Urban Development Strategies in Developing Countries," *Urban Studies, 18* (October 1981), p. 272.

38. Michael P. Todaro, "Urbanization in Developing Nations: Trends, Prospects, and Policies," p. 173.

39. See Abdun Noor, *Education and Basic Human Needs*, Staff Working Paper no. 450 (Washington, DC: World Bank, 1981), pp. 2–4.

40. World Bank, *World Development Report 1980* (Washington, DC: World Bank, 1980). p. 53.

41. World Bank, *World Development Report 1993* (New York: Oxford University Press, 1993), pp. 66–67.

42. Kempe Ronald Hope, Sr., "Urbanization and Economic Development in the Third World," *Cities, 3* (February 1986), p. 50.

43. World Bank, *World Development Report 1979* (Washington, DC: World Bank, 1979), p. 84.

44. Ibid., p. 79.

45. A.G. Tipple, "The Need for New Urban Housing in Sub-Saharan Africa: Problem or Opportunity," *African Affairs, 93* (October 1994), pp. 591–93; and C. Rakodi and P. Withers, "Sites and Services: Home Ownership for the Poor?" *Habitat International, 19,* 3 (1995), pp. 371–89.

46. John F. Turner, "Uncontrolled Urban Development: Problems and Policies," *International Social Development Review, 1* (1966), pp. 123–24; and Ellen M. Brennan, "Urban Land and Housing Issues Facing the Third World," in J.D. Kasarda and A.M. Parnell (eds.), *Third World Cities: Problems, Policies, and Prospects* (London: Sage Publications, 1993), pp. 74–91.

47. Julius K. Nyerere, *On Rural Development,* Address to the Food and Agriculture Organization World Conference on Agrarian Reform and Rural Development, Rome, July 13, 1979, pp. 3–4.

48. P. Coombs and M. Ahmed, *Attacking Rural Poverty: How Non-formal Education Can Help* (Baltimore: Johns Hopkins University Press, 1974), pp. 13–14.

49. Kempe Ronald Hope, Sr., "Agriculture and Economic Development in the Caribbean," *Food Policy, 6* (November 1981), p. 253.

50. See John W. Mellor, *Agricultural Development in the Third World: The Food, Development, Foreign Assistance, Trade Nexus,* Address to the World Food Conference, European Parliament, Brussels, April 6–8, 1988.

51. See David J. King, *Land Reform and Participation of the Rural Poor in the Development Process in African Countries* (Washington, DC: World Bank Conference Papers on Land Reform, 1973).

52. Charles Harvey and others, *Rural Employment and Administration in the Third World: Development Methods and Alternative Strategies* (Geneva: ILO/Saxon House, 1979), pp. 23–25.

53. Julius K. Nyerere, *On Rural Development,* p. 8.

54. Denis Goulet, *The Cruel Choice* (New York: Antheneum, 1971), p. 148.

55. Arthur A. Goldsmith and Harvey S. Blustain, *Local Organization and Participation in Integrated Rural Development in Jamaica* (Ithaca, NY: Rural Development Committee, Cornell University, 1980), pp. 88–89.

56. Peter Hakim, "Lessons from Grass-Root Development Experience in Latin America and the Caribbean," *Assignment Children, 59–60,* 2 (1982), p. 138.

57. See Frances F. Korten, "Community Participation: A Management Perspective on Obstacles and Options," in David C. Korten and Felipe B. Alfonso (eds.), *Bureaucracy and the Poor: Closing the Gap* (West Hartford, CT: Kumarian Press, 1983), pp. 181–200.

58. Ibid.

59. For further discussion, see, for example, Kempe Ronald Hope, Sr., "Self-Reliance and Participation of the Poor in the Development Process in the Third World," *Futures, 15* (December 1983), pp. 455–62; Mohiuddin Alamgir, "Poverty Alleviation through Participatory Development," *Development, 2/3* (1988), pp. 97–102; John Montgomery, *Bureaucrats and People: Grassroots Participation in the Third World* (Baltimore: Johns Hopkins University Press, 1988); and John P. Lewis and contributors, *Strengthening the Poor: What Have We Learned?* ODC Policy Perspectives, no. 10 (New Brunswick: Transaction Books, 1988).

60. A more elaborate discussion of this can be found in Orville Freeman, "Reaping the Benefits: Cash Crops in the Development Process," *International Health and Development, 1* (March–April 1989), pp. 20–23; World Bank, *World Development Report 1986* (New York: Oxford University Press, 1986); and Joachim von Braun and Eileen Kennedy, *Commercialization of Subsistence Agriculture: Income and Nutritional Effects in Developing Countries* (Washington, DC: International Food Policy Research Institute, 1986).

61. Elliot Berg, et al., *Accelerated Development in Sub-Saharan Africa* (Washington, DC: World Bank, 1981), p. 62.

—————— **Chapter 5** ——————

The Growth and Impact of the
Subterranean Sector

The subterranean sector—alternatively referred to as the informal, hidden, underground, shadow, secondary, black, invisible, or parallel economy—now constitutes an important component in the economic activities and process of development in the Third World. Although some Third World governments have tried in the past to minimize its relative importance, the subterranean sector continues to thrive in the Third World, where, generally, foreign-exchange constraints and inefficiency interfere with the normal functioning of the organized or *formal* sector, and therefore disrupts the availability and flow of goods, services, technology, and human resources in and out of those countries. The subterranean sector originally emerged in response to the problems of survival associated with rapid urbanization and unemployment in the Third World. However, this chapter will make it clear that it is *not* now a set of survival activities performed by destitute people on the margins of society.

The Nature of the Subterranean Sector in the Third World

The subterranean sector is defined here as those economic units and workers (both professionals and nonprofessionals) who engage in commercial activities outside of the realm of the *formally* established mechanisms for the conduct of such activities. Included in such activities are barters (exchanging of goods and/or services for other goods and or services); the importation of scarce consumer goods; the importation of production inputs and spare parts; the sale and exchange of hard currency for local currency at black market rates and vice versa; the sale and exchange of certain controlled goods and resources, such as gold, diamonds, and even arms, for hard currency or other goods and services; and unregistered small-scale productive and service activities. It is a process of income generation singularly characterized by the fact that it is unregulated by the institutions of society in an environment where comparable activities are regulated.

The activities of the subterranean sector do not show up in official statistics, although such a sector is widely recognized to be relatively important, autonomous, and self-propelling in almost all Third World countries. Although its exact quantitative magnitude defies any precise estimation, the subterranean sector, by all accounts, operates so "openly" and on such a large scale that any development policy thrust will be senseless unless the subterranean sector is recognized and figured into such policy actions.

Originally, the activities of the subterranean sector were conducted primarily by self-employed and urban-based workers, most of whom were rural migrants with little or no formal education—who became known as either the working poor, traders, higglers, hawkers, or hucksters—and who were engaged primarily in marginal production, service activities, and the importation of scarce consumer goods that were in heavy demand in the urban areas of the Third World. In their original form, the subterranean sector activities constituted a manner in which those individuals and households at the bottom of the socioeconomic system were able to command and accumulate resources. It provided for those without the requisite educational credentials to participate in the national economy and live an independent life. It also provided the wherewithal for those at the bottom of the economic ladder to exploit those above who were in a much more privileged position.

More recently, however, both the activities and the personnel involved have changed considerably. The activities have expanded and the personnel now include the professional and managerial classes, some of whom are even employed in government service or other formal sector activities on a full-time basis and switch between the subterranean and the formal sectors even during the same workday. As a matter of fact, the activities have now expanded to the point where even the formal sector, in some countries, has to conduct business in the subterranean sector in order to acquire hard currency, vital medical supplies, basic goods and services, and spare parts, for example. Also, the formal sector now has no alternative but to subcontract, horizontally or vertically, some of its production and other activities to the subterranean sector to take advantage of the latter's efficient production techniques and access to inputs.

This phenomenal expansion of the subterranean sector has been documented recently in numerous studies and reports. The great majority of that documentation suggests that the evolution of the subterranean economy has taken place because of the failure of the Third World countries formally to make the kind of economic progress that would have allowed for, among other benefits, low urban unemployment rates, a reduction in national poverty rates, wages and salaries that keep pace with inflation, the ready availability of basic goods and services, a functioning infrastructure, and a relatively honest and efficient bureaucracy. Also, in some countries, especially in Africa, government became such a suffocating monster that the private sector went almost completely subterranean to escape it.

The subterranean sector represents, therefore, the populace's spontaneous, yet creative and rational, response to the inability of their individual nation-state to provide the framework to satisfy their basic needs. In that regard, the citizens of the Third World have shown more daring, initiative, and dedication to their nation-state than have the politicians and their policy advisers who seem unwilling and/or unable to think through and implement policy reform that represents their population's changing economic environment and attitudes and desires. A self-reliant and survival network has, consequently, emerged to fill the "vacuum," thereby enhancing and entrenching the subterranean sector.

For some time it was basically accepted that the subterranean sector was a more or less transient phenomenon that would gradually disappear in the process of modernization as the formal sector thrived and absorbed more labor. Such a notion was not only inconsistent with the facts and the emerging trends around the Third World, but also was based essentially on the view (a negative one) taken by the International Labour Organization (ILO), in a 1972 mission to Kenya, that deemed the sector essentially dysfunctional.

More recent analyses, however, including those contained in this chapter, provide evidence that the subterranean sector has not disappeared; rather, it has grown substantially in most parts of the Third World. From a historical perspective, the subterranean sector today is substantially different from what it was two decades ago. It is no longer the exclusive domain of the urban poor. It now includes the professional and managerial classes from the formal sector who, seeing the success of the urban poor, have unleashed their own entrepreneurial spirit to provide a better standard of living for themselves and their families and to attempt to rid themselves of the stigma as victims of the failed and discredited statist/bureaucratic model of development found in their countries.

Among the characteristics of the subterranean sector is the increasing rate of participation of women as an entrepreneurial group, which further increases the trend toward higher rates of female participation in the Third World labor force. The labor force participation rate is simply the labor force measured as a percentage of the population. In Latin America, for example, the labor force participation rate for women increased from 12.6 percent in 1960 to 18.9 percent by 1989, while in Asia it increased slightly from 33 percent to 34 percent for the same period. The labor force participation rate for men declined during the same period in Latin America from 53 percent to 51.3 percent. Female participation in the Latin American subterranean sector is estimated to stand currently at between 35 percent and 39 percent. In urban Tanzania, 50 percent of the employed women work in the subterranean sector; in urban Indonesia this figure is 33 percent; and in Peru it is 33 percent.[1]

Also of significance here, in terms of the characteristics of the subterranean sector, is the fact that its activities have shifted outward from the urban sector and have now become more national in scope, encompassing almost all areas of economic activity. For example, the failure of the formal sector to provide, maintain, and monitor a proper transportation network in the Third World has led to the emergence of ad hoc, but vital, transport systems that link poor neighborhoods with the capital city and other urban areas, usually in the form of music-filled minibuses. In Kenya, these minibuses are called *matatus*; in Senegal, they are called the *car rapides*; in Tanzania, they are known as *dala dalas*; in Abidjan, they are known as *gbakas*; and in Jamaica, they are the *reggae express*.

In Peru, 91 percent of the vehicles used for mass transit are operated in the subterranean sector and are controlled by operators who are succeeding in an area where the state has traditionally failed.[2] Indeed, in the majority of Third World countries, these privately owned vehicles substantially outperform their state-owned counterparts. In cities such as Georgetown, Calcutta, Bangkok, Harare, and Istanbul, with both privately and publicly owned buses, the costs of running private bus services were between 50 percent and 60 percent of the costs of the publicly owned concerns.

Primary Benefits of the Subterranean Sector

The subterranean sector in the Third World has created a new class of entrepreneurs who have been able to use sheer initiative to function in national economies that have been plagued by very serious economic problems. The emergence of the subterranean sector has allowed for the availability of essential goods and services. These essential goods and services obtained in the subterranean sector represent, at one instance, the idea that Third World citizens must be free to choose and have the opportunity to obtain the basic goods and services they desire. In this respect, a thriving retail sector currently exists, dominated in part by street vendors.

At another level, however, the success of the retailing business in the subterranean sector further demonstrates the inefficiency and policy vacuum that exists in the formal sector. In particular, it represents a major indictment of the public enterprises that are responsible for the production and/or importation of such goods and services and further makes the case for their privatization. Because of their own mechanisms for obtaining foreign exchange, the traders and vendors in the subterranean sector find themselves in the position of having to provide essential items that the formal sector is no longer capable of providing. Of course, the vendors and traders find these activities very lucrative, to say the least.

Another major benefit derived through the subterranean sector is employment. Jobs are created cheaply and large numbers of individuals who would otherwise be unemployed and a burden to society are gainfully employed. Studies indicate that the share of the subterranean sector generally exceeded 40 percent of total urban employment in the Third World countries.[3] For Latin America, it was estimated that some 30 percent of the region's urban economically active population, and more than 42 percent of the total economically active population, are engaged in the subterranean sector.[4] In Peru alone, more than 70 percent of the entire work force is engaged full-time in the subterranean sector. In India, almost 45 percent of the urban labor force was found to be engaged in subterranean sector activities.[5] In Bolivia, almost 47 percent of the economically active urban labor force is engaged in subterranean sector activities, while in Colombia about 46 percent of the total labor force is employed in subterranean sector activities.[6]

In Brazil, the subterranean sector accounts for about 38 percent of nonagricultural employment; in Panama, approximately 30 percent of the urban labor market is in the subterranean sector; in Costa Rica, 38.1 percent of household heads and 35.4 percent of secondary household workers are employed in the subterranean sector; in Guatemala, the majority of the urban economically active population is engaged in the subterranean sector (however, of those who are fully employed, 41 percent are in the subterranean sector); in Chile, 21 percent of urban household heads, 26 percent of spouses, and 10 percent of children of household heads are employed in the subterranean sector; in Indonesia, 52 percent of total urban employment is in the subterranean sector; and in Thailand 50 percent of the total urban employment is in the subterranean sector. In Africa, the subterranean sector accommodated about 75 percent of the new entrants into the labor force between 1980 and 1985, and in Pakistan it was 85 percent for the same period. In 1990, the subterranean sector in sub-Saharan Africa employed more than 60 percent of the urban work force, and by the year 2020 it is estimated that 95 percent of African workers will be in the subterranean sector.[7]

The creation of jobs in the subterranean sector demonstrates conclusively that, given a free-enterprise environment, even amid uncontrolled inflation, large numbers of individuals who are able and willing to work would be in a position to do so. What is taking place here are some of the inevitable results of the experience of a free-market situation that encourages risk taking and enterprise regardless of class.

Another benefit of the subterranean sector is its contribution to gross domestic and national product. With the subterranean sector now permeating so much of economic life in the Third World, one would expect that the subterranean sector is now contributing an increasing share to national income in those countries. Overall, the subterranean sector in the Third World covers economic transactions of anywhere between 30 and 70 percent of national product. Several studies have made estimates for individual countries: for example, in Peru it is estimated that the subterranean sector contributes 38.9 percent of GDP;[8] in Bangladesh it is estimated at 33 percent of GDP;[9] in Guyana it is estimated at a range of 7 to 26 percent of GNP;[10] for Kenya it is estimated at 35 percent of GNP;[11] and for South Africa it is estimated at 40 percent of GDP.[12] By the year 2020, it is predicted that the subterranean sector in Africa will grow, while the formal sector will stagnate, resulting in a contribution to GDP from the subterranean sector that will grow from under 50 percent to 66 percent.[13]

One more benefit of the subterranean sector is that it constitutes an important component in the rural financial markets in many Third World countries in Asia, Africa, Latin America, and the Caribbean. It is a dominant source of credit in the rural sector, where the institutional lenders are absent or ineffective and access to formal credit is extremely poor. The numerous types of money lenders and credit suppliers in the subterranean sector include friends, relatives, landlords, commission agents, storekeepers, agricultural produce dealers, traders, and employers of agricultural labor. Of course, interest rates for such credit tend to vary with the economic interests and the nature of the relationship between the borrower and lender. For example, storekeepers may provide interest-free loans as an integral part of their business in order to retain or expand their share in retail trading in the market. Estimates of the percentage of total loans in the rural areas accounted for by the subterranean sector in Sri Lanka, for example, ranged from 57 percent to 79 percent during the period 1978–79 to 1981–82 and 1982;[14] in Zambia for the period 1981–82 it was estimated at 43 percent;[15] in Niger in 1986 it was 84 percent of total loans; in Malaysia it was 75 percent in 1985; in the Philippines it was an estimated 64 percent to 78 percent in the 1970s; while in Thailand it averaged 52 percent in the 1980s; in Gambia it was 80 percent for the period 1987–88.[16] At the national level, the subterranean sector accounts for most of the financial services provided to small-scale producers and enterprises. Informal deposit services are provided through group savings associations, and temporary loans can be arranged. Perhaps the most popular form of subterranean finance is the rotating savings and credit association (ROSCA). The ROSCA has different names in different countries of the Third World. For example, in Guyana it is called *box,* in Trinidad and Tobago it is known as *sou-sou,* in Jamaica it is referred to as *partners,* it is *susu* in Ghana, in India it is *chit fund,* in Mexico it is known as *tanda,* in Barbados it is called *meeting,* in Ethiopia it is called *iqqub,* in Egypt it is *gameya,* in Korea it is *kye,* in Indonesia it is known as *arisan,* in Malawi it is *chiperegani,* in Malaysia and Singapore the common English term for a ROSCA is *tontines,* and in Belize it is referred to as *syndicate.* ROSCA members, ranging from six to forty, pool their money into a fund. The fund is held by a group leader, who is informally selected from among the members of the group and is responsible for periodically collecting a fixed share from each member. The money collected is then given in a rotation as a lump-sum payment to each member of the group, thus allowing some members to finance expenditures much sooner than if they had relied on their own savings efforts.[17]

ROSCAs represent a very popular form of savings among the low- and middle-income groups in the Third World. It has been estimated that in Bolivia about 33 to 50 percent of all adults living in urban areas participate in ROSCAs,[18] while in Zambia the estimate is 80 to 90 percent of the urban population.[19] Although ROSCAs are national in scope in the Third World, in the rural areas they are widespread among all segments of the rural population, while in the urban areas they are more prevalent among the low- and middle-income classes. Funds collected through ROSCAs in urban areas tend to remain there, while a good portion of the funds collected through rural ROSCAs is transferred to urban areas. The reason for this, of course, is that consumer durables are produced and sold primarily in the urban areas. To acquire them requires expenditure in urban areas.

There are two basic reasons for the widespread popularity of ROSCAs in the Third World. First, ROSCAs are highly responsive to the economic and social requirements of their members. For example, they offer a limited number of participants; a specific duration of the savings/credit cycle; considerable individual participation; an agreed upon order of rotation and receipt of funds; absolute freedom of joining; easily understandable rules and procedures; rules and procedures that are consistent with the sociocultural norms of the environment; very good accessibility, and so on. The second reason has to do with the very high economic efficiency of ROSCAs. Transaction costs are low or nonexistent since there are no expenses for office space and personnel, or for assessing creditworthiness; and repayment rates are high since strong cultural norms, social pressures, and cohesion lead to few defaults.

Some Disadvantages of the Subterranean Sector

One obvious disadvantage derives from the fact that the success of the subterranean sector has reduced the pool of skilled labor force entrants in the formal economic sector who are required to administer and/or implement programs or deliver essential public or private services. Basically, job seekers are seeking not work as such, but relatively well paid work, as compared with average opportunities. Moreover, the freedom to be self-employed or to seek other economic opportunities in the subterranean sector, where the derived income and profits can be relatively higher and hidden from taxation, is a rational economic choice. As the subterranean sector thrives, many employees, or potential employees, assess their wages and salaries not in terms of local purchasing power as dictated by the price index, but in terms of the equivalent in U.S. currency, usually at the black market rate.[20] Under such conditions, the equivalent local income that can be derived in the formal sector seems a paltry sum. Hence, many jobs remain available in the formal sector.

What has emerged is a new attitude of no longer wanting to be dependent on paralyzed governments or other players in the formal sector. It embodies, somewhat ironically, the entrepreneurial energy emanating from individuals striving in admirable ways to become successful even without support, and moving away from a formal sector that is currently in disarray.

Another disadvantage of the subterranean sector is that it provides cover for tax evasion, drug trafficking, and smuggling. That state of affairs, however, can only exist where tax administration and law enforcement are inept and/or corrupt. It is perhaps understandable that entrepreneurs in the subterranean sector would attempt to evade all the taxes they can, particularly given that much of the Third World's economy remains in the formal sector where such tax evasion would be more difficult. The problem with such tax evasion is that it reduces the national revenues and therefore reduces the government's ability to spend on national programs. This can lead to additional tax burdens.

Determining the amount of evasion is very difficult in any country; it is particularly so in the Third World countries. It is often heard in many Third World countries that tax evasion is widespread and has reached alarming proportions, but accurate quantification of such evasion is almost impossible. One study on the evasion of the excise tax on cotton goods in India estimated the evasion rate at 28 percent; another study estimated the value-added tax evasion rate for Argentina at 50 percent; another on Jamaica concluded that income tax evasion by the self-employed was approximately 26 percent; another estimated income tax evasion in Guyana at 8 to 20 percent, depending upon the estimation method used.[21] Although the forms of evasion vary widely among countries, the major methods used to evade taxes in the subterranean sector include failure to report all sales, underinvoicing, overstating nontaxable sales, and nondeclaration of commissions retained overseas.

From the days of the first customs duties, smuggling in a great variety of forms has been the primary form of tax evasion. A number of factors may encourage smuggling in Third World countries, including (1) vast stretches of almost unguarded borders and long coastlines, which make a complete patrol impossible—good examples of this are the Bangladesh–India border, the Ghana–Togo border, and the coastlines of the Caribbean islands; (2) the general desire to evade taxes; (3) a desire to get contraband goods into countries where there is a heavy demand and rich dividend for such goods; and (4) the nearby availability of cheap supplies, particularly on islands that are just off the coastlines. Smuggling involving the inflow of goods can expose domestic industry to unfair competition.

Bribery is also a problem associated with the subterranean sector. It stems from the now endemic administrative corruption in the Third World. Bribery is a major cost of functioning in the subterranean sector. Subterranean sector businesses have to devote a large part of their income to bribing the authorities. A study of Peru estimated that subterranean sector businesses paid between 10 and 15 percent of their gross income in bribes and illegal commissions, while businesses in the formal sector paid no more than 1 percent.[22] Bribery has the potential of raising the cost of goods and services, though the payment of bribes also represents the purchasing of security from prosecution, on the one hand, and a sanctioning of the activities conducted in the subterranean sector, on the other.

One disadvantage of the subterranean sector, which can only be corrected through macroeconomic policy, is its contribution to the inflationary spiral in Third World countries. Consumer prices have been increasing at an alarming rate in the Third World, partly in response to the various devaluations of their overvalued currencies, and partly as a result of demand for goods and services that exceeds the available supply—a demand, it must be pointed out, that has arisen in the subterranean sector as a result of the economic deterioration in the Third World nations and the diminished capacity of the individual governments to provide and maintain the expected levels of services, goods, and physical infrastructure. In the 1980s, in the Western Hemisphere, for example, the annual rise in consumer prices exceeded 50 percent with some countries, such as Peru, Brazil, and Argentina exceeding 500 percent. For all Third World countries, the weighted average inflation rate reached 46 percent in 1993, compared with 18 percent during 1970–79, while in the industrial countries during the same period, the inflation rate declined to approximately 3 percent, compared with 8.1 percent during 1970–79.

Policy Conclusions

Experience has shown that the subterranean sector in the Third World is here to stay. Subterranean sector activities are expanding in scenarios of both a contracting formal sector, such as in sub-Saharan Africa, and an expanding formal sector, such as in the newly industrializing countries of Asia and Latin America.[23] Where the formal economy contracts, more individuals are forced into the subterranean sector to earn a living; where the formal economy expands, it generates additional demand for goods and services produced in the subterranean sector, thereby increasing employment in subterranean sector activities.

The subterranean sector in Third World countries has therefore emerged to the point where it is directly responsible for the improvement in the standard of living of a large number of people and, despite some of its shortcomings, contributes significantly to the improvement of life in general in the Third World. Given this generally positive contribution, then the subterranean sector must be regarded and treated as part of the solution to the current economic problems of the Third World nations.

The subterranean sector has exhibited a vibrancy and a resilience that must be enhanced. The sector is an expression of bottom-up initiative that development practitioners now agree is a sine qua non for the success of micro-projects. It must therefore become a matter of national economic policy to acknowledge the subterranean sector so that its contribution to the national economy can be improved even further. The remaining barriers to the functioning of the subterranean sector must be eliminated. This has to be accomplished, however, within a framework that allows for the conduct of business and other activities in a legal manner and thereby minimizes or eliminates altogether the possibility that the subterranean sector will end up with the reputation as a haven for drug traffickers, smugglers, and tax evaders. What is needed, then, is a concerted attempt to accept and to legalize the subterranean sector without allowing it to be absorbed into the bureaucratic and regulatory nightmare of the formal sector, which consists of, but is not limited to, such characteristics as barriers to entry, labor market regulations, controls on marketing and distribution, fiscal regulations, and credit regulations.

Indeed, there is a growing move toward greater flexibility in regulation, brought on primarily by the insistence of some donor agencies on liberalized policy frameworks encompassing the encouragement of local entrepreneurship and private sector activities, among other things. Moreover, it is being accepted more and more that the subterranean sector is both competitive with and complementary to the level of activity of the formal economy. Indeed, there is an increasingly widespread belief in some circles that well-targeted programs of support to the subterranean sector can be far more cost-effective in terms of employment promotion, poverty alleviation, and output than certain large-scale programs of investment in and support to the formal sector.[24]

Among the barriers to the proper functioning of the subterranean sector is inadequate access to credit. This is despite the success of ROSCAs and other types of subterranean sector finance. This means that access to credit must be improved. It has been found that loans to small-scale borrowers are not necessarily more risky. In fact, there is no inverse correlation between the size of a loan and the degree of risk, and the proportion of bad and doubtful debts is not higher among small bank customers.[25] Moreover, the U.S. Agency for International Development (USAID) has found that minimalist direct assistance programs that aim to improve the performance of micro-enterprises by providing short-term credit without attempting to transform the micro-enterprises into more complex businesses have a better record of success to date than do more ambitious programs.[26]

The ability to borrow money to engage in legitimate business activity must therefore be facilitated by the banks and other credit-granting agencies. Creating a more flexible set of rules and regulations under which credit can be granted is a necessary first step in that direction. Providing access to credit further encourages private investment. Given the dismal performance of public enterprises in Third World countries, such private sector initiatives must be soundly supported, as discussed in chapter 7. Moreover, the formal sector in most Third

World nations is now in an advanced stage of decrepitude.

Given the failure and negative impact of subsidized formal finance, as discussed in chapter 2, and the success of group lending to the poor as practiced, for example, by the Grameen Bank in Bangladesh, there are some important lessons here for financial institutions in the formal sector. The World Bank's *World Development Report 1990* indicates that only 5 percent of farms in Africa and 15 percent in Asia and Latin America have had access to subsidized formal credit. In Bangladesh, after more than a decade of subsidies, only 15 percent of small holders and 7 percent of the landless households had received institutional credit. Subsidized credit has become a transfer program for the non-poor while the artificially low interest rates and credit regulations have lent themselves to further patronage and corruption. In Third World subsidized credit programs, loans in arrears range from 30 percent to 95 percent, while the loan programs for the Grameen Bank, for example, have loan recovery rates exceeding 95 percent. Similarly, there are loan recovery rates exceeding 90 percent in the credit programs of the Working Women's Forum in Madras, India. Clearly, credit programs with low transaction costs, market rates, some linkage between repayment and future lending, and more physical accessibility for borrowers from the subterranean sector should be the desired approach in improving the availability of credit. In addition, borrowers must face an incentive structure that induces them to repay their loans.

In general, it is good economic reasoning and makes perfect economic sense to recognize the subterranean sector in national economic policy making in the Third World. As demonstrated here, the subterranean sector has made a major difference between the ability to subsist and abject poverty for large numbers of people in the Third World nations. It has encouraged risk taking and enterprise regardless of class and, perhaps, such a sector would not have existed in a well-working market economy without a public sector. Incentives for the growth of such activities tend to increase with greater state intervention and regulation. Consequently, the subterranean sector needs to be unleashed and the entrepreneurial spirit further nurtured to contribute to the development process. Undoubtedly, the subterranean sector is now a much more efficient system for making goods and services available in the Third World than is the formal sector.

To promote the subterranean sector, Third World governments should consider removing the obvious disincentives to entrepreneurship by creating a liberalized economic environment that minimizes restrictions. In Africa, for example, it was found that local small-scale entrepreneurship increased as the general economic environment became more open.[27] Such an achievement is an example of what can be accomplished if an entire economy is liberalized. The current economic distress in the Third World dictates that business as usual is no longer a viable option and that alternatives to the current approach to economic organization must be implemented. The subterranean sector is one such alternative.[28] The livelihood of millions of Third World citizens depends on its existence, and the future of many Third World societies now depends on its continued evolution and the role now assigned to it in the development process.

Within that scenario, and given the increasing importance of women in the subterranean sector and in the development process generally, the policy framework must also include programs aimed specifically at assisting women. Female entrepreneurship is now an ongoing reality in the Third World and, consequently, all of the discriminatory practices against them based simply on gender must be terminated. Gender inequality in the Third World persists despite some improvements in some societies. In many societies, however, women remain invisible in statistics because little value is attached to what they do.

Gender inequality, moreover, is reinforced in education. For the Third World as a whole, the female literacy rate is now three-fourths that of the male rate despite the fact that increasing numbers of females seek access to education. Women in the Third World must be allowed to participate fully in the development process, with all of the rights and abilities now available to men. The lessons learned during the Decade of the Woman would be useful in informing this strategy. Those lessons suggest that female-oriented policies must be implemented within the context of existing organizational structures, rather than as special, isolated, sporadic, or politically motivated projects.[29]

A great deal more research needs to be undertaken on the subterranean sector so that more can be understood about its internal dynamics and so that a reliable data base can be developed to facilitate optimal decision making. In this regard, the research being undertaken, as well as the advocacy position on behalf of the subterranean sector, by the Institute for Liberty and Democracy in Peru and the African Council of Hawkers and Informal Businesses in South Africa, for example, deserves both special commendation and a recommendation for continued financial support by the international development agencies.

The donor agencies need to extend their support, for promoting the development role of the subterranean sector, to all Third World regions, particularly sub-Saharan Africa, Asia, and the Caribbean, where the need for economic reform is great, where the subterranean sector is expanding rapidly, and where, as others have argued, the role of aid agencies in the economic reform process looms large.[30] This is especially relevant in the Third World environment where the failure of government policy is the primary contributor to the subterranean sector's rapid growth.

In particular, the donor agencies need to continue to tie some of their aid to policy reforms that provide for a much more enabling environment, free of bureaucratic red tape and excessive regulation, for micro-enterprises to flourish. In addition, the donor agencies should follow the lead of USAID by increasing their contributions to programs of direct assistance to the subterranean sector in Third World countries. Many of the subterranean sector enterprises have benefited immensely from an array of technical assistance projects, ranging from basic advice on business management to technology transfer and training. There have also been some small amounts of funding channeled successfully to subterranean sector producers by the ILO/Swiss Cooperation program in Mali, Rwanda, and Togo.

There is also scope for technical cooperation among developing countries in an enabling environment. Through the use of local experts and others who are familiar with the problems of the subterranean sector through hands-on experience, including subterranean sector workers themselves, the cost of technical assistance can be considerably reduced. This could have a much greater impact than exclusive reliance on expensive expatriate experts.

Concluding Remarks

The subterranean sector in the Third World continues to thrive, in spite of the hostile environment in which it must operate. Nevertheless, there are encouraging signs of recent movement toward the further development and implementation of policies in support of the subterranean sector. Governments in many Third World countries are becoming increasingly interested in the subterranean sector because of the large number of people it supports, and donor agencies are showing a willingness to do more in support of the subterranean sector.

The subterranean sector will undoubtedly play a major role in the development process in the Third World in the immediate future and beyond. The magnitude of its contributions, however, will be determined by the extent to which the regulatory framework is diminished.

In any case, the evolution of the subterranean sector in the Third World has provided valuable lessons to those countries that are desperately trying to manage transitions to democratic pluralist and market economic systems.[31] Those involved in subterranean sector activities in the Third World have shown themselves to be among the most innovative entrepreneurial groups in their societies, and this indicates that if they are allowed to function in a nonhostile environment, they would make a much greater contribution not only to their own economic and social progress, but to that of their respective countries as well.

Notes

1. Inter-American Development Bank, *Economic and Social Progress in Latin America: 1990 Report* (Baltimore: Johns Hopkins University Press, 1990), p. 233; and United Nations Development Programme, *Human Development Report 1990* (New York: Oxford University Press, 1990), p. 32.

2. Hernando de Soto, *The Other Path: The Invisible Revolution in the Third World* (New York: Harper and Row, 1989), p. 33.

3. Subbiah Kannapan, "Urban Labour Markets in Developing Countries," *Finance and Development, 26* (June 1989), p. 46.

4. Inter-American Development Bank, *Economic and Social Progress in Latin America: 1987 Report* (Washington, DC: IDB, 1987), p. 125.

5. Tamal Datta Chaudhuri, "A Theoretical Analysis of the Informal Sector," *World Development, 17* (March 1989), p. 351.

6. See José Blanes Jiménez, "Cocaine, Informality, and the Urban Economy in La Paz, Bolivia," pp. 135–49; and Monica L. de Pardo, Gabriel M. Castano, and Alvaro T. Soto, "The Articulation of Formal and Informal Sectors in the Economy of Bogota, Colombia," pp. 95–110, both in Alejandro Portes, Manuel Castells, and Lauren A. Benton (eds.), *The Informal Economy: Studies in Advanced and Less Developed Countries* (Baltimore: Johns Hopkins University Press, 1989).

7. These data are derived from the following papers contained in Gerry Rodgers (ed.), *Urban Poverty and the Labour Market: Access to Jobs and Incomes in Asian and Latin American Cities* (Geneva: International Labour Office, 1989). The papers are: Jorge Jatobá, "Urban Poverty, Labour Markets and Regional Differentiation in Brazil," pp. 35–63; Molly Pollack, "Poverty and the Labour Market in Costa Rica," pp. 65–80; Rene Arturo, Orellana Avila Avila, and Ri-

cardo A. Avila, "Poverty and Labour Market Access in Guatemala City," pp. 81–96; Daniel Camazón, Guillermo Garcia-Huidobro, and Hugo Morgado, "Labour Market Performance and Urban Poverty in Panama," pp. 97–116; Molly Pollack and Andras Uthoff, "Poverty and the Labour Market: Greater Santiago, 1965–85," pp. 117–43; and Hans-Dieter Evers, "Urban Poverty and Labour Supply Strategies in Jakarta," pp. 145–72. Also, World Bank, *World Development Report 1990* (New York: Oxford University Press, 1990), p. 63; *The Economist* (December 8, 1990), p. 71; Nipon Poapongsakoon, "The Informal Sector in Thailand," in A. Lawrence Chickering and Mohamed Salahdine (eds.), *The Silent Revolution: The Informal Sector in Five Asian and Near Eastern Countries* (San Francisco: ICS Press, 1991), pp. 105–44; and UNDP, *Human Development Report 1993* (New York: Oxford University Press, 1993), p. 41.

8. Hernando de Soto, *The Other Path: The Invisible Revolution in the Third World*, p. 12.

9. Sadrel Reza, "The Black Economy in Bangladesh: Some Preliminary Observations," *Savings and Development, 13,* 1 (1989), p. 30.

10. Kempe Ronald Hope, Sr., "The Subterranean Economy in Guyana," *Caribbean Affairs, 3,* 2 (April–June 1990), pp. 100–108.

11. Jeremy Main, "How to Make Poor Countries Rich," *Fortune* (January 16, 1989), p. 101.

12. Graciela D. Testa, "The Invisible Entrepreneurs of South Africa," *International Health and Development, 1* (Summer 1989), p. 22.

13. *The Economist* (December 8, 1990), p. 71.

14. Nimal A. Fernando, "The Interest Rate Structure and Factors Affecting Interest Rate Determination in the Informal Rural Credit Market in Sri Lanka," *Savings and Development, 12,* 3 (1988), p. 249.

15. Mojmir Mrak, "Role of the Informal Financial Sector in the Mobilization and Allocation of Household Savings: The Case of Zambia," *Savings and Development, 13,* 1 (1989), p. 68.

16. World Bank, *World Development Report 1989* (New York: Oxford University Press, 1989), p. 113; Bala Shanmugam, "Development Strategy and Mobilizing Savings through ROSCAs: The Case of Malaysia," *Savings and Development, 13,* 4 (1989), p. 363; P.B. Ghate, "Informal Credit Markets in Asian Developing Countries," *Asian Development Review, 6,* 1 (1988), pp. 64–85; and M. Zeller, J. Von Braun, K. Johm, and D. Puetz, "Sources and Terms of Credit for the Rural Poor in the Gambia," *African Review of Money Finance and Banking, 1/2* (1994), pp. 167–86.

17. Ibid.

18. Ibid.

19. Mojmir Mrak, "Role of the Informal Financial Sector in the Mobilization and Allocation of Household Savings: The Case of Zambia," pp. 65–83.

20. See C.L. Ramirez-Rojas, "Monetary Substitution in Developing Countries," *Finance and Development, 23* (June 1986), pp. 35–38; and Michael Nowak, "Black Markets in Foreign Exchange," *Finance and Development, 22* (March 1985), pp. 20–23.

21. The estimate for India is derived from M.G. Rao and G. Pradhan, *Excise Tax Duty Evasion in Cotton Textile Fabrics* (New Delhi: National Institute of Public Finance and Policy, 1984). The estimate for Argentina is derived from

Vito Tanzi, "The Underground Economy: The Causes and Consequences of the Worldwide Phenomenon," *Finance and Development, 20* (December 1983), pp. 10–13. The estimate for Jamaica is derived from Roy Bahl and Matthew Murray, *Income Tax Evasion in Jamaica,* Jamaica Tax Structure Project Staff Paper 31 (Syracuse: Metropolitan Studies Program, Syracuse University, 1986). The estimate for Guyana is derived from Kempe Ronald Hope, Sr., "The Subterranean Economy in Guyana," pp. 100–108.

22. Hernando de Soto, *The Other Path: The Invisible Revolution in the Third World,* p. 154.

23. Harold Lubell, *The Informal Sector in the 1980s and 1990s* (Paris: OECD Development Centre Studies, 1991), pp. 111–12.

24. ILO, *The Dilemma of the Informal Sector: Report of the Director General* (Geneva: ILO, 1991), pp. 16–17.

25. Kempe Ronald Hope, Sr., *Development Finance and the Development Process* (Westport, CT: Greenwood Press, 1987), pp. 71–72.

26. See USAID, *AID Micro-Enterprise Stock Taking: Synthesis Report* (Washington, DC: USAID, 1989).

27. Walter Elkan, "Entrepreneurs and Entrepreneurship in Africa," *Finance and Development, 25* (December 1988), pp. 41–42; and Graciela D. Testa, "The Invisible Entrepreneurs of South Africa," pp. 22–23.

28. Manuel Castells and Alejandro Portes, "World Underneath: The Origins, Dynamics, and Effects of the Informal Economy," in A. Portes, M. Castells, and L.A. Benton (eds.), *The Informal Economy: Studies in Advanced and Less Developed Countries,* pp. 11–37.

29. Inter-American Development Bank, *Economic and Social Progress in Latin America: 1990 Report,* pp. 236–250; and Jean M. Due, "Experience with Income Generating Activities for Southern African Women," *Savings and Development, 15,* 1 (1991), pp. 79–90.

30. A. Lawrence Chickering and Mohamed Salahdine, "The Informal Sector's Search for Self-Governance," in A. Lawrence Chickering and Mohamed Salahdine (eds.), *The Silent Revolution: The Informal Sector in Five Asian and Near Eastern Countries,* pp. 185–211.

31. Ibid.

Chapter 6

Bureaucratic Corruption and the Administrative Reform Imperative

Widespread bureaucratic corruption has reached epidemic proportions in most Third World countries and is now regarded as a societal norm. The inability of the administrative machinery to comply with reform measures is symptomatic of the endemic nature of the negative ethical values that perpetuate and maintain a system of corrupt activities to the detriment of economic development irrespective of the form of government. Many Third World regimes are corrupt and unable to sustain overall economic development regardless of whether the chief of state is a military dictator who seized power or a constitutionally elected president or prime minister, or whether political parties and the press function freely or are suppressed. Political philosophy and ideology seem to have little or no bearing on standards of morality and ethical behavior in the Third World, despite what the political leaders may claim. There is just as much corruption in statist Zimbabwe as there is in capitalist Bahamas, for example.

By indicating that any given political system in the Third World is vulnerable to corruption, one is forced also to indicate that the will of the people is not reflected in the manner intended. That is to say, corruption in those countries becomes the actual bureaucratic or political order, though an unofficial one. Such a state of affairs therefore demands extremely forceful reform. The prevalence and persistence of bureaucratic corruption are, however, discouraging, for they seem to imply that many policy makers and politicians are unwilling to control such corruption. This seems to be primarily because corruption has self-serving aspects for those in power, not only as a means of accumulating wealth but as a mechanism for political dealing, forging linkages, and even inducing a particular type of political participation.[1]

What Is Bureaucratic Corruption?

Anyone who is familiar with the literature on corruption would be aware that there is no single precise and concise definition of bureaucratic corruption. As a matter of fact, there are many and varying perspectives on corruption. This section attempts to develop a working definition of bureaucratic corruption to provide the framework for the discussions that follow.

With independence, most Third World countries, particularly those in Africa, drifted shamelessly into the transformation from a bureaucratic administration that emphasized good governance to one that emphasized the sovereignty of politics. This resulted in the emergence of a politicized bureaucracy in countries that began to engage in centralized economic decision making and patrimonialism. The new states were not only bureaucratic autocracies, but also political and economic monopolies that were now lacking in accountability, transparency, and the rule of law.[2]

This, then, was the genesis of rampant bureaucratic corruption in the Third World. The politicization of the bureaucracy allowed for the entrenchment of the use of favoritism and patronage as the means through which authority and influence were exercised. The politicians and the bureaucrats forged a dependent patron (politician)–client (bureaucrat) relationship through which administrative decision making occurred. This process, inevitably, led to the abuse of public office for private and personal gains.

Bureaucratic corruption can now be defined against this background. In this work, bureaucratic corruption is, first and foremost, the utilization of bureaucratic official positions or titles for personal or private gain, on either an individual or a collective basis, at the expense of the public good, in violation of established rules and ethical considerations, and through the direct or indirect participation of one or more public officials, whether they are politicians or bureaucrats.

In a somewhat more simplistic sense, bureaucratic corruption may be seen as partisanship that challenges statesmanship.[3] It is an act or acts undertaken with the deliberate intent of deriving or extracting personal and/or private rewards against the interests of the state.[4] Such behavior may entail theft, embezzlement of funds or other appropriation of state property, nepotism and/or the granting of favors to personal acquaintances, and the abuse of public authority to exact monetary benefits or other privileges.

Despite some recent literature that criticizes definitions such as this for placing the emphasis almost entirely on the state sphere and minimizing the behavior of those in the private sector who contribute to the corruption of governmental personnel,[5] the simple truth is that bureaucratic corruption can only occur with the participation of public officials. Whether that participation is direct or indirect is completely irrelevant to the completion of a corrupt act or a set of corrupt acts in which such officials are involved.

Moreover, I see the idea that "bureaucratic corruption" takes place in transactions between private individuals or firms and public officials as a tautology. Thus, as has been implied before, the issue is one of misuse of public office and abuse of public trust by public officials.

Factors Contributing to Bureaucratic Corruption in the Third World

Bureaucratic corruption thrives in the Third World for a number of reasons. In this section we discuss and analyze those primary factors that have contributed, and continue to contribute, to the pandemic of bureaucratic corruption in the Third World. The point of departure for this section is the fact that public accountability is seriously lacking in the great majority of Third World states. Public accountability means holding public officials responsible for their actions. It is also central to good governance.

The first factor is the general absence of a public service "work ethic." Most Third World public officials lack a sense of purpose and commitment to their responsibilities. They do not believe they are serving anyone but themselves, and therefore they exploit their positions for personal gain. There is a general lack of work discipline and an attitude of disrespect for public service rules and regulations. Public servants generally arrive at work late and leave early. They take extra long lunch breaks. They steal public property. They accept bribes for services to which applicants are legally entitled and for the performance of duties that are contractually a part of their responsibilities. They alienate the public by losing files, through excessive review of the issue at hand, or by simply pretending that they have not heard of the matter before. Corruption is aided here by a bureaucratic laxity that results from the lack of a work ethic, which is itself primarily derived from societal norms and poor training and education.

This lack of a work ethic in the bureaucracy partially contributes not only to corruption but to underdevelopment also. In Jamaica, for example, a study commissioned by the government found that public utilities and public enterprises had the lowest level of work effort when compared with other private enterprises and the national average.[6] This suggests not only excess labor capacity that is not being put into the service of greater production and productivity, but also negative attitudes toward work. On the other hand, it is interesting to note that in both those developing and developed states where the bureaucracy performs efficiently and with little or no corruption, the existence of a work ethic is a major contributor to that state of affairs. In Barbados, for example, as in the United States and the United Kingdom, there is a long history of constitutional democracy and a well-educated, highly trained, and disciplined labor force not only in the public sector but also in the private sector.[7] This has, undoubtedly, contributed to the long-term economic stability and development that Barbados has historically experienced.

The second factor has to do with the fact that some Third World countries have been regressing rather than progressing in terms of economic development. This, in turn, has led to a bipolar type of income distribution, creating "haves" and "have-nots." Public servants striving for high social status and to be counted among the "haves," or simply to make ends meet, have tended to pursue corrupt activities. Thus, the incentives to corrupt whatever official purposes public institutions are agreed to have are specifically noticeable in conditions of extreme inequality and deteriorating economic conditions. Economic retardation and inequality force individuals not only to tolerate corruption, but to take advantage of it where it is present and to initiate it where none exists.

A further feature of such inequalities is the practice of extending "favors" to other individuals because of the desire to alleviate their poverty. At other times, such favors may be extended with the objective of extracting future benefits from the recipients. This type of corruption inserts into the transaction between the public official and the client such factors as friendship or family ties and is referred to as "favor corruption." Carino, however, argues that, at least in the case of the Philippines, there are very few instances of pure favor corruption. The majority of corrupt transactions involve some monetary or financial gain.[8] Even in those instances where personal relationships may have influenced the process, it will usually terminate as a market transaction.

The third factor contributing to bureaucratic corruption is the lack of leadership and discipline exhibited by the politicians. Indeed, many studies have shown that administrative corruption tends to be more widespread where significant political corruption exists and/or where the idea of the national interest remains weak. Herein lies the concept of the "soft state." Myrdal has argued that a "soft state" is one where all the various types of social indiscipline manifest themselves in the form of deficiencies in legislation and in the observance and enforcement of law:[9] "The general setting of the "soft state" makes corruption possible, and in turn the prevalence of corruption is a mighty influence keeping these countries as soft states."[10]

The state is often an artificial entity. The disregard of its rules bears little social stigma, and rules are largely disregarded where politicians exhibit weak leadership. In Jamaica, for example, social indiscipline has graduated to the point where it has now become a national disease and a major contributing factor to crime and violence in the society. Thus, there is a growing gap between the symbolic pronouncements of the political leaders and the tangible significance of their actions when it comes to maintaining law and order. Moreover, there is a widespread disobedience by public officials, at various levels, of rules and directives and much collusion with powerful individuals and groups whose conduct they should regulate.

The fourth factor is the expanding role of state activity, which has in turn resulted in an expanding bureaucracy with increasing discretionary power that is abused for personal gain. Planned development in Third World countries has increased government intervention in the socioeconomic sphere and this, in turn, has led to an increased number of regulations and government controls over a wide array of services and goods. These excessive regulations and controls, coupled with greater administrative discretion, provide opportunities for corruption, since the controls and regulations can be used as a bargaining mechanism to induce the payment of bribes.

Many public servants, moreover, do not understand the complexities of such regulations and controls, or do not identify with their purpose. As a result, their loyalty or commitment to the performance of their duties is compromised or diluted. Such a situation provides opportunities for the systematic exploitation of illegal income-earning activities.

In other words, rent-seeking opportunities are enhanced. These opportunities lead to market-clearing responses for inefficiencies from free public goods.[11] Also, they can foster a characteristic of obsessive preoccupation to the point where public officials will do nothing without bribes and payoffs.

The fifth factor has to do with sociocultural norms. Jabbra argues that "bureaucratic corruption is created by attitudes and patterns of behaviour interwoven not only throughout the bureaucratic structures of emerging nations, but also throughout the whole of their social fabric."[12] That is to say, administrative corruption is shaped and conditioned by defective cultural attitudes and behavioral patterns.[13] Bureaucrats are faced with a choice of adhering either to the standards of modern development administration or to the accepted traditional standards. The latter is usually chosen.[14] The meritocratic idea, for example, is negated in favor of personal or sectional interests. One can look at the Africa case in point where the widespread existence of personalism results in significant loyalties toward one's family, tribe, and friends. In many Third World nations, the relationship between the individual and the group—the extended family, the clan, the tribe—differs sharply from that in the West, where the nuclear family dominates. In the West, two complementary but opposite ideas prevail: loyalty to the rules of the state, but also allegiance to the idea of individual liberty. In much of Africa and Asia, the individual is far more thoroughly subsumed into the group; his or her individual rights and personal accountability matter less than his or her loyalties to the group.[15]

Now that we have made the comparison with the West, we need to point out that there is also corruption in the West. The significant difference, however, is that in the West there is no "softness of state," and, as such, corruption is regarded as abnormal and wrong, while in the Third World it is not. Moreover, when corruption is discovered in the West, it is usually dealt with swiftly and severely; that is certainly not the case in the Third World, where there is a gap between verbal condemnation of corruption and action to thwart it. In the West institutions can be depended upon to invoke the law in the national interest. Moreover, a free and vigorous press takes tremendous pride in its investigative journalism and its ability to expose illegal acts, whether in the public or the private sector.

The final factor is the comparatively underdeveloped state of countervailing power in Third World nations; public opinion simply does not exist as a countervailing force. Little power and even less influence exist outside of the ruling party's patron–client network. As a matter of fact, many of the countries do not have freely operating opposition political parties or independent judiciary systems. Many of the legislatures are dependencies of the political leadership and press freedom is also rare. In such circumstances, the bureaucracy is free to act at will in its own economic interest rather than in the interest of the nation. There are usually no effective supervisory or watchdog committees or agencies to monitor administrative performance. In those cases where they do exist, such as the office of the ombudsman, they have very little power or influence.

From the foregoing discussion, it is possible to draw certain conclusions and to indicate why bureaucratic corruption is tolerated in Third World countries. First, many public officials, at all levels, are personally involved, and are reaping significant profits from bureaucratic corruption. When institutions as well as individuals operate corruptly, new recruits are invariably forced to conform to existing patterns of behavior. Second, collective public opinion is weak or apathetic, which militates against demands for positive steps to prevent corruption. Third, many citizens in Third World states accept that, as long as they observe reasonable ethical standards, they do not need to accept responsibility for the conduct of others. They do not see that the control of corruption has anything to do with the preservation of their own economic and political freedom, as well as that of the rest of the citizens. Finally, there are those citizens who genuinely do not believe that corruption has significant negative consequences. They have lived with it for so long that they accept it as a way of life.

The Dysfunctional Effects of Bureaucratic Corruption in the Third World

Bureaucratic corruption in the Third World has become pervasive and is now devouring the economies and polities of many of those nations. Corruption is a universally shameful and despicable phenomenon and, despite the arguments by some authors that corruption may have certain benefits,[16] the evidence and data suggest overwhelmingly that corruption impairs administrative efficiency and has negative effects on the process of socioeconomic and political development. Indeed, bureaucratic corruption is a major contributor to the elusiveness of development in the Third World.

First, there are economic costs. Bureaucratic corruption increases the cost to governments for doing business. Kickbacks and illegal commissions that have to be paid to high-ranking bureaucrats are simply added to the final cost of contracts, equipment, supplies, and so on. This not only increases government expenditures and siphons off scarce funds, but eventually leads to the need to increase revenues either through more taxes or by borrowing or cutting back on other policy programs of greater importance, ultimately leading to a general welfare loss for the affected country. In the Philippines, for example, the economic gain from one corrupt activity in 1983 was roughly equivalent to the national government budget for natural resources, and was 183 percent of that year's budget for social security, labor, and employment.[17] Because of corrupt procurement policies, governments in Third World nations pay 20 to 100 percent more than the price they would pay under noncorrupt situations.[18]

In the area of trade, corrupt activities result in capital flight and price increases at both the wholesale and the retail levels. Corruption in the trade sector is the most systematic and legendary type of corruption in the Third World. The role of trade in these economies and, hence, the importance of the import–export sector loom large, and provide many opportunities for corrupt practices. Bribes have to be paid for the clearance of goods through customs, for obtaining import licenses, for shipping contraband, for exclusion from taxes and fees, and so on. In May 1986, for example, the government of Trinidad and Tobago announced the suspension of a "high official" of the Ministry of Industry and Commerce for issuing licenses for the illegal importation of rice from the United States, thereby defrauding the National Flour Mills—the organization that has the sole authority to import rice. The next month, the *Trinidad and Tobago Mirror* further announced that the police had "unearthed a multi-million bribery racket involving importation of goods banned by the Trinidad and Tobago government." The newspaper claimed that twelve senior officials from the Local Industry Ministry and the Customs Department were under investigation for the collection of over $2 million in bribes to give approval for the importation of goods on the government's "negative list."

In May 1986, U.S. Customs officials discovered $35 million worth of illegal drugs that arrived in a shipment of cement from Jamaica through the fraudulent issuance of a valid Jamaican export license to an unauthorized exporter. In June 1986, the Jamaican and the Indonesian governments announced that, through the use of agents of the Swiss firm Société Général de Surveillance (SGS), they discovered a substantial number of cases of overinvoicing, underinvoicing, and bribery among importers and exporters. It was estimated that such practices added up to $200 million annually in Indonesia. The practice of overinvoicing leads to loss of foreign exchange, while underinvoicing leads to losses of revenue in duties. In early 1989, the U.S. government announced the indictment of the former, now deceased, Philippines President Ferdinand Marcos and his wife, Imelda, for allegedly embezzling several hundred million dollars of funds from the Philippines Treasury—funds obtained primarily as U.S. foreign aid. In that same year the government of Trinidad and Tobago was also successful in freezing, in Canada, the assets of the estate of a former minister of the Trinidad and Tobago government on the grounds of fraud and accepting bribes as a minister of the government. In 1992–93, a number of properties and financial assets belonging to two former presidents of Sierra Leone—Momoh and Stevens—were confiscated by the state on the grounds that they were obtained through plundering of the state treasury. Such examples are abundant.

Corruption also produces detrimental effects on political development. Bureaucratic corruption that is aided and abetted by political corruption generally becomes entrenched in the structure of the state as well as in the structure of all other social institutions. It thus becomes the status quo, the maintenance of which results in the use of repressive tactics, which in turn suppresses political opposition and any possibility of public criticism of the regime's activities. Such repression, however, destroys the necessary means for political development: without the freedoms to organize politically, of speech, and of assembly, life dies out in every public institution and only the bureaucracy remains an active element. In other words, corruption threatens the pillars of democracy and the democratic experience.[19]

Finally, corruption yields effects on administrative development. Bureaucratic corruption hinders administrative development and performance in Third World countries partly because of its institutional spillover effects. It has been found that corrupt bureaucrats and leaders export their corrupt activities to other institutions by exerting influence and pressure on other public officials as a means of sustaining rent-seeking opportunities.[20] Moreover, such corrupt activities can move from a passive to an active phase where public servants do not wait to be approached and bribed, but actively solicit bribes in return for the provision of public services. In India, this is referred to as "speed money"—payment for expediting transactions. In other countries, such as Uganda, Jamaica, and Nigeria, such payments are regarded as necessary and routine, and do not even guarantee that transactions will be expedited. Failure to make payments, however, does guarantee that *no* action whatsoever will be taken on the transactions. In other words, this type of bureaucratic corruption has become the unofficial but operating administrative order.

In Zaire, for example, public servants openly peddle their access to VIPs and their ability to issue official documents. Soldiers hire themselves out as bodyguards to foreign businessmen. As a matter of fact, almost any transaction needs a sweetener. The system has produced the quintessential Zairean kleptocrat, the *protocole,* a professional payer of bribes. The *protocole* will introduce himself whenever any official transaction is to be undertaken. His role is to use his influence to minimize the amount of the bribe; in return, of course, he gets a cut for himself.[21]

Bureaucratic corruption can also affect professionalism in the public service and lead to frustration on the part of honest public servants to the point that it affects their job performance and significantly reduces their productivity. In many instances this frustration leads to emigration, particularly among those who are highly skilled and qualified. This, in turn, contributes to the brain-drain dilemma of Third World countries, thereby further impairing national productivity and output.

The Administrative Reform Imperative

The previous sections lend themselves to the argument that anticorruption campaigns are necessary and must be sustained if bureaucratic corruption is to be rooted out in the Third World. Bureaucratic corruption can only be eradicated, however, when both the politicians and the public make a concerted effort *not* to tolerate it. But, where "softness of state" exists, people are reluctant to uphold laws that get in the way of their personal or sectional interests. The burden therefore falls on the political actors as the only individuals with the power to bring about a stronger allegiance to the state and, hence, a commitment to the national interest.[22] This, however, would require that the citizenry develop confidence and trust in their public institutions. This, in turn, would require first that those institutions be reformed. Of course, after several decades of entrenched bureaucratic corruption in the Third World states, it would be very difficult to eradicate it totally. It can, however, be minimized, and its negative effects significantly reduced.

When corruption is institutionalized, systemic, or an intrinsic part of everyday life, it cannot be effectively contained or eliminated by legal measures or through the use of the police singly. Only when the vast majority of citizens spontaneously accept the laws, even when they disagree with them, can those laws be a tool for community direction and reform. In the absence of such reform, the morality and loyalty of the citizens may become further factionalized.[23]

Administrative reform can be defined as specially designed and deliberate efforts to induce fundamental change in both the structure and procedures of the public bureaucracy and the attitudes and behavior of the administrators involved in order to promote organizational effectiveness and achieve national development goals.[24] The process is designed to adjust the relationship between a bureaucracy and other elements in society or within the bureaucracy itself. It has a moral content in that it seeks to create a better system by eliminating faults and imperfections. It is usually undertaken to change the status quo for the better.[25] It involves, therefore, the reorganization of the machinery of government from both a technical and a practical standpoint.

Many Third World countries have organized major administrative reform programs in the past, and many now have such programs being implemented and funded, by such agencies as the World Bank, as a major new thrust, through the understanding that development cannot proceed unless there is a reasonably good and honest administrative machinery. The notion of administrative reform has important practical advantages, although others have argued that it is a concept in disrepute.[26]

Administrative Reform Strategies

The major interacting ingredients of administrative reform are training of public servants, decentralization of administrative functions, an enhanced commitment of the political leadership to an effective and efficient administration, and a smaller and better-paid public service. However, for administrative reform to be successful, it must be adaptable to the specific cultural environment and related to clearly defined contingencies. Its goals and objectives must be consistent and boundaries must be established, political commitment must be garnered, the mode of implementation and sustained follow-up measures must be clear-cut, and the staff and consultants charged with this task must be of the highest possible caliber.

Developing strong and efficient public institutions in Third World countries requires the injection of new ideas and new people, in a new combination of tasks and relationships, into the policy and administrative process. Some previous attempts at administrative reform have succeeded in establishing new administrative structures but have often failed to improve efficiency or change bureaucratic behavior. This indicates that governments need to define their reform boundaries and direct their efforts toward them so as to ensure long-term institutional development.

Administrative reform strategies should therefore focus on certain specific issues. First, personnel planning and training are usually necessary. The effective performance of public administration depends, to a great extent, on the capability of its personnel. The behavior and performance of public personnel are a dominant factor determining productivity and confidence in the public sector. This means that there must be proper personnel planning and assessment. The size and scope of public personnel systems tend to increase each year and, as such, personnel planning and assessment must go far beyond the mere tabulation of demand and supply indices, to take into consideration the broad spectrum of problems of public personnel development. Public personnel planning is necessary in the Third World to ensure the adequate supply of human resources for public organizations to meet the quantitative, qualitative, and time requirements of national development objectives. It also provides the basis for planning training requirements at various levels. Moreover, the lack of systematic personnel planning has, in many cases, generated problems such as duplication of work, multiplication of agencies, impairment of efficiency, and low morale.

Training is necessary because no matter how well qualified a person may be at the time of recruitment, how to become an effective and efficient public servant must be taught and inculcated, not assumed. This is why in some countries a person who is newly recruited into the public service must go through a period of training before being assigned to specific duties. Administrative training may be defined as the act or process of developing the capacities and potentialities of the public service for a more efficient and effective discharge of the service's current and future responsibilities.[27] It should *not* be viewed as merely a technocratic exercise, and its objectives must include the creation of a commitment in public servants to the national goals and values, including ethical behavior, and a thorough understanding of the environment to which the specific skills learned are to be adapted.

Equally important is in-service training. In many Third World states national training institutions or administrative staff colleges have been established, for the most part, to provide in-service training at the lower- and middle-management levels. Such institutions, however, have very limited scope, since a dominant feature of public service training in most Third World states is its concentration on preservice and immediate postservice courses for administrative élites, to the neglect of in-service training and the needs of lower-level bureaucrats. It should be recognized, however, that some form of tutelage and on-the-job training is indispensable in the public services, and that self-development and learning from experience and mistakes have an important function. Another critical factor in the effectiveness of in-service training programs pertains to their content. In-service training, by its very nature, tends to be very general and invariably not geared to any specialized career development. To make in-service training productive, measures must be undertaken that would meaningfully relate training to the career development of civil servants and to the process of probationary periods, postings, and promotions.

It is important to distinguish clearly between the mere availability of training programs and their effectiveness in promoting development objectives. It has been found that the quality of most public service training in the Third World is very low.[28] Formal training programs, both preservice and in-service, in many nations are excessively theoretical and frequently of little operational value. Some are only for system maintenance and are not change-oriented. Some are traditional and not development-oriented. Some are borrowed, without modification, from highly developed nations and are therefore irrelevant to the Third World environment. Some programs are run by trainers who elaborate on their own skills rather than on the skills and knowledge of the trainees, or they use training material that is not career- or country-specific.

The fundamental differences between developed and Third World nations suggest three basic orientations necessary for training public service personnel in the Third World.[29] There is need for a different kind of knowledge, a need to promote creative abilities and innovational attitudes, and to promote motivation and commitment for change. A different type of knowledge is needed if the knowledge imparted to the trainees is to be relevant and thus functional. Moreover, relevance of the knowledge gained promotes interest and enthusiasm. The need to develop a sense of creativity and an innovative attitude arises from the fact that some public servants will have to reconstruct the theories they learn abroad to adapt them to the situation in their own nations. They need to be innovative in order to successfully accommodate the ever growing and changing interests and demands. The need to promote motivation and commitment stems from the fact that bureaucratic performance and the rate of development will depend largely on the enthusiasm of the bureaucracy.

Despite the role training can play in reorienting bureaucratic behavior and performance, evidence suggests that public service training still receives less emphasis in Third World countries than in developed countries.[30] Most Third World nations have no policies and plans for public service training. Management training programs in Third World countries are attended more frequently by employees from the private sector. In contrast, the United States and Japanese governments, for example, offer training opportunities to nearly one-quarter of their employees each year.[31] Furthermore, the significance of training can be gleaned by looking at the emphasis placed on it in successful private corporations. Surveys indicate that all managers in those corporations receive at least forty hours of mandatory training each year.[32]

The second aspect of reform has to do with decentralization. Strategies of administrative reform must seek to reduce or eliminate altogether the excessive centralization of the administrative machinery in Third World countries in order to reduce overload and congestion and improve the channels of communication and the level of coordination both within and among various departments. One of the worst features of a centralized bureaucracy is the time wasted on routine administrative duties and an overenthusiasm for "paper chasing."

Decentralization can be broadly defined as the transfer of planning, decision making, or administrative responsibility from the central government to its field units, local administrative bodies, semiautonomous or parastatal organizations, local governments, or nongovernmental organizations.[33] There are four major forms of decentralization: (a) deconcentration—the transfer of some resources and administrative responsibilities or a redistribution of administrative authority within the central government; this has been the most frequently used form of decentralization in the Third World since the 1970s; (b) devolution—the relinquishing of certain functions to autonomous units of government such as local governments or the creation of new units of government outside the direct control of the central government; (c) delegation—the transfer of managerial responsibility and decision making for specific functions to organizations, such as public corporations, regional planning authorities, farmer cooperatives, trade unions, and credit unions, that are outside the regular bureaucratic structure and not under the direct control of the central government; this type of decentralization has been used extensively in Third World countries primarily through the creation of public enterprises; (d) privatization—the transfer of some planning and administrative responsibilities or public functions from government to voluntary, private, or nongovernmental institutions. This generally takes the form of divestiture or the selling of public enterprises to the private sector. Public enterprises, however, still proliferate in the Third World as discussed in chapter 1.

Administrative decentralization promotes participation, access, and responsiveness. Through administrative decentralization, national standards can be emphasized to deal with problems that are national in scope, while at the same time allowing for adjustments to meet particular regional needs. Such decentralization should extend both to the lower units in the central hierarchy and to units at the lower levels of governments, especially local governments. Apart from improving the efficiency of administration, administrative decentralization can bring public administrators and citizens closer together. A centralized administration tends to appear faceless as well as monolithic to the populace, who therefore feel helpless against it. On the other hand, evidence and experience have shown that administrative decentralization results in less alienation and better understanding as well as increased cooperation between public administrators and citizens.

To date, the most successful decentralization strategies have been in the area of integrated rural development, particularly in Asia and Africa, where implementation of rural development programs is increasingly in the hands of paraprofessionals and local government officials.[34] Decentralization was the preferred mode in rural service delivery because the complexity and uncertainty that characterize the environments of the Third World now greatly exceed what centralized bureaucratic organizational structures can cope with. Moreover, decentralization was necessary because the involvement of the rural beneficiaries was perceived to be useful. Building on the experience gained from the integrated rural development projects, decentralization can be made a more useful tool of the administrative reform process, and a measure to combat corruption, by resulting in greater sharing of authority and responsibility and by limiting the scope of decisions of any one person or a select group of persons.

The next aspect of administrative reform is political commitment and leadership. The World Bank's *World Development Report 1983* states:

> When political leaders are recognized for their integrity, vision, and concern for the public welfare, these qualities can be reflected in the ethos and performance of the public service and will have a profound effect on all sections of society. But if corruption is rife, public bureaucracy is likely to become demoralized and self-serving.[35]

This passage clearly indicates the concern in official international circles about the role of political leadership in promoting ethical behavior, which scholars have been debating for some years. The improvement of a nation's administrative capability is highly dependent on support from the political leadership. The role of the political leadership is indeed the most crucial factor in the process of national development and, hence, in the improvement of the administration of development. Political leadership is *the* arbiter, rather than one participant or factor among many, of the process of national development. Lending support to administrative change and reform requires, therefore, commitment on the part of the political leadership. Commitment here involves a sustained determination to promote rationality, an increase in productivity, social equity, and ethical behavior.

If a nation's leadership shows little interest in administration, downgrades administration in national priorities, and is ambivalent about reform, then reform agencies find themselves conducting technical exercises that have little impact on administrative performance.[36] Political commitment is needed for three reasons. First, strong political support is needed to promote and articulate strategy in national policies, legislation, and administrative directives. Second, political support is needed to ensure high priority for the goals and objectives of administrative reform. This is important for the transformation of plans into beneficial programs of action. Finally, political commitment is needed to break barriers and settle territorial disputes among competing interests, including external actors, which may hamper and frustrate the reform process.

The political universe is the context of actions of political leadership; the political system is the instrument that broadly defines the behavior of political leadership; and politics is the means through which political leadership performs its role. Society develops or fails to develop to the extent that its political leadership is intelligent, creative, skillful, committed, and able to enlist support, to induce loyalty, and to inspire confidence.[37] Without this requisite aspect of political leadership, there will be no change in administrative performance and behavior. It is impossible, however, to construct a workable model made up of all the virtues deemed basic to the ideal political leader, since certain patterns of leadership apply to some, but not all, situations. A political leader may be successful in one situation but fail in another. Leadership, however, that takes the form of detailed bureaucratic regulation or that exists in a system of centralized authority is more likely to retard than to enhance administrative efficiency and socioeconomic development. In short, excessive intervention breeds corruption.[38]

The final aspect of administrative reform pertains to pay/grading and downsizing of the public service. The public service in most Third World countries is much larger than those countries require, more costly than they can absorb, and significantly less effective and productive than they need. In several of the countries, the public service contains many who are superfluous and none who are paid well; and the ministries and departments in which they work tend to be poorly structured.[39] The reform of pay and grading has therefore taken on considerable significance in recent years.

As an administrative reform measure, to be used in the fight against bureaucratic corruption, pay and grading usually have five objectives: (1) to increase overall real pay levels; (2) to decompress pay scales to improve the competitiveness of public service pay at higher levels; (3) to establish a new grading system based on job evaluation; (4) to introduce performance-based pay; and (5) to improve pay policy making and administration.[40] The experience of pay and grading reform in the Third World suggests some successful outcomes to date, which over the medium term ought to effect some reduction in bureaucratic corruption.

The other item in this final aspect of administrative reform is the need to downsize Third World public services and thereby eliminate surplus employees. A number of methods are available, including enforcement of mandatory retirement ages, abolition of job guarantees for high school and university graduates, attrition through hiring freezes, introducing voluntary departure schemes, outright dismissals, and elimination of "ghost" (fictitious) employees from the payroll. The experience of Africa suggests some success in this area.[41] Such success needs to be sustained into the future to prevent the public services from again becoming both bloated and a haven for corruption.

Implementing Administrative Reform

The most significant constraint to administrative reform in Third World countries is the extent of implementation. Implementation is perhaps the most important aspect of administrative reform, since the manner in which it is done will dictate and determine not only the pace of administrative reform but also its overall success. There are several ingredients to successful implementation. One of them, the commitment of political leadership, has been discussed above. Before we discuss others, it may be useful to put the concept of implementation in perspective.

Implementation is taken here to mean the management of resources (human, physical, and financial) and institutions for the achievement of previously specified and sustained reform goals and objectives. It is usually facilitated through an organizational setting, such as an administrative reform commission or secretariat.

A major obstacle in the implementation process is that reform goals and objectives may be ambiguous, undefined, or simply unobtainable in the framework in which they are cast. This is referred to as "a bad beginning."[42] A good beginning is worth a great deal since it can take a reform program through some of the difficult periods. Goals and objectives must, therefore, be clearly defined and achievable as stated.

Another ingredient for successful implementation is innovation. Too many Third World nations in the past have attempted to implement administrative reform by imitating what has been done elsewhere—the "copy-cat syndrome." Administrative systems, however, tend to differ from country to country and the reform measures must be tailored to suit individual cases. Moreover, the whole cultural milieu and personnel systems have to be considered unique, which they are, and reform efforts must take this into consideration. In other words, the administrative environment must be correctly assessed. Furthermore, the solutions and techniques used to accomplish administrative reform must be adaptable to public sector organizations. Too often, organization development models used in the private sector are adopted mechanically, but these are business administration models and they are not always appropriate for the complexities of public administration, and may, in turn, exacerbate the administrative problems and generate confusion in the reform process.[43]

Also important is the need for comprehensiveness and integration. Many attempts at administrative reform have failed because the programs were of an isolated nature, concentrating on the improvement of specific practices rather than linking that improvement to increased efficiency in the entire administrative machinery. As a consequence, reform plans consisted merely of shifts in functions between different public agencies without simultaneous attention to other important areas, such as training and the process of decision making. In this regard, feedback becomes important. Feedback means any information about the impact of past and present system performance and policy choices that can be used to improve future system performance and make new decisions about future policy directions. When feedback is lacking, institutions cannot respond to mistakes quickly enough to avoid their adverse consequences. Feedback is enhanced through monitoring of reform agents and the beneficiaries of the reform process to ensure there is no misinterpretation of the reform intent or that the process is not being sabotaged by those who are opposed to reform. Adequate feedback has beneficial impacts on motivation in general, effort, goal setting, goal attainment, and performance improvement.[44]

The final ingredient for successful implementation is support from the public and other interest groups such as the trade unions and public servants themselves. This support can best be realized through a conscious attempt to elicit their participation in the reform process. In recent years much has been written about the benefits of such participation, and the general consensus is that it must be encouraged to ensure sustained program benefits. Participation improves the channels of communication and stimulates a greater acceptance of program outcomes. It also can help overcome lack of sensitivity to beneficiary needs and views and, hence, can result in better outcomes and more accurate feedback information.

Concluding Remarks

Bureaucratic corruption is endemic in the Third World, and sweeping administrative reform measures need to be implemented to increase not only the administrative performance and efficiency of public servants and institutions, but also ethical behavior. Ethical behavior is a beneficial mode of behavior for both the individual and society in general. The general population as well as public officials must be concerned with the welfare of others rather than trying to maximize their personal gain. Given what is known about the nature and causes of bureaucratic corruption in the Third World, however, it may be wishful thinking to advocate that such corruption can ever be totally eradicated in those nations. Indeed, in the West, where there is a strong emphasis on ethical behavior in both the public and the private sectors, corrupt activity is exposed from time to time. It may be possible, however, to reduce bureaucratic corruption in the Third World, as advocated here, and thereby to diminish its dysfunctional effects on the development process.

Dealing with bureaucratic corruption through comprehensive administrative reform can have a greater positive impact than piecemeal measures simply to punish wrongdoers. However desirable punishment may be, it merely satisfies a social demand for retribution. It is not and never has been a deterrent. The best anticorruption campaigns must emphasize the creation and maintenance of a moral and accountable administration. This can only be accomplished through administrative reform. The capacity of a nation's political system to prevent, detect, and control the abuse of power is of major significance here since, in the final analysis, ethical and accountable behavior among public servants is a reflection of similar behavior among the political leaders.[45] Public officials in Third World nations will only accept the challenge to live up to the highest standards when codes of behavior that enhance ethical conduct are exemplified and enforced.

The experiences of the World Bank suggest that administrative reform programs must aim also at installing personnel information and management systems that are more tightly linked to payrolls, improved training systems, simplification of the legal framework governing the civil service, and providing stronger incentives to attract and retain higher-caliber, and presumably more ethical, public servants.[46] The World Bank may need to place greater emphasis on some of these factors in its economic recovery programs for Third World countries.

Notes

1. Robert Klitgaard, *Controlling Corruption* (Berkeley: University of California Press, 1988), pp. 2–3.

2. Mamadou Dia, *A Governance Approach to Civil Service Reform in sub-Saharan Africa* (Washington, DC: World Bank, 1993), p. 12.

3. Herbert H. Werlin, "Revisiting Corruption: With a New Definition," *International Review of Administrative Sciences, 60,* 4 (1994), p. 547.

4. Kempe Ronald Hope, Sr., "Administrative Corruption and Administrative Reform in Developing States," *Corruption and Reform, 2,* 2 (1987), pp. 127–47; and Kempe Ronald Hope, Sr., "Politics, Bureaucratic Corruption and Maladministration in the Third World," *International Review of Administrative Sciences, 51,* 1 (1985), pp. 1–6.

5. See, for example, Ernest Harsch, "Accumulators and Democrats: Challenging State Corruption," *Journal of Modern African Studies, 31,* 1 (1983), pp. 31–48.

6. See Carl Stone, *Work Attitudes Survey: A Report to the Jamaican Government* (Kingston, Jamaica: Earle Publishers, 1982).

7. It is argued that this "work ethic" is a major contributory factor to the generally capable economic management of the Barbados public authorities and the overall business-like attitudes of the Barbados work force. See, for example, Kempe Ronald Hope, Sr., *Economic Development in the Caribbean* (New York: Praeger, 1986), p. 208; and Inter-American Development Bank, *Economic and Social Progress in Latin America: 1983 Report* (Washington, DC: IDB, 1983), p. 161.

8. Ledivina V. Carino, "The Politicization of the Philippines Bureaucracy: Corruption or Commitment," *International Review of Administrative Sciences, 51,* 1 (1985), pp. 13–18.

9. See Gunnar Myrdal, *The Challenge of World Poverty* (London: Penguin, 1970).

10. Ibid.

11. N. Vijay Jagannathan, "Corruption, Delivery Systems and Property Rights," *World Development, 14,* 1 (1986), pp. 127–32; and Harendra Kanti Dey, "The Genesis and Spread of Economic Corruption: A Microtheoretic Interpretation," *World Development, 17* (April 1989), pp. 503–11.

12. J.G. Jabbra, "Bureaucratic Corruption in the Third World," *Indian Journal*

of Public Administration, 22 (October–December 1976), pp. 673–91.

13. Ibid.

14. Gerald E. Caiden and Naomi Caiden, "Administrative Corruption," *Public Administration Review, 37* (May–June 1977), pp. 302–9.

15. *The Economist* (February 4, 1984), pp. 13–14; and K.K. Prah, "Socio-Cultural Dimensions of Ethics and Accountability in African Public Services" in S. Rasheed and D. Olowu (eds.), *Ethics and Accountability in African Public Services* (Nairobi: ICIPE Science Press, 1993), pp. 49–62.

16. See, for example, Tevfik F. Nas, Albert C. Price, and Charles T. Weber, "A Policy-Oriented Theory of Corruption," *American Political Science Review, 80* (March 1986), pp. 107–19; and R.O. Tilman, "Emergence of Black-Market Bureaucracy: Administration, Development and Corruption in New States," *Public Administration Review, 27* (September–October 1968), pp. 437–44.

17. Ledivina V. Carino, "The Politicization of the Philippine Bureaucracy: Corruption or Commitment," pp. 13–18.

18. Robert Klitgaard, *Controlling Corruption*, p. 39.

19. Simcha B. Werner, "The Development of Political Corruption: A Case-Study of Israel," *Political Studies, 31* (December 1983), pp. 620–39.

20. David J. Gould and Jose Amaro-Reyes, *The Effects of Corruption on Administrative Performance: Illustrations from Developing Countries*, World Bank Staff Working Paper no. 580 (Washington, DC: World Bank, 1983), pp. 27–35.

21. *The Economist* (December 17, 1994), p. 43.

22. Kempe Ronald Hope, Sr., "Politics, Bureaucratic Corruption and Maladministration in the Third World," pp. 1–6; and Robert Klitgaard, *Tropical Gangsters: One Man's Experience with Development and Decadence in Deepest Africa* (New York: Basic Books, 1990), pp. 146–49.

23. Ibid.; and Simcha B. Werner, "New Directions in the Study of Administrative Corruption," *Public Administration Review, 43*, 2 (1983), pp. 146–54.

24. Jon S.T. Quah, "Administrative Reform: A Conceptual Analysis," *Philippine Journal of Public Administration, 20* (January 1976), pp. 50–67.

25. Kempe Ronald Hope, Sr., *The Dynamics of Development and Development Administration* (Westport, CT: Greenwood Press, 1984), pp. 79–94.

26. Hammergren, for example, erroneously asserted that administrative reform "is today in so much disrepute that it has all but disappeared from the vocabulary of development theory." See Linn A. Hammergren, *Development and the Politics of Administrative Reform: Lessons from Latin America* (Boulder, CO: Westview Press, 1983), p. 15.

27. A.R. Tyagi, "Administrative Training: A Theoretical Postulate," *International Review of Administrative Sciences, 40*, 2 (1974), pp. 155–70.

28. See World Bank, *World Development Report 1983* (New York: Oxford University Press, 1983), p. 107.

29. Metin Heper, "Notes on Public Administration 'Training' for the Potential Bureaucratic Elites of the Transitional Societies," *International Social Science Journal, 27*, 1 (1975), pp. 163–73.

30. Selcuk Ozgediz, *Managing the Public Service in Developing Countries: Issues and Prospects*, World Bank Staff Working Paper No. 583 (Washington, DC: World Bank, 1983), p. 2

31. Samuel Paul, *Training for Public Administration and Management in Developing Countries: A Review,* World Bank Working Paper no. 584 (Washington, DC: World Bank, 1983), p. 2.

32. Selcuk Ozgediz, *Managing the Public Service in Developing Countries: Issues and Prospects,* p. 29.

33. Dennis A. Rondinelli and G. Shabbir Cheema, "Implementing Decentralization Policies: An Introduction," in G. Shabbir Cheema and Dennis A. Rondinelli (eds.), *Decentralization and Development: Policy Implementation in Developing Countries* (Beverly Hills: Sage, 1983), p. 18.

34. United Nations, *Changes and Trends in Public Administration and Finance for Development: Second Survey 1977–1979* (New York: United Nations, 1982), pp. 6–7.

35. World Bank, *World Development Report 1983,* pp. 5–6.

36. Gerald E. Caiden, "The Vitality of Administrative Reform," *International Review of Administrative Sciences, 54* (September 1988), pp. 331–57.

37. Kempe Ronald Hope, Sr., *The Dynamics of Development and Development Administration,* pp. 90–92.

38. Ibid.; and World Bank, *World Development Report 1991* (New York: Oxford University Press, 1991), p. 131.

39. World Bank, *The Reform of Public Sector Management: Lessons from Experience* (Washington, DC: World Bank, 1991), p. 14.

40. Louis de Merode and Charles S. Thomas, "Implementing Civil Service Pay and Employment Reform in Africa: The Experiences of Ghana, the Gambia, and Guinea," in D. Lindauer and B. Nunberg (eds.), *Rehabilitating Government: Pay and Employment Reform in Africa* (Washington, DC: World Bank, 1994), pp.160–94.

41. Ibid.

42. Gerald E. Caiden, "Implementation—The Achilles Heel of Administrative Reform," in A.F. Leemans (ed.), *The Management of Change in Government* (The Hague: Martinus Nijhoff, 1976), pp. 145–48.

43. Nasir Islam, "Filling the Implementation Gap: How to Strengthen the Administrative Capacity at the Periphery," *Public Administration Review* (Pakistan), *19,* 2, (1981), pp. 1–19.

44. Kempe Ronald Hope, Sr., "The Administrative Reform Imperative in Developing Nations," *Public Administration, 60* (December 1988), pp. 7–18.

45. O.P. Dwivedi, "Ethics and Values of Public Responsibility and Accountability," *International Review of Administrative Sciences, 51,* 1 (1985), pp. 61–66.

46. Barbara Nunberg and John Nellis, *Civil Service Reform and the World Bank,* Staff Working Paper 422 (Washington, DC: World Bank, May 1990), pp. 24–29.

Chapter 7

Can the Third World Develop?
An Optimistic Viewpoint

The preceding chapters have examined and analyzed what were considered the primary issues pertaining and contributing to elusive development in the Third World, and advocated some policy responses which, in the author's opinion, can lead to an improvement in the *prospects* for development in those countries. This chapter offers an optimistic point of view with respect to the future development possibilities in the Third World. It also elaborates and clarifies the discussion with regard to appropriate policy responses.

Elusive development in the Third World has resulted in, among other things, tremendous public sector deficits, unmanageable debt, diminished living standards, an obsolete and deteriorating physical infrastructure, rapid urbanization, corrupt bureaucracies, widespread poverty, high rates of unemployment, and spiraling inflation. In addition, development planning and other state interventionist policies have crowded out what were once vibrant private sectors and led to the ascendancy of inefficient public enterprises that are unprofitable and impose a budgetary burden upon the Third World governments.

The negative consequences of the elusiveness of development in the Third World, however, go far beyond the purely economic. Currently, the development crisis has thrown the population of the great majority of those nations into severe poverty, and the hope for human progress now seems extremely bleak. Moreover, government spending on physical infrastructure has been dramatically reduced as resources continue to be limited. During the last decade, for example, the proportion of government expenditure devoted to health has fallen in most of the countries of sub-Saharan Africa, in more than half the countries of Latin America and the Caribbean, and in half the nations of Asia. In the thirty-seven poorest nations of the world, spending per person on education has declined by nearly 50 percent and on health care by nearly 25 percent during the last ten years. In almost half of the 103 Third World nations from which there is current information, the proportion of six- to eleven-year-olds enrolled in primary school is now falling. Also, throughout most of Africa and much of Latin America, average incomes fell by 10 to 25 percent during the 1980s.[1] Currently, about one-third of Latin America's population and about one-half of the population of sub-Saharan Africa live in dire poverty. These and other varied and comparable socioeconomic indices that characterize the development process and the human condition depict, in the great majority of cases, a situation of despair.

If one is *not* optimistic about the future prospects for some improvement in the socioeconomic situation and standards of living in the Third World nations, then one would also need to argue that all foreign aid programs should be dismantled (which, of course, some *have* argued, as discussed in chapter 3), and that all of the international agencies and nongovernmental organizations (NGOs) concerned with and engaged in the promotion of economic development should be disbanded. This, however, is not only myopic and nonsensical, but, as an argument, it is indefensible. Granted, some of the international development agencies (IDAs) suffer from some of the same ills that they have diagnosed in the Third World—overstaffing, excessive patronage, misplaced budgetary and program priorities, and so on. However, the existence and respective mandates of those agencies have allowed them to intervene in many Third World nations and to cooperate with the policy makers there to prevent a total collapse of the economies of those countries, as well to as provide emergency relief in times of other disasters, and, by so doing, to maintain some semblance of hope for their citizens and their future generations. Moreover, the developed countries and the IDAs have, in recent years, insisted on the implementation of macroeconomic reform programs by the Third World countries. Indeed, both bilateral and multilateral assistance nowadays are almost always tied to the demand for economic and, in some instances, political liberalization within recipient nations.

Undoubtedly, a considerable store of knowledge and skills exists in both the IDAs and the NGOs, and that augurs well for making future economic progress a reality in the Third World. In that regard, the point made by the late former executive director of the United Nations Children's Fund, in his 1989 report, warrants repetition here: "Resources will continue to be limited, but the crucial factor is that the ratio of resources to results can be vastly improved."[2] This ratio *has* to be vastly improved if there is to be shared optimism about the future of Third World development. The improvement in this ratio applies equally to both internal and external resources as well as to results. In other words, the Third World nations would also need to streamline their national development efforts and implement policies that are complementary to the endeavors of the IDAs and NGOs on their behalf.

Toward a Modified Policy Framework for Third World Development

By now it should be obvious that a number of modifications would have to be made to Third World development policy. The development objective requires that the indigenous policy framework be modified to take into consideration the experiences of the past as well as the current economic climate. Also significant is the need for flexibility to respond to changes in both the domestic and the international economic environment. Economic history and its impact are essential here to aid understanding of the nature of the present elusive development and the imperative to avoid repetition of policies that have resulted in such a situation.

Flexible Market-Oriented Planning

First in this policy framework is the requirement for flexible market-oriented planning (FMOP). FMOP is short-term planning that is geared to emphasizing the market mechanism. It is enlightened state intervention to provide guidance in the allocation of scarce resources and designed as an alternative to the deficiencies of past conventional planning where state intervention was frequently particularistic, promoting the interests of such special groups as the military, landowners, the urban as against the rural population, and so on.[3] The emphasis of FMOP is on the benefits of markets. The record of development and the increasing store of empirical research have heightened recognition of the importance of markets and incentives and of the limits of government intervention and central planning.[4]

FMOP represents relevant planning to the extent that some kind of planning may have to be undertaken in the Third World. Conventional approaches to planning, with rigid time frames, the breakdown of planning tasks into sectors and regions, and a centralized and technocratic perspective on plan formulation and implementation, did not work during the past three decades and are unlikely to be effective in this time of economic crisis.[5] FMOP, as envisaged here, entails a short-term policy framework (one to two years) that emphasizes the role of the private sector and delineates private sector initiatives, along with the required interconnections between public sector activities, which are necessary, and the budget.

The FMOP approach is guided by the principle that governments should leave consumers, producers, and the price mechanism as free as possible to allocate resources. Some necessary activities for state intervention, however, would have to be included in the FMOP. The best current representation of this is in the supply of infrastructure, such as roads. Left to itself, the market would be at something of a loss to say what roads should be built and where. It would be the task of the state to say whether a particular road were needed at all, to choose the route, to set the rules for contracts for construction, and so on.

FMOP would also eliminate the need for an extensive planning bureaucracy. What would be needed, rather, is a planning committee and an appropriate technical staff. The planning committee should be composed only of those individuals engaged in socioeconomic planning from the relevant ministries and government agencies. The committee, through its chairperson, who would be appointed by the cabinet, would report directly to the cabinet or to the pertinent cabinet subcommittee. The planning committee has to be free of all interference, however, to conduct its work once the planning process begins for each given planning period. Development planning done in this fashion will offer the greatest degree of efficiency with respect to plan formulation and implementation. It debureaucratizes the process without centralizing it, and at the same time maintains some of the flexibility the process requires for rapid responses.

Privatization and Private Sector Activity

In concert with the FMOP, as well as being among its goals, are the requirements that Third World nations deregulate their economies, privatize their public enterprises, and promote and sponsor initiatives that enhance private sector activities, particularly foreign direct investment. Such policy actions, in turn, will further improve the business climate by allowing market forces to offset themselves, which, in turn, will have beneficial multiplier effects for the Third World countries and thereby help to stem their current intensive and rapid economic decay.

Without a viable private sector, Third World governments would not be able to stimulate or sustain economic growth, and their economies would remain in crisis indefinitely, thereby contributing to all sorts of negative externalities. It is worth repeating here that public enterprises in the Third World should be privatized, and further private sector initiatives need to be put in place not only to benefit from the subterranean economy but also to encourage additional domestic and foreign private investment in general. It is essential to stress here, however, that privatization does not necessarily imply termination of government responsibility for any essential services or for the general welfare of the citizenry.

Privatization is defined here as the transfer of ownership and control from the public to the private sector, with particular reference to asset sales. It is therefore equated with total or partial denationalization. The growing appeal for privatization in the Third World nations derives from the economic case for such privatization. That economic case is made by the fact that public ownership is much more extensive than can be justified and sustained in terms of the development role of public enterprises in Third World countries, the poor economic performance of the public enterprises when compared with private enterprises, and the built-in characteristics of public ownership—such as political interference and bureaucratic failure—that give rise to economic inefficiency.[6] Undoubtedly, some of the worst excesses of public ownership would be diminished by a shift to private ownership. Simply taking public enterprise decision making out of the political arena and withdrawing financial backing will eliminate much of the inefficiency. If such a change involves the mere transfer of a public monopoly to the private sector, however, with its monopoly power left intact and no change in the regulatory regime, such gains will be limited.

Before we look at the privatization policy framework, it may be useful to review some quantitative evidence on the performance, or lack thereof, of the public enterprises in the Third World. This performance varies from region to region as well as from sector to sector, with Asian countries showing fewer problems than Latin American nations, which, in turn, perform better than the countries of sub-Saharan Africa. In those few cases where performance is profitable, it is usually due to noninterference by the politicians and/or because the enterprises enjoy monopoly or near-monopoly status. In general, many public enterprises that were expected to generate surpluses, for use by state planners in the development process, now lose rather than make money and impose a budgetary burden on Third World treasuries.

In Africa, for example, Kenya had a rate of return of only 0.4 percent on the $1.4 billion invested in the public enterprises sector between 1963 and 1984. Of sixteen major Kenyan agricultural and agroindustrial public enterprises, aggregate losses for the years 1977–84 totaled $183 million. In West Africa, 62 percent of the public enterprises in twelve countries had net losses and 36 percent had negative net worth. In Egypt, during 1986–87, the authorities were unable to collect profit transfers from public enterprises equivalent to their target return of 2.6 percent on the government's investment. In Tunisia, total government financial support to the public enterprise sector has ranged from 5 to 7 percent of GDP in the period 1983–86. Included were subsidies to cover operating deficits (10 to 20 percent of the total), capital transfers for investment and debt repayment (20 to 40 percent of the total), and new capital injections in the form of equity participation and lending (30 to 50 percent of the total).[7]

In Guyana, 71 percent of the enterprises composing the Guyana State Corporation were unable to transfer dividends and pay taxes to the central government during the period 1980–88.[8] In India, from the late 1960s to the mid-1980s, the rate of return on total assets employed by public enterprises was between 2 and 3 percent while the corresponding rate for private sector enterprises was between 9 and 12 percent. Similarly, in South Korea in the early 1980s the public enterprise rate of return was only 7.8 percent, compared with a private sector rate of 27.5 percent. In Nigeria, it was estimated that the national airline was losing $8.6 million per month and its debts exceeded $450 million.[9]

Rarely in history has an innovation in economic and financial policy caught on as quickly as privatization. Privatization requires the reassigning of the state's development role, or convincing officials that they can achieve development with less state intervention. As a policy framework, privatization became popular because of its potential and actual contributions to the development process as an alternative to public enterprises. The basic methods of privatization include the public offering of shares, the private sale of shares, the sale of assets, joint ventures, management/employee buyouts, and leases.[10] Privatization today is being driven by a spirit of pragmatic reaction to at least three decades of failed experiments in public enterprise activity. Such policy shifts that question the ideological base and appropriateness of state intervention in the economy are rare.[11] Privatization is in part, therefore, a response to the need for fiscal austerity and responsibility, and it is easier to implement than had been originally thought because the austerity and equity costs are relatively small compared with those of the broader structural adjustment process.[12]

Hence, a pervasive dissatisfaction with the performance of public enterprises is at the center of the appeal of privatization in the Third World nations. Privatization can cut government expenditures and help restore budgetary balance. This fiscal justification for privatization is certainly plausible, particularly for the poorer Third World nations. Privatization can also be justified in terms of economic efficiency.[13] There are three kinds of efficiency gains that can be potentially derived from privatization. These are gains in allocative efficiency, productive efficiency, and nonmarket efficiency.[14] However, despite the fiscal, efficiency, and other benefits of privatization, there are those who argue for caution in its implementation while others categorically exhibit no enthusiasm for it whatsoever and, in fact, condemn it.

The arguments for caution seem to be based on the notion that privatization is unlikely to overcome the kinds of economic and political forces that undermined public production activities in the first place. Consequently, the most likely opponents to privatization are usually found in the state apparatus itself, who do not want to lose cultivated rents and prerogatives, or the political support base.[15] At another extreme, the arguments against privatization are couched in the need to promote a new arrangement of the status quo public, state, and private interests which will, somehow, be more functional. The argued purpose is not the dismantling of the present system of regulations and the state-controlled productive apparatus, but rather its rationalization—in a gradual and clearly understood way—so as to improve the overall efficiency of the economy, in both its public and its private sectors.[16] It is also argued, moreover, that state ownership does not necessarily result in poor enterprise performance since the determinants of an enterprise's success or failure are not related to who owns it but, rather, the enterprise's success or failure is a function of the extent and direction in which its owners exercise the authority that comes with ownership and the efficiency with which managers carry out their jobs.[17]

It has also been suggested that the problems of public enterprises may be a consequence of their control systems, which are usually excessive in quantity but rather deficient in quality. They interfere in day-to-day activities but provide little or no strategic direction.[18] This, combined with inappropriate motivation and reward systems, has led to the development of dysfunctional organization cultures. The remedy therefore is not one of simply changing the ownership of public enterprises but of reforming their culture.[19]

The above arguments in favor of public enterprises, however, all neglect the crucial importance of efficiency and other proven economic benefits of private sector activity. Privatization represents a rational economic response to the ills and negative economic impact of more than two decades of state ownership of productive enterprises. One of the factors indiscriminately overlooked by the opponents of privatization is the fiscal burden that public enterprises in the Third World impose upon governments. That fiscal burden increases budget deficits and leads to even further economic deterioration. Essentially, and for the most part, the public enterprise mode of production has been an economic disaster in the Third World and should now be abandoned, except in those very few cases where it is abundantly clear that other interests, social impact and so on, must supersede economic considerations. The track record of public sector investment in the Third World has not been an inspiring one and it is time that we accept this reality.

Through privatization and private sector initiatives, it is indeed possible to expose Third World economies to market forces and thereby to promote greater choice, competition, and efficiency. By deregulating their economies, the Third World nations would be in a position to offer a wider array of opportunities to both local and foreign investors. In spite of the fact that, in the past, misplaced nationalism fueled opposition to foreign investors, Third World countries must now come to grips with the overall negative results of such actions. The policy makers of many of those countries are therefore now coming to the realization that the more foreign investors they can interest in their country's prosperity, then so much the better, since with such investment comes goodwill and, ultimately, the Third World countries would obtain some influence over the foreign investors, and not the foreign investors over them.

Foreign investment benefits the host country in many ways. As a matter of fact, direct foreign investment has multiple effects on the economy of a host country in terms of production, employment, access to finance and markets, income, the balance of payments, and general welfare. These sources of capital help to modernize factories, create jobs, produce a greater choice of quality goods at competitive prices, bring new technology and management techniques, and earn desperately needed foreign exchange for the Third World countries. Foreign investment is also likely to bolster competition in domestic markets. During the 1980s, foreign direct investment in Third World nations was relatively stable, averaging $10 billion to $15 billion a year (about 10 to 15 percent of total capital inflows). However, from 1986 to 1993, foreign direct investment in the Third World increased from $10 billion to $56 billion.[20]

For the Third World countries to encourage more foreign investment, they will have to further liberalize their policies toward such investment, particularly with respect to entry restrictions, screening procedures, sectors open to investment, ownership restrictions, investment incentives, and repatriation of profits.[21] Indeed, a number of Third World countries have already either revised or introduced investment codes. In sub-Saharan Africa alone, for example, more than twenty countries have done so since 1982.

Many countries have also eased entry restrictions; for example, Argentina has opened up oil exploration and exploitation to foreign investors, while Decision 220 of the Andean Pact (May 1987) now allows the member countries of Latin America to regulate the sectoral entry of foreign investment at the national level, replacing the more stringent regional restrictions that had been in effect. Other examples include simplified and streamlined procedures for screening applications for foreign investment by creating one-stop investment agencies, as in Guyana, Ghana, and Kenya; relaxed rules governing the share of enterprises that may be owned by foreign investors, in Ghana, Guyana, and Mexico; new fiscal incentives for foreign investment, as in India and Ghana; abolition of restrictions on the repatriation of profits by foreign investors, as in Colombia, Guyana, Zaire, and Venezuela; and new or expanded domestic securities markets in Brazil, India, and Malaysia.[22]

Despite these developments, a great deal more needs to be done, particularly in the area of investment promotion to attract foreign direct investment. Promotion efforts need to be regularly undertaken by the political leaders and appropriate trade teams to inform potential investors that their respective nations are open for new and/or additional business. This is particularly important in those nations where there is no organized capital market or where such capital markets are weak.

It is believed that underdeveloped capital markets have hindered privatization efforts in countries as varied as Sri Lanka, Malaysia, and Ghana.[23] More compelling and convincing arguments, however, have been made elsewhere to show that privatization can lead to opportunities for the development and/or improvement of capital markets. As pointed out by Waters,[24] for example, there is really no point in complaining that the organized local financial markets do not exist in many of the Third World nations since the process of raising funds for privatization can be the vehicle for recognizing the existence of unofficial financial markets and can provide an opportunity to create the missing organized financial structures. This was clearly borne out in the case of Jamaica, where measures were used to compensate for the weakness of capital markets. In Jamaica's privatization of the National Commercial Bank, the government launched an elaborate information campaign about the public share offer and developed a distribution mechanism that ultimately resulted in the offering being oversubscribed by a factor of 2.7.[25] Clearly, then, the promotion and dissemination of information on the enterprises to be privatized play a key part in the magnitude and timeliness of the response to privatization efforts.

To further encourage private direct foreign investment, the Private Sector Development Review Group of the World Bank has recommended that the Bank pay more attention, in its policy-based lending, to overcome factors that deter private direct investment. A new Bank agency, the Multilateral Investment Guarantee Agency (MIGA),[26] has been created and is now providing advice on how countries can attract investment, along with guarantees to investors against noncommercial risks.

Another consideration, in the modified policy framework, ought to be the further simplification and decentralization of the government bureaucracy, with an eye toward ultimately deregulating, or depoliticizing, national productive life in the Third World. Decentralization promotes participation, access, and responsiveness. Through decentralization, new national standards can be emphasized to deal with problems that are now national in scope. Deregulation in this context means increasing the responsibilities and opportunities of private individuals and reducing those of the state. Deregulation involves depoliticizing the economy in order to protect the economic sphere and to reduce the negative consequences of the burden of government, including the impairment of economic growth and social efficiency.[27]

The economic sphere in the Third World needs to be freed from the grip of parasitic public enterprises and the arbitrary influence of political decision making and ideological turf battles that do nothing but retard development. In order to produce wealth, it is necessary that the state's actions not obstruct the actions of those who are serious about investing, in any magnitude, in the Third World countries. The Third World governments must further adjust to the idea that they must limit themselves to functioning only in those necessary areas in which private industry cannot or will not function. All of the remaining vestiges of the paralyzing central government control and state planning must be eliminated. In other words, politicians must decide to withdraw themselves and the administrative machinery from detailed intervention in their respective economies and concentrate their attention on the kinds of policy making, some of which are advocated in this book, that both historical experience and contemporary evidence have shown to be vital to economic success.

Debt Management and Control

The debt crisis began to attract international attention in the early 1980s when it became apparent to the world that Mexico would never be able to pay its foreign debt. In the early 1980s, the debt crisis was thought of as a liquidity problem; today it is widely regarded as a problem of insolvency. As such, there is now greater international cooperation in working toward and implementing debt relief. In particular, the creditor country governments have formulated varying plans to assist with debt relief, which include debt reduction or the writing off of portions of the total debt.

For the Third World nations, the net transfer of financial resources (net capital or resource flow minus the net payment of interest and dividends) turned positive in 1990, having been negative since 1984 and with a net outflow of at least $38 billion during 1984–88. The situation in the 1980s had a direct relationship with the debt problem because the part of the capital flow that had shrunk was the credit flow, and the part of the investment income payment that had grown was the interest paid. The problem primarily affected the seventeen largest debtors. As a matter of fact, the negative transfer of resources of the aggregate of Third World countries in the 1980s was largely a reflection of the transfer from that group of seventeen.[28] When the net transfer for all the capital-importing countries combined turned negative in the 1980s, large amounts of domestically earned foreign exchange had to be transferred abroad instead of being used at home.

In addition to the above contributory factors, the Third World nations, having accumulated totally excessive debt burdens, have been unable to grow out of them. The total Third World debt (including short-term debt) outstanding now exceeds $1 trillion and represents approximately 32 percent of the aggregate GNP of those countries and more than 150 percent of their export earnings. The debt ratios suggest that the total debt now overwhelms the economic size and export earnings capacity of the majority of the Third World nations and, although measures have been taken to increase the flow of resources from official sources, the decline in private flows has rendered the total volume of financial flows to those countries inadequate to meet the needs for economic growth, poverty alleviation, structural adjustment, and the very resolution of debt difficulties.

Reluctance on the part of commercial banks to increase their exposure in the Third World nations has, consequently, resulted in financial stagnation. Virtually the only Third World nations with easy access to external borrowing are the more successful East Asian exporters of manufactures, and, at least in the short run, they have little need for foreign capital and little willingness to borrow new money. For all other Third World nations, significant efforts would have to be made, in addition to other measures advocated in this work, to increase capital flows and to reduce the fiscal burden of the state if those nations are to be able to service their debt in the future, in a manageable manner. In that regard, there are two sets of policies that are important in a modified policy framework.

First, the Third World nations need to adhere to their debt-ceiling limitations. These limitations should not be exceeded unless such actions are accompanied by economic adjustment policies and/or Paris Club debt restructuring. Adhering to debt-ceiling limitations would require that Third World nations strengthen their debt management by measures directly designed to assure control and surveillance of the total external debt. These measures would include screening procedures to ascertain that foreign loans are being contracted only for high-priority projects, prior authorization procedures for public loans, and central registration procedures for private loans.[29]

This system for central debt recording enables a country continually to check its overall indebtedness and service obligations, and can be accomplished through the establishment of a Debt Management Unit, appropriately staffed, in the Ministry of Finance or the Central Bank. The establishment of such a unit is particularly important and critical in those Third World nations with a large number of state-owned enterprises capable of contracting foreign loans with a government guarantee.

In concert with such debtor–creditor collaborative debt-relief measures as debt–equity swaps, buybacks, and debt–debt swaps, Third World nations need to implement, as the second suggested policy here, measures to lure flight capital back and to keep it at home. It has been suggested that the more than $170–$300 billion of flight capital belonging to residents of Third World countries lies at the heart of the debt problem of those countries, and that without such capital, Latin American countries—and other indebted nations—will not be able to grow their way back to creditworthiness.[30] Consequently, this financial hemorrhaging effect on the Third World countries must be halted.

Capital flight entails the movement of private nonbusiness capital to other countries in order to diversify portfolios, to hedge against expected devaluations of national currencies, to get better yields, to avoid taxes or confiscation, to seek anonymity, or generally to respond to political or financial crises. Capital flight from the Third World has intensified in recent years, partly because the incentives for such movements became greater (national economic mismanagement, overvalued exchange rates, negative real interest rates, big budget deficits, high inflation, inefficient capital markets, and so on), and partly because the opportunities for these outward movements of capital were encouraged through the active solicitation of these funds by banks in the creditor nations,[31] the same banks to which some of the Third World nations are heavily indebted. The explanations for and the reasons underlying capital flight in the Third World point to serious weaknesses in the economic framework of those countries. Capital flight from the Third World is bad because it destabilizes interest rates and exchange rates, reflects discrepancies between private and social rates of return, contributes to erosion of the domestic tax base, reduces domestic investment, and necessitates increases in foreign borrowing, which, in turn, increases the national cost of borrowing.[32]

Encouraging the repatriation of capital to the Third World would necessarily entail sound financial policies and incentives. Flight capital has been a missing link in the fight to break the vicious circle of declining growth and increasing debt. If flight capital could be lured back, it would provide more funds than the banks are now able or willing to provide. History and evidence suggest that luring flight capital back and keeping it at home require sufficiently high real interest rates and avoiding overvalued currencies. In addition, eliminating the tax liability on returning money can be a tremendous boost to the return of flight capital. Whenever currencies are overvalued and interest rates are kept below equilibrium levels, capital will fly away.

It is now imperative that the Third World countries drastically reduce their military expenditures and thereby reduce their external debt. During the past three decades there has been a rapid increase in Third World military spending, despite the faltering economic circumstances in most of those countries during the same period. Military expenditures of the Third World countries have increased by 7.5 percent per year during the past twenty-five years, and the military debt now accounts for more than one-third of the total debt for many of the Third World nations. Although the industrial nations reduced the share of their GDP allocated to the military by one-half from 6.3 percent in 1960 to 3.2 percent in 1992, the Third World countries as a whole only decreased their share from 4.2 percent in 1960 to 3.8 percent in 1992. However, the poorest Third World nations increased the percentage share of their GDP from 2.1 percent to 5.9 percent, while the countries of sub-Saharan Africa also increased their share of military expenditure from 0.7 percent of GDP to 3 percent of GDP over the same period. In 1992, the total military expenditure of the Third World was estimated in 1985 prices to be almost US$137 billion.[33] Clearly, this is excessive, given their current economic circumstances and the now apparent end to the Cold War and, hence, the end of the need for country alignments to one or another superpower.

Exchange Rate Flexibility

A country's residents will not, however, repatriate capital if by doing so they lose flexibility in its use thereafter. This suggests, therefore, that there needs to be a simultaneous liberalization of the exchange rate with attempts to move toward high positive real interest rates in order to provide the strongest incentive for reversing capital flight and supporting the balance of payments in the short term.[34] Moreover, exchange rate flexibility is necessary, as a general policy, because controls or misalignments of the exchange rate have imposed severe losses of welfare and efficiency and, hence, are economically counterproductive. Exchange-rate misalignments usually are accomplished by a number of severe exchange and trade controls designed to reduce the drainage of foreign-exchange reserves. These trade and exchange controls, however, introduce large inefficiency costs that tend to be even greater than those resulting from the misalignment itself. For example, smuggling and black markets for goods and currencies have flourished.[35]

In general, trade (usually import) controls lead to a lower price of foreign exchange in terms of domestic currency, because there tends to be an excess demand for foreign exchange.[36] This undervaluation of foreign currency or overvaluation of domestic currency tends to discourage the earning of foreign exchange through increased exports and would require further rigid foreign exchange and import controls to deal with the excess demand for foreign exchange. The overvaluation of the domestic currency effectively undervalues the price of the imports and thus underestimates the real social cost of a country's imports. Such a situation only misleads the public into demanding more imports than can be financed with the available foreign exchange.

Currency overvaluation imposes an extra burden on export-oriented industries and to a large extent inhibits their growth in small Third World countries. A lower valued currency in those countries would encourage more export-oriented or outward-looking policies and thus support the exporting industries in their efforts to enter world markets and become more competitive in the long run. It would also discourage the importation of certain commodities and make some domestic industries more competitive. The overvaluation of currency also allows for a distortion in the capital–labor ratio in production activities. Since imported goods are usually made more cheaply, production processes with high import content would be selected. Such a situation tends to reduce the employment effects of an import control policy.[37]

Realigning the exchange rates to be consistent with fundamental economic circumstances, and to maintain their flexibility in Third World nations, requires the use of the devaluation mechanism in concert with other macroeconomic policies. Nominal devaluation has the immediate objective of reducing or eliminating the misalignment of the real exchange rate by generating a real devaluation, which would improve the international competitiveness of Third World nations and ultimately improve their external payments position. Devaluation has three primary effects on an economy. The first is that it reduces expenditures. By increasing domestic prices, devaluation lowers the real value of assets denominated in domestic currency, including domestic money. The result is a negative wealth effect.[38] This means that the real value of cash balances also declines, thereby inducing an excess flow demand for cash balances matched by an excess flow supply of real goods. To the extent that the negative wealth effect dominates any positive wealth effect, expenditure on all goods will decline, and the trade deficit will also decline.

The second effect of devaluation is that it increases the supply of final goods. By increasing the domestic price of imported inputs, devaluation increases the price of final goods, thereby reducing their demand and shifting their supply schedule upward. Finally, devaluation tends to diminish the share of imported goods in total consumption by raising import prices in relation to domestic prices. This switching of expenditure will improve the external position.

Devaluation has been found to be successful, however, only when accompanied by a package of consistent macroeconomic policies. The available evidence confirms that price elasticities of supply in Third World countries are generally positive, but that in the short run such elasticities can be fairly low in comparison with long-run elasticities. As a result, a real exchange-rate realignment, once in place, must be sustained, unless the basic circumstances change.[39] This requires the implementation of other macroeconomic policies. Currently, the data suggest that considerable progress has been made in achieving exchange-rate flexibility. By 1987, the real exchange rate for fifteen Third World countries had, on average, depreciated by about 40 percent relative to the 1965–81 level. Two immediate benefits of this realignment have been an increase in the export volumes of those countries and the virtual elimination of the premium in their currency black markets.[40]

Trade Liberalization

An appropriate exchange-rate regime, during the liberalization process, and the maintenance of fiscal stability are essential for a sustainable liberalization program. Trade liberalization can be defined as any change that moves a country's trade system toward greater neutrality. If a trade system operates as it would in the absence of government interference, it is considered to be neutral. Trade liberalization seeks to reform a country's international commercial policies in order to improve economic welfare by achieving a better allocation of resources in the long term.[41] For trade liberalization to be successful, it has to be linked to the conduct of macroeconomic policy, including the implementation of a flexible exchange rate, appropriate fiscal and monetary policies, a relevant credit and wage policy, and so on.

Trade liberalization manifests itself in two ways. First, it shows up through a change in the price system that alters relative prices in the economy. A move toward neutrality lowers the average level and reduces the dispersion within the system of protection rates. The second manifestation is a change in the form of market intervention from controls through government regulation to the use of the price system.[42] Over the long term, the primary benefit of trade liberalization should be an increase in exports at the expense of import-competing activities. At the same time, trade liberalization encourages some activities at the expense of others. During this process the transition costs and delays in moving resources from the losing to the gaining sectors may induce some short-term unemployment. The multicountry evidence, however, suggests that the impact of trade liberalization on unemployment has been very small.[43]

Trade liberalization in the Third World, however, is likely to be influenced considerably by economic conditions in the world economy. Liberalization would be much more successful during a period of growth in the world economy (which would tend to increase demand for exports) than during a period of downturn. In addition, a substantial nominal devaluation at the inception and a strict adherence to a menu of constrained fiscal and monetary policies have been advocated as crucial aspects, under the majority of initial conditions, for the eventual success of a policy of liberalization.[44]

Liberalizing trade in Third World countries offers an excellent opportunity for those nations to enhance their foreign-exchange earnings and to take advantage of the various opportunities provided for them to increase their exports without significant barriers—such opportunities as provided, for example, by the industrial nations under the Generalized System of Preferences (GSP), by the European Community (EC) to the African, Caribbean, and Pacific (ACP) group of countries through the Lomé Convention, or by the United States to the nations in the Caribbean Basin through the Caribbean Basin Initiative (CBI). These are preferential schemes that guarantee markets for certain exports and, consequently, the earning of foreign exchange. Undoubtedly, a liberal trade regime is superior to a highly restrictive one in generating economic efficiency and growth and requires the prompt attention of Third World governments. Postponing this type of adjustment program can only result in increased black market premia, inflation, and current account deficits.

Concluding Remarks

Moving toward economic development in the Third World means, essentially, modifying current economic policy to draw upon what actually works as well as new approaches, some of which are advocated in this work, that are consistent with the present economic problems and circumstances in those countries. If the policy framework is not modified, then development will remain elusive in the Third World ad infinitum. On the other hand, if the policy framework is modified, development is quite achievable for many of the Third World countries.

Understandably, and given the varying levels of development that have been achieved among the Third World countries as well as their varied past approaches to development, the modified policy framework advocated here would be of greater significance to some countries than to others. Clearly, the "four-tigers"—Hong Kong, Singapore, Taiwan, and South Korea—stand out in any comparison of economic performance. Their high economic growth rates, low inflation, improved life expectancy, and higher literacy levels contrast sharply with the economic and social stagnation in many of the other Third World countries.[45]

The East Asian countries posted growth rates exceeding 8 percent during the past two decades. On the other hand, the living standards of millions in Latin America are now lower than in the early 1970s. In most of sub-Saharan Africa living standards have fallen to levels last seen in the 1960s. The Latin America and Caribbean growth rates in the 1970s averaged 5 percent, compared with 2.8 percent in 1992, while in sub-Saharan Africa the growth rates for similar periods were 2.7 percent and 1.2 percent, respectively. The successful East Asian countries have pursued, and continue to pursue, many of the economic policies discussed in this book.

Third World states can be viewed as a group of self-regarding individuals and groups interacting strategically with private agents.[46] The state is then seen as seeking to maximize its own utility (including incomes, perquisites, and power), and not necessarily the welfare of its citizens.[47] The state is, in effect, a predator, a role that is alien and inimical to the process of development. Such a situation requires action to deregulate state activity. Moreover, the efficiency of the state would be enhanced by limiting its role in the economy. Through deregulation and economic liberalization, the state would be concerned less with intervention and more with creating the basic conditions and environment necessary for development.[48]

Economic development is a complex process that involves more than just economic factors. Consequently, the choice of policies must, obviously, be based on the particular circumstances of individual countries. Nonetheless, given the generally similar characteristics of the economic problems now faced by the majority of Third World nations, there are some general implications for policy. In any case, the basic thrust of any attempt to make a sustained effort to promote economic development must contain elements of the modified policy framework suggested here. In addition, committed effort must be made to incorporate the subterranean sector into national economic policy. The national economic significance of the subterranean sector in Third World economies now necessitates that it not be dismissed, but, rather, that it be integrated and promoted.

If development in the Third World is viewed, as suggested, in terms of profits and losses, then it will be found that most losses come from the state sector and its accompanying redistributive system, while profits are derived from competitive activities.[49] As the ensuing economic crisis gains momentum in the Third World, economic liberalization then becomes an inevitable policy solution. Economic liberalization becomes necessary to redirect economies away from unnecessary governmental control, intervention, and repression. One of the ironic effects of past economic policy in many Third World countries has been that attempts to exercise political control over ever-increasing areas of economic life have often led to a decrease of the government's effective areas of control regarding private agents, as represented primarily by the subterranean sector, who find numerous ways of avoiding them. In effect, there now appears to be "a sort of 'Laffer curve' of government intervention, so that after a certain stage, increased government intervention, instead of increasing the area of government control, diminishes it."[50] Economic liberalization then becomes obligatory because the costs to the state of both intervention and its resulting negative effects are far greater than the short-term costs of liberalizing the economy.

It must be noted, however, that attention would have to be given to the order in which the modified policy framework is implemented—that is, to the sequencing of economic liberalization in the Third World. This is an important issue that seems to have become blurred in the noise on adjustment programs. Sequencing is important, however, to the ultimate success of liberalization programs since inappropriate sequencing may result in more severe distortions than those they were initially designed to eliminate. Two possible sequencing paths have been advocated in the literature on economic liberalization. The first, based primarily on Latin American experience, advocates the control of the fiscal deficit before reforming the domestic capital market and the external current account and then opening up the capital account.[51]

The second path advocates first reducing the fiscal deficit, while removing domestic capital market distortions, and then eliminating the exchange controls and freely floating the exchange rate, accompanied by an announcement and the implementation of a phased program for removing commodity market distortions.[52] Which of these two paths is chosen depends on the nature of the distortions and the immediate results required. However, for those countries particularly concerned with capital flight, it would seem that the first path should be chosen, since if interest rates are repressed, the liberalization of the capital account will most definitely encourage capital flight.

Finally, we can gauge further from this work that there are three sets of reasons contributing to the current development crisis in the Third World and the current imperative to move toward economic liberalization.[53] The first is that, during most of the twentieth century, Third World governments have increased the scope of their involvement in their economies and in the lives of their citizens. Whether through regulation, taxation, or expropriation, the growth in government was sustained and relentless, taking place with no distinction between democracies and dictatorships. The second is that government mismanagement and inefficiencies manifested themselves in increased costs of government services. This, inevitably, resulted in higher government expenditures and larger deficits, which in turn led to more borrowing and higher taxes. Third is the fact that some governments grew more rapidly than others. The market economies were better able to limit government growth than were their socialist counterparts. Consequently, by the early 1980s, the countries with the highest rates of economic growth and prosperity were those that emphasized market-oriented policies, while those with serious economic problems were those that had emphasized state intervention and regulation of their economies.

Notes

1. James P. Grant, *The State of the World's Children 1989* (New York: Oxford University Press, 1989), p. 1.
2. Ibid., p. 37.
3. Tony Killick, *A Reaction Too Far: Economic Theory and the Role of the State in Developing Countries* (London: Overseas Development Institute, 1989), p. 18.
4. World Bank, *Research News, 6* (Summer 1985), p. 1.
5. Francisco R. Sagasti, "National Development Planning in Turbulent Times: New Approaches and Criteria for Institutional Design," *World Development, 16,* 4 (1988), p. 437.
6. Richard Hemming and Ali M. Mansoor, *Privatization and Public Enterprises*, Occasional Paper 56 (Washington, DC: IMF, January 1988), pp. 1–3.
7. This information and all of the preceding data in this paragraph are derived from John Nellis and Sunita Kikeri, "Public Enterprise Reform: Privatization and the World Bank," *World Development, 17* (May 1989), pp. 659–72; and Peter S. Heller and Christian Schiller, "The Fiscal Impact of Privatization, with Some Examples from Arab Countries," *World Development, 17* (May 1989), pp. 757–67.
8. Kempe Ronald Hope, Sr., *An Assessment of the Economic Performance of the Guyana State Corporation Group of Corporations,* report prepared for UNIDO/UNDP, Technical Assistance Project GUY 86/008, October 1988.
9. John Nellis and Sunita Kikeri, "Public Enterprise Reform: Privatization and the World Bank," p. 664; and Henry Bienen and John Waterbury, "The Political Economy of Privatization in Developing Countries," *World Development, 17* (May 1989), p. 630.
10. For a more elaborate discussion of these privatization methods and their implementation, see Charles Vuylsteke, *Techniques of Privatization of State-Owned Enterprises:* Volume I: *Methods and Implementation,* World Bank Tech-

nical Paper no. 88 (Washington, DC: World Bank, July 1988).

11. Raymond Vernon, *The Promise of Privatization: A Challenge for U.S. Policy* (New York: Council on Foreign Relations, 1988), pp. 18–19.

12. Henry Bienen and John Waterbury, "The Political Economy of Privatization in Developing Countries," pp. 618–19.

13. Nicolas Van de Walle, "Privatization in Developing Countries: A Review of the Issues," *World Development, 17* (May 1989), pp. 602–3.

14. Ibid., pp. 604–6.

15. Henry Bienen and John Waterbury, "The Political Economy of Privatization in Developing Countries," pp. 623–29; and Nicolas Van de Walle, "Privatization in Developing Countries: A Review of the Issues," pp. 608–11.

16. Juan M.F. Martin, "Interactions between the Public and Private Sectors and the Overall Efficiency of the Economy," *CEPAL Review, 36* (December 1988), pp. 101–16.

17. Heidi Vernon-Wortzel and Lawrence H. Wortzel, "Privatization: Not the Only Answer," *World Development, 17* (May 1989), pp. 633–41.

18. Ravi Ramamurti, "Controlling State-Owned Enterprises," *Public Enterprise, 7* (March 1987), pp. 99–117.

19. Heidi Vernon-Wortzel and Lawrence H. Wortzel, "Privatization: Not the Only Answer," pp. 639–40.

20. World Bank, *World Development Report 1989* (New York: Oxford University Press, 1989), p.23; and World Bank, *Annual Report 1994* (Washington, DC: World Bank, 1994), p. 27.

21. Kempe Ronald Hope, Sr., *Development Finance and the Development Process* (London: Greenwood Press, 1987), pp. 72–74; and David Goldsbrough, "Foreign Direct Investment in Developing Countries," *Finance and Development, 22* (March 1985), pp. 31–34.

22. Guy P. Pfeffermann, *Private Business in Developing Countries: Improved Prospects,* Discussion Paper no. 1 (Washington, DC: International Finance Corporation, 1988), pp. 27–33; Guy P. Pfeffermann and Dale R. Weigel, "The Private Sector and the Policy Environment," *Finance and Development, 25* (December 1988), pp. 25–27; and David Gill and Peter Tropper, "Emerging Stock Markets in Developing Countries," *Finance and Development, 25* (December 1988), pp. 28–31.

23. Guy P. Pfeffermann, *Private Business in Developing Countries: Improved Prospects,* p. 21.

24. A.R. Waters, "Privatization: A Viable Policy Option?" in *Privatization: Policies, Methods and Procedures* (Manila: Asian Development Bank, 1985).

25. Charles Vuylsteke, *Techniques of Privatization of State-Owned Enterprises:* Volume I: *Methods and Implementation,* p. 142; and Roger Leeds, "Privatization through Public Offerings: Lessons from Two Jamaican Cases," in R. Ramamurti and R. Vernon (eds.), *Privatization and Control of State-Owned Enterprises* (Washington, DC: World Bank, 1991), pp. 86–125.

26. The international convention establishing the MIGA took effect on April 12, 1988. The objective of the MIGA is to encourage the flow of investments for productive purposes among its member countries, in particular, to Third World countries. MIGA is intended to enhance mutual understanding and confidence between host governments and foreign investors and to heighten awareness of

investment opportunities. To fulfill its purposes, MIGA will guarantee eligible investments against losses resulting from noncommercial risk and will also carry out research and promotional activities.

27. Edwin S. Mills, *The Burden of Government* (Stanford, CA: Hoover Institution Press, 1986), pp. 154–56.

28. United Nations, *World Economic Survey 1988* (New York: United Nations, 1988), p. 52.

29. Kempe Ronald Hope, Sr., "External Borrowing and the Debt Problems of the Developing Nations," *International Journal of Development Banking, 2* (January 1984), pp. 22–24; and Marilyn J. Seiber, *International Borrowing by Developing Countries* (New York: Pergamon Press, 1982), p. 76.

30. *The Economist* (August 12, 1989), pp. 16, 64.

31. Jacques J. Polak, *Financial Policies and Development* (Paris: OECD Development Center Studies, 1989), p. 115; Mohsin S. Khan and Nadeem ul Haque, "Foreign Borrowing and Capital Flight," *IMF Staff Papers, 32* (December 1985), p. 608; and Alain Ize and Guillermo Ortiz, "Fiscal Rigidities, Public Debt, and Capital Flight," *IMF Staff Papers, 34* (June 1987), pp. 311–32.

32. John T. Cuddington, *Capital Flight: Estimates, Issues, and Explanations,* Princeton Studies in International Finance no. 58 (Princeton University, December 1986), pp. 10–15.

33. All of the data in this paragraph are derived from United Nations Development Programme, *Human Development Report 1990* (New York: Oxford University Press, 1990), pp. 76–78; and United Nations, *Human Development Report 1995* (New York: Oxford University, 1995), p. 171.

34. Peter J. Quirk, "The Case for Open Foreign Exchange Systems," *Finance and Development, 26* (June 1989), pp. 30–33.

35. For a greater elaboration of these costs, see Sebastian Edwards, *Exchange Rate Misalignment in Developing Countries,* World Bank Occasional Papers no. 2/New Series (Baltimore: Johns Hopkins University Press, 1988), pp. 21–46; and C.L. Ramirez-Rojas, "Monetary Substitution in Developing Countries," *Finance and Development, 23* (June 1986), pp. 35–38.

36. See Kempe Ronald Hope, Sr., and D. Misir, "Import-Substitution Strategies in Developing Countries: A Critical Appraisal with Reference to Guyana," *Foreign Trade Review, 16* (July–September 1981), pp. 153–65.

37. Henry J. Bruton, "The Import-Substitution Strategy of Economic Development: A Survey," *Pakistan Development Review, 10* (Summer 1970), p. 131.

38. Sebastian Edwards, *Exchange Rate Misalignment in Developing Countries,* p. 27.

39. For further analysis of this idea, see Omotunde E.G. Johnson, "Currency Depreciation and Imports," *Finance and Development, 24* (June 1987), pp. 18–21; and Omotunde E.G. Johnson, "Currency Depreciation and Export Expansion," *Finance and Development, 24* (March 1987), pp. 23–26.

40. Vinod Thomas and Ajay Chhibber, "Experience with Policy Reforms under Adjustment," *Finance and Development, 26* (March 1989), pp. 28–30; and John Roberts, "Liberalizing Foreign-Exchange Rates in Sub-Saharan Africa," *Development Policy Review, 7* (June 1989), pp. 115–42.

41. Michael Mussa, "Macroeconomic Policy and Trade Liberalization: Some Guidelines," *The World Bank Research Observer, 2* (January 1987), p. 61.

42. Michael Michaely, Armeane Choski, and Demetris Papageorgiou, "The Design of Trade Liberalization," *Finance and Development, 26* (March 1989), pp. 2–5.

43. Ibid.

44. Ibid.

45. See, for example, Lawrence J. Lau (ed.), *Models of Development: A Comparative Study of Economic Growth in South Korea and Taiwan* (San Francisco: ICS Press, 1990); Bela Balassa and Associates, *Development Strategies in Semi-Industrial Economies* (Baltimore: Johns Hopkins University Press, 1982); and World Bank, *World Development Report 1990* (New York: Oxford University Press, 1990).

46. T.N. Srinivasan, "Neo-Classical Political Economy, the State and Economic Development," *Asian Development Review, 3,* 2 (1985), pp. 38–58.

47. Deepak Lal, "The Political Economy of Economic Liberalization," *The World Bank Economic Review, 1* (January 1987), p. 277.

48. Hernando De Soto, *The Other Path: The Invisible Revolution in the Third World* (New York: Harper and Row, 1989), pp. 247–52.

49. Ibid., p. 256.

50. Deepak Lal, "The Political Economy of Economic Liberalization," p. 281.

51. Sebastian Edwards, "Sequencing Economic Liberalization in Developing Countries," *Finance and Development, 24* (March 1987), pp. 26–29.

52. Deepak Lal, "The Political Economy of Economic Liberalization," pp. 286–88.

53. Similar arguments and analysis can be found in Ronald D. Utt, "Shifting the Balance toward Growth," *International Health and Development, 1* (Summer 1989), pp. 4–7; Gerald W. Scully, "The Institutional Framework and Economic Development," *Journal of Political Economy, 96* (June 1988), pp. 652–62; and Keith Marsden, "Private Enterprise Boosts Growth," *Journal of Economic Growth, 1,* 1 (1986), pp. 17–28.

Chapter 8

Policy Reform and Governance: Concluding Comments

This book has examined the problem of elusiveness of development in the Third World and has provided a framework and evidenciary justification for initiating specific economic reform policies in those countries. By so doing, the book has also exposed the progressive socioeconomic decay of the Third World nations and the consequent deepening agony it brings to their citizens, which, in turn, provides the imperative for economic liberalization—an imperative that requires immediate action on the part of Third World leaders, and further action where such reform has already been initiated.

When there is no development, there is hopelessness; and where there is hopelessness, there is no effort to work toward development. The circle is complete. Unfortunately, elusive development in the Third World has made life in those countries an endless series of vicious circles spreading economic suffering in a now concentrated fashion. Elusive development represents a historical tragedy, and the historical evidence now suggests the circumstances under which development can be fostered. The policy experimentation and blunders of the past must now give way to much more sober thinking that can only result in much desired economic progress.

The Third World's catastrophic encounter with centralized economic decision making has provided a painful but critically important lesson. State intervention is fundamentally in conflict with the process of economic development. Economic progress blossoms best when economic freedom, expressed through the marketplace, is promoted and enhanced. The precipitating cause of the elusiveness of development in the Third World is the manifest irrelevance of centralized economic decision making. State intervention is now equated with economic retardation and has consequently become a discredited policy framework. The significant truth is that bad government is the biggest single reason for poverty in the Third World, and less government is the most effective single remedy.

Third World leaders must eschew state ownership and intervention in favor of market-oriented policies. State intervention in economic affairs has not resulted and cannot result, for reasons discussed in this book, in a dependable relationship between economic development and economic management. Consequently, state intervention as a policy option must be terminated, except in very special circumstances, as alluded to in this work. Even in the former Soviet Union this was recognized, albeit perhaps too late, and exhibited in "perestroika" (restructuring) and "glasnost" (overtness). Indeed, many Third World nations are now attempting to reduce government control over their economies and leave behind the dismal failure of statism. The World Bank has reported, for example, that there were 2,162 cases of privatization in the Third World countries between 1980 and 1991. Of that total, 122 were in Asia, 373 were in sub-Saharan Africa, and 804 were in Latin America and the Caribbean.[1]

Just as political expediency in the past three decades reinforced the somewhat intellectually fashionable preference for some form of centralized state socioeconomic decision making as the basis for nation building and as the means toward modernization, it is now necessary to disengage from such a policy framework and implement liberalized economic policies. After a quarter-century (and in some cases more) of independence and the right to develop and implement policy indigenously, the majority of Third World nations are now poorer than they were at the outset. The experimentation associated with postindependence socioeconomic policy in the Third World has brought disastrous results—so disastrous, as a matter of fact, that it seems incredible that the model was viewed as attractive and worthy of imitation by so many nations. However, like so many of the Third World nations, those policies are now considered "bankrupt," and it is now time to attempt to eradicate the whirlpool of despair they have created.

Economic policy reform, then, is a matter of urgency in order for the Third World nations to move toward achieving the rising levels of growth necessary to sustain an improved standard of living and create an atmosphere that is *not* antidemocratic, antisocial, antiprogress, or antientrepreneurial. Economic policy reform creates opportunities for people to make their own choices. Where people are allowed to make choices, a nation's economy can respond more quickly to the ever-changing world economy and even take advantage of the opportunities that such change may offer. Economic reform may be difficult, but it is absolutely essential in order to produce the growth that Third World nations must have if they are to meet the needs of their citizens. Reform represents the initial steps in the long journey toward sustainable economic progress.

Evidence of the benefits of economic reform is most glaring in Africa, where growth in gross domestic product (GDP) for the reforming countries increased from an average of 1 percent in 1980–84 to nearly 4 percent in 1986–87, while GDP for nonreformers grew at only 1.5 percent for the same period. Agricultural production and export performance were also affected. In those countries that initiated economic reforms, agricultural production grew at twice the rate of those that did not. Likewise, exports grew by 5 to 6 percent in reforming countries, compared with only 1 to 2 percent in the nonreforming African countries. More recent evidence also suggests that the reforming countries continue to have better economic performance than the nonreforming ones.[2]

In Latin America, economic liberalization has resulted in significant benefits. For example, the Inter-American Development Bank (IDB) reports that the net inflow of capital to the Latin American countries was $16.4 billion in 1990—the first time in almost a decade that more money flowed into the region than flowed out. The IDB also estimated direct foreign investment in 1990 at $9 billion with a prediction that it could reach $22 billion annually by the year 2000. The four countries that have benefited the most are Chile, Colombia, Mexico, and Venezuela. They account for approximately 70 percent of the capital inflow. Not surprisingly, this has resulted from the fact that all four countries have opened their economies to foreign trade and investment, have cut back on burdensome government regulations, have reduced government expenditures, and have begun to privatize their public enterprises.

Implementing economic policy reform requires that Third World leaders assume a stance of leadership. Good leadership can assure good government, which in turn can assure stability and continuity, without which investment and production will continue to falter. Good government or governance, taken here to mean the exercise of legitimate power and authority in the management of national affairs, can provide the environment to facilitate economic progress. The dimensions of good governance are political, technical, and institutional; it is good government and also implies political accountability, bureaucratic transparency, freedom of association and participation, freedom of information and expression, and capacity-building capability.[3] In addition, it requires a professionally competent and honest public service and sound fiscal management.

The reform policies a government pursues will also determine the pace of economic development. The behavior of government plays as important a role in stimulating, or impeding for that matter, economic progress, as does the behavior of entrepreneurs, for example. Thus, the creativity and skill of the Third World leadership, and their advisers, play a key role in the process of economic development.

Many Third World governments have caused remarkable damage to the development process by suppressing markets.[4] Without a working price mechanism, producers and investors (both foreign and domestic) can only move blindly forward. Judging future risks and returns, therefore, becomes guesswork. The results have been declining investment and slow growth. By these standards, the governments in the industrialized and newly industrializing nations are models of good sense. Their economies are, by and large, market economies, so they work. Third World governments must accept the importance of markets in their policy frameworks as they move through the 1990s. Not to do so would only result in prolonged economic stagnation through the 1990s and beyond.

In the majority of Third World nations, the only price system that works is that found in the subterranean sector, particularly in the hard currency markets. Once Third World governments engage in policies to steer their economies in the government's preferred direction, economic chaos results. As soon as such chaos and its resultant uncertainty become visible, a chain reaction begins that ultimately produces severe instability. For example, in Latin America, it was observed that capital flees abroad, plunging countries into foreign-exchange crises. That leads, in turn, to expectations about currency devaluations, which drives capital away faster, and increases expectations about further inflation. These fears then become reality as workers demand more pay to offset the impact of inflation and producers increase their prices for similar reasons.[5] Eventually, a thriving subterranean sector emerges as national currencies become worthless and a hard currency (usually the U.S. dollar) price system takes effect.[6] In addition to those effects, there are also the issues of brain drain and systemic corruption, for example.

Generally, those Third World nations that have grown fastest and have been successful in making economic progress are the ones with governments that encouraged private enterprise and entrepreneurship, reduced government control over the economy, allowed the price of agricultural produce to rise or change with market demands, kept the rates of interest for savings above the inflation rate, reduced the rate of growth of the money supply, realigned overvalued exchange rates for national currency, promoted exports primarily by liberalizing trade; and kept inflation under control by pursuing prudent monetary and fiscal policy.

Clearly, government policies and the effectiveness with which they are pursued are crucial to the development process. The desire to ensure the occurrence of sustained development would significantly influence the process through which leaders apply priorities in shaping policies, and the people, institutions, and practices they use to execute those policies.[7] Leaders can, by their example, contribute to changed popular expectations and the development process by living simply, by dealing civilly with their opposition, and by pursuing liberalized reform policies. The appeal of nationalism should be directed toward the accomplishment of socioeconomic advancement rather than toward a desire to maintain political office regardless of the national cost.

Some research has shown that growth rates in societies that circumscribe or proscribe political, civil, and economic liberty are about half of those in societies where individual rights are protected.[8] Put another way, in those nations where individual rights are preserved, economic growth rates are about twice those accomplished by those nations where such rights are restrained. On average, open societies were found to grow at a compound real per capita rate of 2.53 percent per year, compared with a 1.41 percent growth rate for closed societies. Moreover, societies that subscribe to the rule of law were found to grow at a rate of 2.75 percent, compared with a rate of 1.23 percent in those societies where the state intervenes in resource allocation.[9] Consequently, the structure of rights is a most important phenomenon in the development process and must also be incorporated in the economic reform policy framework required in the Third World.

Undoubtedly, policy reform, good governance, and development are directly correlated, as this book shows. As a matter of fact, many of the international development agencies, some of which had previously shown a contempt for economic liberalization, are also increasingly acknowledging that the role of the state needs to be redefined in order for it to provide an enabling policy environment for efficient production and equitable distribution, but it should not intervene unnecessarily in the workings of the market mechanism.[10] On the other hand, the World Bank has been assisting Third World countries to adopt a supportive, or enabling, environment for private sector development so that they can obtain the advantages of private initiative and market discipline in promoting efficient development.[11] Such initiatives should be intensified.

Government intervention has retarded economic development and progress in most Third World states and has exacerbated poverty in those economies. The time is now past due for policy reform and good governance to become operational aspects of the functioning of Third World governments. Poverty and economic retardation need not be a permanent state for the majority of Third World inhabitants and their future generations.

Notes

1. Sunita Kikeri, John Nellis, and Mary Shirley, *Privatization: Lessons of Experience* (Washington, DC: The World Bank, 1992), pp. 22–24.

2. Charles Humphreys and William Jaeger, "Africa's Adjustment and Growth," *Finance and Development,* 26 (June 1989), pp. 6–8; World Bank, *Adjustment in Africa: Reforms, Results, and the Road Ahead* (New York: Oxford University Press, 1994), pp. 131–59; see also the papers in David E. Sahn (ed.), *Adjusting to Policy Failure in African Economies* (Ithaca, NY: Cornell University Press, 1994).

3. Edgardo Boeninger, "Governance and Development: Issues and Constraints," in Lawrence H. Summers and Shekhar Shah (eds.), *Proceedings of the World Bank Annual Conference on Development Economics* (Washington, DC: The World Bank, 1991), pp. 267–87; Pierre Landell-Mills and Ismail Serageldin, "Government and the Development Process," *Finance and Development,* 28 (September 1991), pp. 14–17; and John Healey and Mark Robinson, *Democracy, Governance and Economic Policy: Sub-Saharan Africa in Comparative Perspective* (London: Overseas Development Institute, 1992).

4. One good example of this damage, in addition to others discussed in this book, can be found in the Third World agricultural crisis which is brilliantly discussed, for example, in George B.N. Ayittey, "Why Can't Africa Feed Itself?" *International Health and Development, 1* (Summer 1989), pp. 18–21; and Orville Freeman, "Reaping the Benefits: Cash Crops in the Development Process," *International Health and Development, 1* (March–April 1989), pp. 20–23.

5. Clive Crook, "A Survey of the Third World: Poor Man's Burden" *The Economist* (September 23, 1989), Survey section, p. 10.

6. Kempe Ronald Hope, Sr., "The Growth and Impact of the Subterranean Economy in the Third World," *Futures, 25* (October 1993), pp. 864–76.

7. For a further thorough presentation of this assertion, see Lawrence E. Harrison, *Underdevelopment Is a State of Mind* (Cambridge, MA: The Center for International Affairs, Harvard University, 1985).

8. See, for example, Gerald W. Scully, "Liberty and Economic Progress," *Journal of Economic Growth, 3,* 2 (1989), pp. 7–8.

9. Ibid.

10. See United Nations Development Programme, *Human Development Report 1990* (New York: Oxford University Press, 1990), p. 6; and United Nations Development Programme, *Human Development Report 1991* (New York: Oxford University Press, 1991), p. 21.

11. World Bank, *Annual Report 1990* (Washington, DC: World Bank, 1990), p. 68; and World Bank, *World Development Report 1991* (New York: Oxford University Press, 1991), pp. 128–47.

12. World Bank, *World Development Report 1991,* pp. 31–51.

——————— Select Bibliography ———————

Ahamed, Liaquat. "Stabilization Policies in Developing Countries." *The World Bank Research Observer, 1* (January 1986).

Alam, M.S. "Some Economic Costs of Corruption in LDCs." *Journal of Development Studies, 27* (October 1990).

Alam, M. Shahid. *Governments and Markets in Economic Development Strategies.* New York: Praeger, 1989.

Arndt, H.W. "Economic Development: A Semantic History." *Economic Development and Cultural Change, 29* (April 1981).

———. "The Role of Political Leadership in Economic Development." *Canadian Journal of Development Studies, 5,* 1 (1984).

———. *Economic Development: The History of An Idea.* Chicago: University of Chicago Press, 1987.

———. "Market Failure and Underdevelopment." *World Development, 16* (February 1989).

Ayittey, George B.N. "The Political Economy of Reform in Africa." *Journal of Economic Growth, 3* (Spring 1989).

———. "Why Can't Africa Feed Itself?" *International Health and Development, 1* (Summer 1989).

———. *Africa Betrayed.* New York: St. Martin's Press, 1992.

———. "The Failure of Development Planning in Africa." In Peter J. Boettke (ed.), *The Collapse of Development Planning.* New York: New York University Press, 1994.

Bates, Robert H. *Markets and States in Tropical Africa.* Berkeley: University of California Press, 1981.

Bauer, Peter T. *Dissent on Development.* London: Weidenfeld and Nicolson, 1972.

———. *Equality, The Third World and Economic Delusion.* Cambridge: Harvard University Press, 1981.

———. *Reality and Rhetoric: Studies in the Economics of Development.* Cambridge: Harvard University Press, 1984.

Bienen, Henry, and John Waterbury. "The Political Economy of Privatization in Developing Countries." *World Development, 17* (May 1989).

Bird, Richard M. "The Administrative Dimension of Tax Reform in Developing Countries." In Malcolm Gillis (ed.), *Tax Reform in Developing Countries.* Durham, NC: Duke University Press, 1989.

———. *Tax Policy and Economic Development.* Baltimore: Johns Hopkins University Press, 1992.

Bird, Richard M., and Susan Horton, eds. *Government Policy and the Poor in Developing Countries.* Toronto: University of Toronto Press, 1989.

Blejer, Mario I., and Mohsin S. Khan. "Government Policy and Private Investment in Developing Countries." *IMF Staff Papers, 31* (June 1984).

Boeninger, Edgardo. "Governance and Development: Issues and Constraints." In Lawrence Summers and Shekhar Shah (eds.), *Proceedings of the World Bank Annual Conference on Development Economics*. Washington, DC: The World Bank, 1991.

Boettke, Peter J., ed. *The Collapse of Development Planning*. New York: New York University Press, 1994.

Bouchet, Michael Henri. *The Political Economy of International Debt*. Westport, CT: Greenwood Press, 1987.

Bruton, Henry J. "The Search for a Development Economics." *World Development, 13,* 10 (1985).

Brzezinski, Zbigniew. *The Grand Failure: The Birth and Death of Communism in the Twentieth Century*. New York: Scribners, 1989.

Burki, Shahid Javed, and Robert L. Ayres. "A Fresh Look at Development Aid." *Finance and Development, 23* (March 1986).

Caiden, Gerald E. "The Vitality of Administrative Reform." *International Review of Administrative Sciences, 54* (September 1988).

Cassen, Robert. "The Effectiveness of Aid." *Finance and Development, 23* (March 1986).

Cheema, G. Shabbir, and Dennis A. Rondinelli, eds. *Decentralization and Development: Policy Implementation in Developing Countries*. Beverly Hills: Sage Publications, 1983.

Chickering, A. Lawrence, and Mohamed Salahdine, eds. *The Silent Revolution: The Informal Sector in Five Asian and Near Eastern Countries*. San Francisco: ICS Press, 1991.

Cline, William. *The International Debt Problem*. Cambridge: MIT Press, 1983.

Collins, Paul D. "Strategic Planning for State Enterprise Performance in Africa: Public versus Private Options." *Public Administration and Development, 9,* 1, 1989.

Cowan, L. Gray. *Privatization in the Developing World*. New York: Praeger Publishers, 1990.

David, Wilfred L. *Conflicting Paradigms in the Economics of the Developing Nations*. New York: Praeger, 1986.

———. *Political Economy of Economic Policy: The Quest for Human Betterment*. New York: Praeger, 1988.

De Soto, Hernando. *The Other Path: The Invisible Revolution in the Third World*. New York: Harper and Row, 1989.

Dornbusch, Rudiger. "The Case for Trade Liberalization in Developing Countries." *Journal of Economic Perspectives, 6* (Winter 1992).

Dornbusch, Rudiger, and F. Helmers, eds. *The Open Economy: Tools for Policymakers in Developing Countries*. New York: Oxford University Press, 1988.

Dornbusch, Rudiger, and Steve Marcus, eds. *International Money and Debt: Challenges for the World Economy*. San Francisco: ICS Press, 1991.

Eberstadt, Nick. *The Poverty of Communism*. New Brunswick: Transaction Publishers, 1987.

Edwards, Michael, and David Hulme, eds. *Making a Difference: NGOs and Development in a Changing World*. London: Earthscan Publications, 1992.

Edwards, Sebastian. "Sequencing Economic Liberalization in Developing Countries." *Finance and Development, 24* (March 1987).

————. *Exchange Rate Misalignment in Developing Countries.* Baltimore: Johns Hopkins University Press, 1988.

————. *Real Exchange Rates, Devaluation, and Adjustment: Exchange Rate Policy in Developing Countries.* Cambridge: The MIT Press, 1989.

Fields, Gary S. *Poverty, Inequality, and Development.* New York: Cambridge University Press, 1980.

Findlay, R. "Trade, Development and the State." In Gustav Ranis and Theodore P. Schultz (eds.), *The State of Development Economics: Progress and Perspectives.* New York: Basil Blackwell, 1988..

Finsterbusch, Kurt, and Warren A. Van Wicklin, III. "Beneficiary Participation in Development Projects: Empirical Tests of Popular Theories." *Economic Development and Cultural Change, 37* (April 1989).

Fischer, Bernhard. "Savings Mobilization in Developing Countries: Bottlenecks and Reform Proposals." *Savings and Development, 13,* 2 (1989).

Fischer, Stanley. "Recent Debt Developments." In Rudiger Dornbusch and Steve Marcus (eds.), *International Money and Debt: Challenges for the World Economy.* San Francisco: ICS Press, 1991.

Friedmann, John. *Empowerment: The Politics of Alternative Development.* Cambridge: Blackwell, 1992.

Gemmell, Norman, ed. *Surveys in Development Economics.* New York: Basil Blackwell, 1987.

Gillis, Malcolm, ed. *Tax Reform in Developing Countries.* Durham, NC: Duke University Press, 1989.

Glickman, Harvey, ed. *The Crisis and Challenge of African Development.* Westport, CT: Greenwood Press, 1989.

Goldsbrough, David. "Foreign Direct Investment in Developing Countries." *Finance and Development, 22* (March 1985).

Gordon, Richard K., Jr. "Income Tax Compliance and Sanctions in Developing Countries." *Bulletin for International Fiscal Documentation, 42* (January 1988).

Grant, James P. *The State of the World's Children 1989.* New York: Oxford University Press, 1989.

————. *The State of the World's Children 1991.* New York: Oxford University Press, 1991.

Greene, Joshua. "The Debt Problem of Sub-Saharan Africa." *Finance and Development, 26* (June 1989).

Grindle, Merilee, and John W. Thomas. *Public Choices and Policy Change: The Political Economy of Reform in Developing Countries.* Baltimore: Johns Hopkins University Press, 1991.

Guha, Ashok S. *An Evolutionary View of Economic Growth.* New York: Oxford University Press, 1981.

Gulhati, Ravi. *The Making of Economic Policy in Africa.* Washington, DC: World Bank, 1990).·

Hancock, Graham. *Lords of Poverty: The Power, Prestige, and Corruption of the International Aid Business.* New York: The Atlantic Monthly Press, 1989.

Hanke, Steve H., ed. *Privatization and Development.* San Francisco: ICS Press, 1987.

Hansenne, Michel. *The Dilemma of the Informal Sector.* Geneva: ILO, 1987.

Hellinger, Stephen, Douglas Hellinger, and Fred M. O'Regan. *Aid for Just Development: Report on the Future of Foreign Assistance.* Boulder, CO: Lynne Rienner Publishers, 1988.

Hirschman, Albert O. *Essays in Trespassing: Economics to Politics and Beyond.* New York: Cambridge University Press, 1981.

———. "The Rise and Decline of Development Economics." In M. Gersovitz, C.F. Diaz-Alejandro, G. Ranis, and M.R. Rosenzweig (eds.), *The Theory and Experience of Economic Development.* London: Allen and Unwin, 1982.

———. *The Strategy of Economic Development.* Boulder, CO: Westview Press, 1988.

Hope, Kempe Ronald, Sr. "Taxation in Developing Countries." *Bulletin for International Fiscal Documentation, 31* (November 1977).

———. "Development and Development Administration: Perspectives and Dimensions." *Administrative Change, 7* (July–December 1979).

———. *Development Policy in Guyana.* Boulder, CO: Westview Press, 1979.

———. "The Role of Domestic Savings in the Financing of Economic Development in Developing Countries." *Economic Affairs, 25* (November 1980).

———. "The Concept of Economic Development: Toward a New Interpretation." *Man and Development, 3* (June 1981).

———. "Improving Public Enterprise Management in Developing Countries." *Journal of General Management, 7* (Spring 1982).

———. "The New International Economic Order, Basic Needs, and Technology Transfer: Toward and Integrated Strategy for Development in the Future." *World Futures, 18,* 3 and 4 (1982).

———. "Some Problems of Administering Development in Developing Nations." *Indian Journal of Public Administration, 29* (January–March 1983).

———. "Basic Needs and Technology Transfer Issues in the New International Economic Order." *American Journal of Economics and Sociology, 42* (October 1983).

———. "Self-Reliance and Participation of the Poor in the Development Process in the Third World." *Futures, 15* (December 1983).

———. "Self-Reliance as a Development Strategy: A Conceptual Policy Analysis." *Scandinavian Journal of Development Alternatives, 3* (December 1984).

———. "External Borrowing and the Debt Problem of the Developing Nations." *International Journal of Development Banking, 2* (January 1984).

———. *The Dynamics of Development and Development Administration.* Westport, CT: Greenwood Press, 1984.

———. "Politics, Bureaucratic Corruption and Maladministration in the Third World." *International Review of Administrative Sciences, 51,* 1 (1985).

———. *Guyana: Politics and Development in an Emergent State.* Oakville, Ontario: Mosaic Press, 1985.

———. "Urbanization and Economic Development in the Third World." *Cities, 3* (February 1986).

———. *Urbanization in the Commonwealth Caribbean.* Boulder, CO: Westview Press, 1986.

———. *Economic Development in the Caribbean.* New York: Praeger, 1986.

———. "Administrative Corruption and Administrative Reform in Developing States." *Corruption and Reform, 2,* 2 (1987).

————. *Development Finance and the Development Process.* Westport, CT: Greenwood Press, 1987.

————. "The Administrative Reform Imperative in Developing Nations." *Public Administration, 60* (December 1988).

————. "Private Direct Investment and Development Policy in the Caribbean." *American Journal of Economics and Sociology, 48* (January 1989).

————. "Managing Rapid Urbanization in the Third World: Some Aspects of Policy." *Genus, 45,* 3–4 (1989).

————. "The Subterranean Economy in Guyana." *Caribbean Affairs, 3,* 2 (1990).

————. "Privatization and the Quest for Economic Revival in Guyana." *Caribbean Affairs, 5,* 2 (1992).

————. "Development Theory and Development Policy in the Third World." *South African Journal of Economics, 60* (December 1992).

————. "The Subterranean Economy in the Third World: Evidence from Latin America and the Caribbean." *Journal of Developing Societies, 9,* 2 (1993).

————. "The Subterranean Economy and the Role of Private Investment in Developing Countries." *Journal of Social, Political and Economic Studies, 18* (Summer 1993).

————. "The Growth and Impact of the Subterranean Economy in the Third World." *Futures, 25* (October 1993).

————."Managing Development Policy in Botswana: Implementing Reforms for Rapid Change," *Public Administration and Development, 15* (February 1995).

Hope, Kempe Ronald, Sr., and Aubrey Armstrong. "Toward the Development of Administrative and Management Capability in Developing Countries." *International Review of Administrative Sciences, 46,* 4 (1980).

Hope, Kempe Ronald, Sr., and D. Misir. "Import-Substitution Strategies in Developing Countries: A Critical Appraisal with Reference to Guyana." *Foreign Trade Review, 16* (July–September 1981).

Humphreys, Charles, and William Jaeger. "Africa's Adjustment and Growth." *Finance and Development, 26* (June 1989).

Imbeau, Louis M. *Donor Aid: The Determinants of Development Allocations to Third World Countries: A Comparative Analysis.* New York: Peter Lang Publishing, 1989.

Jagannathan, N.V. "Corruption, Delivery Systems, and Property Rights," *World Development, 14,* 1 (1986).

————. *Informal Markets in Developing Countries.* New York: Oxford University Press, 1987.

James, William E., Seiji Naya, and Gerald M. Meier. *Asian Development: Economic Success and Policy Lessons.* Madison: University of Wisconsin Press, 1989.

Jenkins, Jerry, ed. *Beyond the Informal Sector: Including the Excluded in Developing Countries.* San Francisco: Institute for Contemporary Studies, 1989.

Johnson, Omotunde E.G. "Currency Depreciation and Export Expansion." *Finance and Development, 24* (March 1987).

————. "Currency Depreciation and Imports." *Finance and Development, 24* (June 1987).

Kannappan, Subbiah. *Employment Problems and the Urban Labor Market in*

Developing Nations. Ann Arbor: Graduate School of Business Administration, University of Michigan, 1983.

————. 1989. "Urban Labor Markets in Developing Countries." *Finance and Development, 26* (June 1989).

Khan, Mohsin S. "Macroeconomic Adjustment in Developing Countries: A Policy Perspective." *The World Bank Research Observer, 2* (January 1987).

Khan, Mohsin S., and Nadeem ul Haque. "Foreign Borrowing and Capital Flight." *IMF Staff Papers, 32* (December 1985).

Khan, Mohsin S., and J. Saul Lizondo. "Devaluation, Fiscal Deficits, and the Real Exchange Rate." *World Bank Economic Review, 1* (January 1987).

Killick, Tony. *A Reaction Too Far: Economic Theory and the Role of the State in Developing Countries*. London: Overseas Development Institute, 1989.

Kindleberger, Charles P. "Capital Flight: An Historical Perspective." In Donald R. Lessard and John Williamson (eds.), *Capital Flight and Third World Debt*. Washington, DC: Institute for International Economics, 1987.

Kletzer, Kenneth. "External Borrowing by LDCs: A Survey of Some Theoretical Issues." In Gustav Ranis and T. Paul Schultz (eds.), *The State of Development Economics: Progress and Perspectives*. New York: Basil Blackwell, 1988.

Klitgaard, Robert. *Controlling Corruption*. Berkeley: University of California Press, 1988.

————. *Adjusting to Reality: Beyond "State versus Market" in Economic Development*. San Francisco: ICS Press, 1991.

Krauss, Melvyn B. *Development without Aid: Growth, Poverty and Government*. New York: McGraw-Hill, 1983.

Krueger, Anne O. *Exchange Rate Determination*. New York: Cambridge University Press, 1983.

————."Aid in the Development Process." *The World Bank Research Observer, 1* (January 1986).

————. "Government Failures in Development." *Journal of Economic Perspectives, 4* (Summer 1990).

————. *Perspectives on Trade and Development*. Chicago: University of Chicago Press, 1990.

Krueger, Anne O., C. Michalopoulos, and V. Ruttan. *Aid and Development*. Baltimore: Johns Hopkins University Press, 1989.

Lal, Deepak. *The Poverty of "Development Economics."* London: Institute of Economic Affairs, 1983.

————. "The Political Economy of Economic Liberalization." *The World Bank Economic Review, 1* (January 1987).

Landell-Mills, Pierre, Ramgopal Agarwala, and Stanley Please. *Sub-Saharan Africa: From Crisis to Sustainable Growth: A Long-Term Perspective Study*. Washington, DC: World Bank, 1989.

Larrain, Felipé, and Marcelo Selowsky, eds. *The Public Sector and the Latin American Crisis*. San Francisco: ICS Press, 1991.

Lau, Lawrence J., ed. *Models of Development: A Comparative Study of Economic Growth in South Korea and Taiwan*. San Francisco: ICS Press, 1990.

Lessard, Donald R., and John Williamson, eds. *Capital Flight and Third World Debt*. Washington, DC: Institute for International Economics, 1987.

Lewis, W. Arthur (Sir). *Development Planning*. London: Allen and Unwin, 1966.

————. *The Evolution of the International Economic Order.* Princeton: Princeton University Press, 1978

————. "The State of Development Theory." *American Economic Review, 74* (March 1984)..

————. "Reflections on Development." In Gustav Ranis and T. Paul Schultz (eds.), *The State of Development Economics: Progress and Perspectives.* New York: Basil Blackwell, 1988.

Little, Ian M.D. *Economic Development: Theory, Policies and International Relations.* New York: Basic Books, 1982.

Loup, Jacques. *Can The Third World Survive?* Baltimore: Johns Hopkins University Press, 1983.

Lubell, Harold. *The Informal Sector in the 1980s and 1990s.* Paris: OECD Development Centre Studies, 1991.

Main, Jeremy. "The Informal Route to Prosperity." *International Health and Development, 1,* 1 (1989).

Maizels, Alfred, and Machiko Nissanke. "Motivations for Aid to Developing Countries." *World Development, 12,* 9 (1984).

Marsden, Keith. "Private Enterprise Boosts Growth." *Journal of Economic Growth, 1,* 1 (1986).

Mathur, H.M. *Administering Development in the Third World: Constraints and Changes.* Beverly Hills: Sage Publications, 1986.

Mauri, Arnaldo, ed. *Mobilization of Household Savings: A Tool for Development.* Milan: Finafrica Foundation, 1989.

McCarthy, Stephen. *Africa: The Challenge of Transformation.* London: I.B. Tauris, 1994.

McGreevey, William Paul. *Third World Poverty.* Lexington, MA: Lexington Books, 1980.

McKee, David L. *Growth, Development, and the Service Economy in the Third World.* New York: Praeger, 1988.

Meier, Gerald M. *Emerging from Poverty: The Economics That Really Matters.* New York: Oxford University Press, 1984.

————. ed. *Politics and Policy Making in Developing Countries: Perspectives on the New Political Economy.* San Francisco: ICS Press, 1991.

Michaely, Michael, Armeane Choski, and Demetris Papageorgiou. "The Design of Trade Liberalization." *Finance and Development, 26* (March 1989).

Mills, Edwin S. *The Burden of Government.* Stanford, CA: Hoover Institution Press, 1986.

Moran, Theodore, and contributors. *Investing in Development: New Roles for Private Capital,* ODC Policy Perspectives no. 6. New Brunswick: Transaction Books, 1986.

Morton, James. *The Poverty of Nations: The Aid Dilemma at the Heart of Africa.* London: British Academic Press, 1994.

Mosley, Paul. *Overseas Aid: Its Defence and Reform.* Brighton, UK: Wheatsheaf Books, 1987.

Murdoch, William W. *The Poverty of Nations.* Baltimore: Johns Hopkins University Press, 1980.

Nellis, John, and Sunita Kikeri. "Public Enterprise Reform: Privatization and the World Bank." *World Development, 17* (May 1989).

Newberry, David, and Nicholas Stern, eds. *The Theory of Taxation for Developing Countries.* New York: Oxford University Press, 1987.

Nixson, Frederick. "Economic Development: A Suitable Case for Treatment?" In Barbara Ingham and Colin Simmons (eds.), *Development Studies and Colonial Policy.* London: Frank Cass, 1987.

North, Douglass C. *Institutions, Institutional Change and Economic Performance.* New York: Cambridge University Press, 1990.

Nowak, Michael. "Black Markets in Foreign Exchange: Their Causes, Nature, and Consequences." *Finance and Development, 22* (March 1985).

Osterfeld, David. *Prosperity versus Planning: How Government Stifles Economic Growth.* New York: Oxford University Press, 1992.

Perkins, Dwight H., and Michael Roemer, eds. *Reforming Economic Systems in Developing Countries.* Cambridge: Harvard Institute of International Development, 1991.

Pirie, Masden. *Dismantling the State: The Theory and Practice of Privatization.* Dallas: National Center for Policy Analysis, 1985.

Polak, Jacques J. *Financial Policies and Development.* Paris: OECD Development Center, 1989.

Preston, P.W. *Rethinking Development: Essays on Development and Southeast Asia.* London: Routledge, 1987.

Quirk, Peter J. "The Case for Open Foreign Exchange Systems." *Finance and Development, 26* (June 1989).

Ramirez-Rojas, C.L. "Monetary Substitution in Developing Countries." *Finance and Development, 23* (June 1986).

Ranis, Gustav, and J.C.H. Fei. "Development Economics: What Next?" In Gustav Ranis and T. Paul Schultz (eds.), *The State of Development Economics: Progress and Perspectives.* New York: Basil Blackwell, 1988.

Ranis, Gustav, and T. Paul Shultz, eds. *The State of Development Economics: Progress and Perspectives.* New York: Basil Blackwell, 1988.

Ravenhill, John, ed. *Africa in Economic Crisis.* New York: Columbia University Press, 1986.

Riddell, Roger. "The Ethics of Foreign Aid." *Development Policy Review, 4* (March 1986).

———. *Foreign Aid Reconsidered.* Baltimore: Johns Hopkins University Press, 1987.

Riely, Frank Z. *Third World Capital Flight: Who Gains, Who Loses?* Policy Focus no. 5. Washington, DC: Overseas Development Council, 1986.

Rodgers, Gerry, ed. *Urban Poverty and the Labour Market: Access to Jobs and Incomes in Asian and Latin American Cities.* Geneva: International Labour Office, 1989.

Roemer, Michael, and Christine Jones, eds. *Markets in Developing Countries: Parallel, Fragmented, and Black.* San Francisco: ICS Press, 1991.

Roth, Gabriel. *The Private Provision of Public Services in Developing Countries.* New York: Oxford University Press, 1987.

Ruttan, Vernon. "Why Foreign Economic Assistance." *Economic Development and Cultural Change, 37* (January 1989).

Ryrie, William (Sir). "Capitalism and Third World Development." *International Economic Insights, 2, 3* (1991).

Sahan, David E., ed. *Adjusting to Policy Failure in African Economies.* Ithaca, NY: Cornell University Press, 1994.

Sanbrook, R. "The State and Economic Stagnation in Tropical Africa." *World Development, 14* (March 1986).

Scott, Maurice, and Deepak Lal, eds. *Public Policy and Economic Development: Essays in Honor of Ian Little.* New York: Oxford University Press, 1990.

Shirley, Mary, and John Nellis. *Public Enterprise Reform: The Lessons of Experience.* Washington, DC: The World Bank, 1991.

Simmons, Colin. "Economic Development and Economic History." In Barbara Ingham and Colin Simmons (eds.), *Development Studies and Colonial Policy.* London: Frank Cass, 1987.

Streeten, Paul. "Development Ideas in Historical Perspective." In K.Q. Hill (ed.), *Toward a New Strategy for Development: A Rothko Chapel Colloquium.* New York: Pergamon Press, 1979.

———. *Development Perspectives.* London: Macmillan, 1981.

———. ed. *Beyond Adjustment: The Asian Experience.* Washington, DC: International Monetary Fund, 1988.

Summers, Lawrence. "The Challenges of Development: Some Lessons of History for Sub-Saharan Africa." *Finance and Development, 29* (March 1992).

Thomas, Vinod, Ajay Chhibber, Mansoor Dailami, and Jaime de Melo, eds. *Restructuring Economies in Distress: Policy Reform and the World Bank.* New York: Oxford University Press, 1991.

United Nations Development Programme. *Human Development Report 1990.* New York: Oxford University Press, 1990.

———. *Human Development Report 1991.* New York: Oxford University Press, 1991.

———. *Human Development Report 1993.* New York: Oxford University Press, 1993.

———. *Human Development Report 1994.* New York: Oxford University Press, 1994.

Van de Walle, Nicolas. "Privatization in Developing Countries: A Review of the Issues." *World Development, 17* (May 1989).

Vickers, John S. "Economics of Predatory Practices." *Fiscal Studies, 6* (August 1985).

Wellisz, S., and R. Findlay. "The State and the Invisible Hand." *The World Bank Research Observer, 3* (January 1988).

Wheeler, Joseph C. "The Critical Role for Official Development Assistance in the 1990s." *Finance and Development, 26* (September 1989).

Whitaker, Jennifer Seymour. *How Can Africa Survive?* New York: Council on Foreign Relations Press, 1988.

Whynes, D.K., and R.A. Bowles. *The Economic Theory of the State.* Oxford: Martin Robertson, 1981.

World Bank. *Annual Report 1988.* Washington, DC: World Bank, 1988.

———. *World Development Report 1988.* New York: Oxford University Press, 1988.

———. *Annual Report 1989.* Washington, DC: World Bank, 1989.

———. *World Development Report 1989.* New York: Oxford University Press, 1989.

————. *Annual Report 1990.* Washington, DC: World Bank, 1990.

————. *World Development Report 1990.* New York: Oxford University Press, 1990.

————. *Annual Report 1991.* Washington, DC: World Bank, 1991.

————. *World Development Report 1991.* New York: Oxford University Press, 1991.

————. *The East Asian Miracle: Economic Growth and Public Policy.* New York: Oxford University Press, 1993.

————. *Annual Report 1994.* Washington, DC: World Bank, 1994.

————. *Adjustment in Africa: Reforms, Results, and the Road Ahead.* New York: Oxford University Press, 1994.

————. *World Development Report 1994.* New York: Oxford University Press, 1994.

World Bank and United Nations Development Programme. *Africa's Adjustment and Growth.* Washington, DC: World Bank, 1989.

Index

——————— About the Author ———————

Kempe Ronald Hope, Sr., is a United Nations Chief Technical Adviser to the Government of Botswana and Professor of Development Studies at the University of Botswana. He has vast experience as an adviser on development policy to several developing-country governments. His books include *Development Finance and the Development Process* (1987), *Economic Development in the Caribbean* (1986), *Urbanization in the Commonwealth Caribbean* (1986), and *The Dynamics of Development and Development Administration* (1984).